LOCK
DOWN

LOCK DOWN

CHIP LE GRAND

Lockdown
© Copyright 2022 Chip Le Grand
All rights reserved. Apart from any uses permitted by Australia's *Copyright Act 1968*, no part of this book may be reproduced by any process without prior written permission from the copyright owners. Inquiries should be directed to the publisher.

Monash University Publishing
Matheson Library Annexe
40 Exhibition Walk
Monash University
Clayton, Victoria 3800, Australia
publishing.monash.edu

ISBN: 9781922633446 (paperback)
ISBN: 9781922633460 (epub)

Editor: Paul Smitz
Design: Philip Campbell Design
Typesetter: Cannon Typesetting
Proofreader: Gillian Armitage
Printed in Australia by Ligare Book Printers

A catalogue record for this book is available from the National Library of Australia.

The paper this book is printed on is in accordance with the standards of the Forest Stewardship Council®. The FSC® promotes environmentally responsible, socially beneficial and economically viable management of the world's forests.

CONTENTS

1	This Is Australia	1
2	The Man from Wuhan	26
3	Woefully Unprepared	56
4	An Unconscionable Delay	86
5	The Lonely Run	117
6	Dementor's Kiss	144
7	Vaxxed and Vexed	174
8	Out of Living Memory	203
	Acknowledgements	229
	Notes	230

CHAPTER 1
THIS IS AUSTRALIA

On 4 July 2020, Melbourne became *that* city. We'd seen people snatched off streets and barricaded into apartments in Wuhan. We'd seen heavily armed Carabinieri patrolling deserted villages in northern Italy. We'd assured ourselves such things could never happen here. Then they did, without warning or precedent. On a Saturday afternoon, at a time when kids are coming in from playing at the park and parents are starting to get dinner on the stove, images broadcast around the world showed hundreds of police surrounding high-rise housing commission buildings on the edge of central Melbourne. By 4 p.m., nearly 3000 people were effectively under house arrest, having committed no crime. That night, we were the city other people gawked at on their television screens, wondering what on earth was going on. Inside the towers, people stared down from their windows at a city they no longer recognised as their own.

Saeed Ali is sitting in the same place he was that day. It's a meeting room inside a disused warehouse in North Melbourne that a local Islamic community group, the Australian Muslim Social Services Agency (AMSSA), uses as a mosque and community drop-in centre.

Through the window, the Alfred Street commission flats rise above a post-industrial landscape now largely gentrified, with spruced-up workers' cottages that used to house meat workers and their families selling for $1.5 million. Like many of the people who live in the flats, Ali was born in Somalia in East Africa. He fled the civil war there, heading west into Kenya and then travelling to Australia, on his own, when he was fourteen years old. He was twenty-one on the night that Victoria Police, carrying out detention orders issued by the state's acting chief health officer, sealed off Alfred Street and eight other housing commission towers. People in the building, panicked and frightened, starting calling him, asking what was going on and what they should do.

Ali was one of only a few people who had known that an intervention of some kind was coming. An hour and a half earlier, he'd been called to a meeting of local government and community members at the nearby North Melbourne Football Club and told of the government's intention to quarantine residents inside their flats to contain an outbreak of COVID-19, the novel coronavirus causing disease, death and community disruption around the world. No-one seemed to know how long the quarantine would last or how it would work. The meeting went for an hour and, as Ali recalls it, little was agreed to. By the time he got back to the AMSSA office, the familiar figure of Victorian Premier Daniel Andrews was on the television announcing a 'complete lockdown' of the towers, including Alfred Street. As he made the announcement, the premier described it as the most challenging issue faced by his government during the pandemic. To this date, it also remains the most confronting. No government in Australia, before or since, has implemented such a draconian restriction of liberty to control the spread of the virus.

While Andrews was talking to the television cameras, Ali looked out of the window of the meeting room and across Boundary Road, and saw busloads of police arriving in the car park of the tower building. He'd expected to see police but imagined it would only take a handful of cops to instruct people to stay in their homes and answer their questions. Instead, it looked like a police response to a terror attack or a natural disaster. This stirred deep disquiet in communities that, since arriving in Australia from countries plagued by violent conflict, had never had reason to entirely trust Victoria Police. It was also closer to the truth than Ali or any of the tower residents understood. The lockdown, ordered by the state's most senior public health official, was nominally overseen by Victoria's then Department of Health and Human Services (DHHS, which in February 2021 was split into the Department of Health and the Department of Families, Fairness and Housing). This is what you would expect in a public health intervention to contain an infectious disease. In practice, Victoria Police were running the show. Such was the haste with which the government decided to act that afternoon, a high-ranking Victoria Police officer was seconded to the health department to quickly throw together an operational plan. Mick Hermans is the assistant commissioner responsible for counterterrorism. He had spent the previous summer directing the evacuation of Victorian families cut off by bushfires. Now he was being asked to organise, within a matter of hours, something that had never before been attempted in Victoria. 'I think anywhere in the world would have struggled to respond to what we did there,' says Chief Commissioner Shane Patton.

Victoria Police called it Operation Benessere, an Italian word which loosely translated means 'welfare'. The tower residents didn't see it in these terms. Some of them hadn't done their weekly shopping and were nearly out of food when the police arrived and blocked the entrances to the towers. Some needed medicine. Others were caught short of critical items like nappies, sanitary pads, baby food and toilet paper. Some were caught on the wrong side of the police cordon and prevented from entering their own homes—they stayed with friends or family, and in some cases slept rough in their cars, until health authorities permitted them to return to their own beds.[1] The government had locked people into a building where it knew the virus was circulating but hadn't yet provided them with masks or hand sanitiser to stop them from getting sick. It had promised them food and whatever support they needed, but as darkness fell over the towers, no-one seemed to know when or how these things would be delivered. The North Melbourne and Flemington commission flats, home to some of the state's most disadvantaged people, were Jenga towers of anxiety.

Barry Berih, a 27-year-old youth worker, was on the fifth floor of the Alfred Street towers, inside the apartment he shares with his mum and younger brother, when he heard the premier on TV. He has lived his entire life in Australia and is a community leader for the Eritrean diaspora who came to Melbourne during their country's thirty-year War of Independence against Ethiopia. From his apartment window, Berih could see that police were already massing on the ground below. He knew from past dealings with government agencies that the tower residents couldn't wait for help to come but would need to make things happen themselves. He started calling other young people in the building, and his contacts in the broader community, to see what they knew. He set up a WhatsApp group and a Facebook page to circulate any information that could be gathered. In those first chaotic hours, there wasn't much. Then his mother Kubra called. She works as a cleaner at the Royal Melbourne Hospital's Centre for Medical Research and had arrived home from her Saturday shift to find her apartment building surrounded by police. They refused to let her in: her driver's licence had an out-of-date address on it and the police wouldn't accept her word that she lived upstairs with her two adult sons. For the next two weeks she was unable to return to her own home and family. 'When I look back, it was just scary,' Berih says. 'It was terrorising.'

It soon became clear, both to tower residents inside the police cordon and community members trying to help them on the outside, that the government had locked down the towers without a clear plan about how to provide necessities that even prisoners in maximum-security jails are entitled to: proper food, medical attention, daily access to fresh air and exercise. There were no food deliveries by government agencies on that first night, and when the supplies did arrive, some of the food was out of date or contained pork products that couldn't be eaten by Muslim residents. An information hotline was established by DHHS but without provision for residents who didn't speak English. Increasingly, residents started calling AMSSA to request essential supplies and find out what was going on.

Over the next two weeks, AMSSA became a lifeline to the outside world for the residents of Alfred Street. Within a few hours of lockdown, community donations of food, face masks and other essentials started arriving at the front door of the warehouse. By Monday, the community response had developed into a well-organised operation, with tailored care packages prepared for each tower household according to what they needed. In effect, two relief operations were running in parallel: one backed by government agencies which the residents didn't trust, and the community response which they did. One of the frustrations for tower residents and community organisations like AMSSA was that, even after DHHS recognised the work they were doing, volunteers still had to run a police gauntlet to get supplies into the building. Sometimes police would let them through, sometimes they wouldn't. Barry Berih says he experienced this first-hand one night when he tried to receive some medicine for another resident and became involved in a heated altercation with a police officer.

Arron Wood, a former City of Melbourne councillor and deputy lord mayor, was one of the few government figures who saw the lockdown unfold through the eyes of the local community. Wood lives near the Alfred Street flats and, throughout his time on council, worked closely with community organisations to secure funding for The Venny, a nearby adventure playground and community centre.

When the lockdown was announced, he knew AMSSA would be at the centre of the community response, so he called his contacts there and offered to help. For the next week, he spent his days packing up boxes of food in the warehouse and calling in favours to get more supplies. He also witnessed rising tensions between the young volunteers and Victoria Police.

Wood explains that, in contrast to some older community leaders, the AMSSA volunteers weren't willing to be told what to do by government agencies, whom they saw as well resourced, well paid and largely inept. They felt their community was being deliberately targeted by an unnecessarily heavy-handed government response. 'I was seeing a community that had been treated pretty badly and had a fear of authority to the point that, when anyone tried to come into the mosque, there was open animosity from the largely young people who were coordinating on the ground,' Wood says. 'We had individual bags packed with exactly what community members needed. We were getting them to the foot of the towers, and DHHS didn't have any way of getting into the towers. There was either a lack of understanding or a disrespect for the knowledge and ability of the community to help each other.'

One incident in particular has stayed with Wood. During the first week of lockdown, television news crews came to the AMSSA mosque to film a story about the community response. While they were setting up their cameras, a man bolted from out of the Alfred Street towers pursued by police, who caught the man and threw him to the ground. AMSSA volunteers started angrily remonstrating with police. 'It was hair on the back of the neck stuff,' he says. 'It felt like everything was just out of control.'

On 9 July, the inhabitants of eight of the nine housing towers were released from home detention. Testing had detected 158 COVID cases in seven of the apartment towers. Two of them hadn't recorded a single case. The greatest concentration of cases, about one-third, was at Alfred Street. While the residents of the other towers celebrated their release, the Alfred Street residents learned they would remain in lockdown for another week. To soften the blow, Daniel Andrews announced that the public health orders were being changed so that residents could leave their apartments and go outside into the fresh air, at least once a day, for 'supervised daily exercise'. Although the announcement was welcome news within the tower building, there was one hitch: no-one within DHHS, the government agency responsible for managing the tower lockdown, knew what the premier was talking about. It was not until the next day that bureaucrats hastily started to develop a plan for 600 residents to be let out for a walk.[2]

On a brilliant late summer's day in Melbourne, Hava Buday takes me to where they put 'the pen'. This is how she and her fellow Alfred Street residents referred to a temporary, cyclone-fenced enclosure that government contractors erected at the back entrance of their apartment block a week into the lockdown. As best as anyone can tell, the episode was a cock-up. As DHHS officials later explained to an investigation conducted by the Victorian Ombudsman, they had arranged for temporary fencing around the perimeter of the housing estate car park. Instead, they got something that resembled a cage right at the back door of the building. Less than twenty-four hours after it went up, the pen was taken down. For residents, the fact it was erected at all is symbolic of what they describe as humiliating treatment. For the day that the fencing stood, residents were escorted by police from their apartments to the pen. Then, under police supervision, they were allowed to walk around the damp, grassless enclosure for their allotted fresh-air time.

'It was sad to watch,' Buday says. 'When you know these people and what type of characters they are, to see them put into that position was so heartbreaking. You are like, "These people don't deserve this shit, they really don't." It wasn't saving our lives, it was making our lives worse. If anything, it made people more sick. Sometimes we sit and wonder, "What did they think they were dealing with?"

Humans need fresh air, humans need to be in the sun, humans need to be out.' Saeed Ali is similarly scathing: 'It shows you what they think of these people. It is like we are animals.'

How did a city like Melbourne arrive at a place where we would strip people of all agency, and finally, their dignity, in the name of public health?

The tower lockdown came four months after the Australian Government declared the SARS-CoV-2 virus a pandemic—beating the World Health Organization (WHO) to the punch by two weeks—and the Victorian Government gazetted a state of emergency, a step necessary to enact extraordinary powers, including mandatory detention, to protect public health. By this stage of the pandemic, we were all getting used to the exercise of those powers. Australia had already spent two months in lockdown, when our work lives shifted to Zoom, kids were kept home from school, and restaurants and cafes were limited to takeaway only, to ride out our first and mercifully small wave of COVID cases. But this was something different. This was the first time the government had detained a sizeable population in the name of public health, and it did so without giving them any time to prepare for a major disruption to their lives. Three days later, when stay-at-home orders were reintroduced across Melbourne, everyone was given until midnight the following night to stock up and get ready.

Inner Melbourne Community Legal, an organisation that provides legal advice and other support to local housing commission residents, was blunt in its assessment of this dual standard in a submission to the Ombudsman: 'That public housing residents were being treated differently speaks volumes about the Victorian Government's view of the people living in these buildings ... To our knowledge no other group or community was policed as intensively as public housing residents were in North Melbourne and Flemington.'³

The reason for this, put plainly, is that the Victorian Government didn't trust them. As senior government figures privately said at the time, and the Ombudsman's investigation later established, they thought that if they gave the residents time to prepare, some would use it as an opportunity to bolt from their bedrooms and evade lockdown. Saeed Ali says the only thing worse than the chaos created by the lack of notice was the message it sent: 'They viewed the people that live here as people from another country, people they can't trust. The idea was just lock them down, they are criminals anyway.'

Hava Buday remembers the panicked call she received from her grandmother on the first night. Her grandma is seventy-three and has lived in the Alfred Street flats for thirty years. Buday stayed with her throughout the tower lockdown. 'She loves this country,' Buday says as she walks her grandmother's dogs outside the flats. 'For her to see something like that was so disheartening. She kept asking me questions and I kept telling her I don't have the answers. It is sad. This is Australia. This is not what we do here.'

The notion of what we do in Australia, particularly when confronted by a crisis, has undergone a dramatic revision since 25 January 2020, when Melbourne's first case of COVID-19 was confirmed in a 58-year-old man recently arrived from Wuhan, capital of China's Hubei Province. Who would have predicted before the pandemic that state and federal governments would prevent Australian citizens from returning to their own country, or that state governments would deploy police to stop families crossing state borders to come home from a beach holiday or a funeral or a visit with their grandparents? That people would be prevented from saying goodbye to dying loved ones, and children would be separated from parents, and sick people from medical treatment? That playground equipment would be taped off like a crime scene to deter children from playing outside and their mums and dads from lingering over a takeaway coffee?

That we would be subjected to a night-time curfew and questioned by police if we strayed 5 kilometres from home without one of four 'permitted' reasons?

The self-isolation of an entire continent for nearly two years fits awkwardly with the outward-looking, globally engaged ethos of modern Australia. Within this Fortress Australia, Melbourne's pandemic was a singular experience. For 262 days, a city of five million people was cocooned by stay-at-home orders. Businesses were forcibly closed, classrooms shuttered, and all community and social life relegated to an impersonal online world. In the space of two years, we went from the world's most liveable city to its most locked down. The purpose of this book is to examine why this happened, what the consequences have been, and whether there was another way open to us that could have protected lives and allowed people to live.

Australia's great success throughout the pandemic is that fewer people came into contact with the virus, fewer people got critically sick and fewer people died compared with most other countries. The contrast is particularly stark across the Anglosphere where, by the end of February 2022, the United States, United Kingdom, South Africa and Canada had recorded death rates between five and fourteen times greater than Australia's. Victoria's death rate, while very low by global standards, was nearly twice the national average. About one in four Australians live in Victoria, and by the start of 2022, one in two of Australia's COVID fatalities had been recorded in this state. The Victorian approach, particularly the social and economic consequences for people who live in Melbourne, remains a bitterly contested story. Josh Frydenberg, Australia's treasurer throughout the pandemic, describes it as 'the biggest public policy failure by a state government in living memory'. The Victorian Government, backed by modelling done by some of the same researchers who informed the NSW response, insists its actions saved tens of thousands of lives. In November 2021, when Daniel Andrews announced that Victoria was finally opening up, the premier was emphatic: 'We have saved lives, we have kept people safe.'

Debate about how Victoria responded to the pandemic and what Melbourne endured as a consequence has been largely framed as a binary proposition: either you supported protracted lockdowns in pursuit of 'COVID-zero'—an epidemiological nirvana where you have no local transmission of the virus—or you supported no public health interventions at all. When put in the hands of an effective political communicator, this false choice is readily presented as no choice—unless you backed the government approach or you were happy for the virus to kill old people. In an echo of the national security arguments used by federal government ministers to shield counterterrorism and hardline border policies from scrutiny, journalists, epidemiologists and rival parliamentarians who questioned the Victorian Government's approach were accused of undermining public health and putting people's lives at risk. Scientists who provided modelling for the government were told not to publicly discuss their work.

This framing obscures a more complex picture. Preventing people from becoming infected with COVID before the arrival of vaccines, particularly the old and those already sick, was universally accepted as a public health goal. Not even Sweden, the country cited by advocates and opponents of a more laissez-faire response to the pandemic, let the virus rip. When Melbourne was entering its second-wave lockdown in July 2020, Swedes were being urged to work from home and avoid public transport, public access to nursing homes was restricted, and bars and restaurants were limited to table service.[4] The question facing governments around the world was not whether to try to reduce the spread of the virus, but rather how best to achieve this. The idea of locking down an entire city for months on end to stop anyone getting sick—the intersection between the ready use of precautionary lockdowns and a COVID-zero goal—is a radical policy prescription.

One of the WHO's special envoys on COVID, Imperial College London's Institute of Global Health Innovation Co-Director Dr David Nabarro, repeatedly made the point throughout 2020 that, although lockdowns can be necessary to delay the peak of an epidemic, they should be used sparingly because of the damage they do. He argued that the social and economic impacts of lockdowns, particularly on poor people, means they should be used as a last resort and for the shortest duration possible. He urged governments to do everything possible to avoid lockdowns as a primary means of containing COVID. He tells me: 'Why on earth are people always going on about lockdown as though that is the best thing a government can do when, in my judgement, it was a failure of narrative and a failure of policy?'

The Victorian Government did not enter the pandemic planning to use lockdowns to eliminate the virus. The idea that this was possible, much less something the government should do, only took shape through our long COVID winter of 2020. There was concern over this epidemiological mission creep within senior ranks of the government, and misgivings were held by public health officials about the implications and ethics of such a response. Around the government's Crisis Council of Cabinet, the state's peak decision-making body through the first year of the pandemic, senior ministers challenged the advice and assumptions that were being relied upon to justify such drastic steps. The final decision to 'go for zero', as Victoria's Chief Health Officer Brett Sutton described the new strategy, was not easily reached. More than two years later, the government's justification for its approach is both powerful and simple: if not for the measures it took, many more people would have died.

'What we could have had was 20 000 dead from COVID,' says infectious-disease expert Allen Cheng, an influential figure within Victoria's public health response. 'There is probably no other situation where it is so obvious what could have happened.'

This counterfactual is an essential consideration in any fair assessment of Melbourne's pandemic experience. But it doesn't justify everything.

As the first chill of winter blew across Melbourne in 2020, a relieved city slowly exhaled. Having been told to prepare for the onslaught of a deadly virus and, potentially, scenes of the kind witnessed in New York City, where hospitals and morgues were overwhelmed and unclaimed bodies were buried in communal graves on Hart Island, our first wave of COVID infections ended up being little more than a ripple. A massive, emergency logistical operation overseen by the Victorian Government had prepared us for the worst. Thousands of ventilators had been ordered in, and plans were drawn up to transform the cavernous Melbourne Convention and Exhibition Centre into a 1000-bed intensive-care hospital and temporary morgue. Epidemiological modelling commissioned by the Andrews government predicted that, in the absence of strict social distancing and other mitigating measures, as many as 36 000 people could die in the state. Instead, nineteen people died in Victoria from COVID-19 in the first wave of infections.

Across all of Australia, the first-wave epidemic peaked at just under 300 cases a day. There were difficult outbreaks in New South Wales, where the virus escaped from a cruise ship and leached into nursing homes, including Newmarch House in Penrith. But remarkably, by the end of the first wave, only 113 lives had been lost to the virus across the nation. Inside the intensive-care units (ICUs) of big-city hospitals, well-prepared nurses waited for sick people who never arrived. Australians, not for the first time, counted ourselves lucky and, perhaps, an exception to global rules. Was the pandemic something that overran hospitals and caused mass loss of life only in other countries? Premier Andrews announced that stay-at-home orders, in force since 30 March, would be lifted and pubs reopened. Kids were told to get ready for school. As our case numbers dropped to near zero, a mild strain of hubris spread through our pandemic response. We didn't know that a more deadly second-wave epidemic had already begun.

On 9 May, a family of four arrived in Melbourne from Bangladesh, a country that since late March had been on forced 'holiday' to keep kids away from school and workers out of factories. They were already infected with COVID-19 when they checked into the Rydges on Swanston, a private hotel which had agreed to house returned travellers under the Victorian Government's hotel quarantine program. By 25 May, staff and security guards at the hotel had contracted the virus. They took it home to their families, who in turn spread it to their friends, local schools and other workplaces. This chain of events would have profound implications for everyone living in the state.

By the beginning of July, 484 people were registered as residents at the Alfred Street housing commission flats, with another 100 people living there unofficially or visiting at the time of the lockdown. The tower, constructed in 1968 in the shape of a three-point star, was the largest and last apartment block built on what is known as the North Melbourne estate. This was the culmination of a 'war on slums' declared by the Victorian Government thirty years earlier,[5] when squalid shacks running off bluestone laneways in North Melbourne, Carlton, Collingwood and Richmond housed families in abject poverty. The Victorian premier whose reforms led to the construction of the towers, Sir Albert Dunstan, was a wheat farmer and grazier from near Swan Hill who entered parliament representing the Victorian Farmers Union and eventually led the wartime government of the United Country Party. Described as a 'short, stocky man with shrewd blue eyes and a "curiously frog-like mouth"',[6] Dunstan was renowned as a straight-talking political pugilist with a knack for quickly assessing complex situations. It is said that when Dunstan toured Melbourne's inner-city slums in 1936 with social reformer Frederick Barnett, an accountant and devout Methodist, he was so disturbed by what he saw that he couldn't sleep for days. That experience prompted Dunstan to establish the Slum Abolition Board, and two years later the Victorian Housing Commission, which oversaw the construction of about fifty high-rise towers across postwar Melbourne.

As the second-wave epidemic spread across Melbourne's northern and western suburbs, Victoria's public health officials kept an increasingly nervous watch on the towers. At 33 Alfred Street, there are 152 residential apartments spread across twelve floors. These are connected by two central lifts and four staircases, and residents share a laundry. The apartments are not well ventilated and don't have balconies. Although nearly half the residents are children who are at small risk of getting seriously sick with COVID, the towers are also home to elderly people and others in poor health. The largest flats have three bedrooms but some house families with six or seven children. Annaliese van Diemen, a communicable diseases expert who at the time was in charge of Victoria's public health interventions, says she was frightened of where the outbreak in the towers could lead: 'I was quite terrified, to be honest, that we would see within a week many hundreds of cases if we continued and so it was a very, very difficult decision.'[7]

Van Diemen's fear was based, in part, on Hong Kong's experience with a much deadlier pathogen nearly twenty years earlier. The SARS (severe acute respiratory syndrome) epidemic which, like COVID, emerged out of China, infected more than 8000 people globally and killed 774. Among those killed by the highly virulent coronavirus were forty-two people who lived in the Block E building of the Amoy Gardens apartment complex in Hong Kong. Unlike Melbourne's housing commission towers, Amoy Gardens was privately owned and maintained. In March 2003, due to an unlikely combination of aerosol physics and the neglected maintenance of an ageing sewerage system, it became a death trap.

An investigation commissioned by the Hong Kong Government traced the outbreak to a man from mainland China who visited his brother's apartment in Block E. Subsequent studies have concluded that, from there, the virus entered the sewerage system, escaped back into the man's apartment in aerosol form through dried seals in the plumbing, and travelled through an air shaft into upper-floor apartments.[8] Zeb Jamrozik, a Melbourne-based infectious disease ethicist who worked for Victoria's health department in the second year of the pandemic, says that notwithstanding the differences between SARS and COVID, and the peculiar method of transmission at Amoy Gardens, the idea of entire apartment buildings becoming infected with the virus was a hot-button concern within the state's public health team. Australia's most senior public health official, Chief Medical Officer Paul Kelly, supported the lockdown of the Melbourne housing commission towers, describing them as 'vertical cruise ships', a reference to Sydney's infamous outbreak during the country's first wave of infections—officials from DHHS used the same phrase in their defence of the tower lockdown.

The cruise ship analogy evokes two things. The first is the public health crisis that unfolded in March 2020 at Sydney's Circular Quay, when 2650 passengers aboard the just-arrived *Ruby Princess* ocean liner were allowed to disembark despite there being suspected COVID cases on board. That sequence of events was eventually linked to more than 700 COVID infections and sixty deaths among passengers, crew, or people who got the virus from someone who'd been on the ship. The second is the political crisis that ensued. The *Ruby Princess* episode exposed the complexity and, at times, confusion that exists in policy areas where federal and state responsibilities overlap, and the furious blame-shifting likely to accompany any significant COVID outbreak. A special commission of inquiry was established by the NSW Government, and its findings were damning. Although it found no systemic failures, it attributed the outbreak to a series of serious, inexcusable and inexplicable errors made by NSW health officials. In response, NSW premier Gladys Berejiklian issued a public apology to the families of everyone who fell sick or died. In Victoria, there was immense pressure on the Andrews government and its senior health officials not to make a similarly catastrophic mistake.

Four days before the tower lockdown was announced, Brett Sutton provided Daniel Andrews with devastating news. For the previous month, the government's COVID response team had been tracking with increasing concern what looked like a new wave of infections. They weren't certain where the outbreak had started and whether it had been seeded by a single source or many. To get a better idea of what they were dealing with, DHHS commissioned a group of cold-case investigators, scientists who work for the Doherty Institute's Microbiological Diagnostic Unit Public Health Laboratory, to trace the origins of all cases recorded in Victoria since the start of the pandemic. Using genomic tracing techniques—a type of analysis which maps the entire DNA code of a viral sample retrieved by a test swab—the investigators were able to distinguish separate strands of transmission. When this was combined with information already gathered by DHHS contact tracers through their interviews with confirmed cases, Professor Sutton and Victoria's COVID response team had a map showing where each outbreak began and who passed the virus to whom. They discovered that nearly every case recorded in Victoria since the end of May, including the cases recorded in the housing commission towers, could be traced back to two quarantine hotels.

Although quarantine is traditionally a federal government responsibility, the Victorian Government had offered to run the hotel quarantine program, as agreed at a meeting of first ministers of all states and prime minister Scott Morrison. The political implication for the Andrews government, whether fair or not, was inescapable: whatever the toll from Victoria's second wave of COVID, the state government would be blamed. This was not lost on Daniel Andrews, a skilled political operator who had led the Labor Party to two election victories, or on his Cabinet ministers, when they took the decision to place the towers immediately into lockdown.

When Annaliese van Diemen rose early on 4 July after a restless night, she also understood what was at stake. There were twenty-three confirmed COVID cases at 33 Alfred Street and thirty-four cases in total across the nine towers. Van Diemen, in addition to her role as public health commander, was filling in that day for Brett Sutton as acting chief health officer. This meant that, if any emergency measures were to be taken, they would require her signature on legally binding public health orders. The previous night, van Diemen had sent a message to one of the state's most senior bureaucrats, DHHS secretary Kym Peake, expressing her concern about the risk of the virus spreading exponentially through the towers and into surrounding suburbs. She flagged the prospect of things needing to move very quickly the next day. This ensured that Premier Andrews and his political advisers were also briefed on the emerging crisis. Two months earlier, Andrews had personally appointed Peake, a rising star of the Victorian Public Service, to lead the bureaucratic response to the health emergency. She was given a direct line to the premier, and her instructions were clear. 'In this role, you are accountable to me,' he told her.

Van Diemen's idea was for a cordon sanitaire to be established around the towers. Cordons sanitaires, a seventeenth-century French term for isolating a geographical area to prevent the spread of an infectious disease, had been used in medieval Europe to stop the spread of the plague, in nineteenth-century America to contain yellow fever, and more recently in Zaire (now the Democratic Republic of the Congo) to control an Ebola outbreak. It is a contentious intervention because, although it protects the broader community, it can victimise the people trapped inside the cordon. This risk is heightened when you are locking up migrant communities, like those who live at 33 Alfred Street. As Saeed Ali points out, it was only six weeks earlier that George Floyd's murder beneath the knee of a Minneapolis police officer had sparked global demonstrations against racial injustice. 'The Black Lives Matter movement was going crazy and they were locking down a community of predominantly black people,' he says. 'The community viewed the police as the enemy and the measures taken at the time showed them they were right.'

When considering Victoria's approach to the pandemic and the decisions of the Andrews government, it is important to acknowledge that everyone charged with responding to this global health crisis—political leaders, bureaucrats, public health officials and epidemiologists—wanted the same thing: to limit the sickness, death and social damage wrought on communities all over the world by a novel coronavirus. As Peter Doherty, Australia's Nobel prize–winning immunologist, succinctly puts it: 'COVID-19 is a story of a bad virus, not bad guys.' There is no evidence that the government agencies which responded to the tower outbreak were motivated by malice. It seems particularly unlikely that the public health orders signed by Annaliese van Diemen, a woman who provoked the ire of conservative commentators by comparing the impact of white settlement on Indigenous Australians to the arrival of SARS-CoV-2, contained racist intent. There is no question, however, that the tower residents were treated differently. They felt it acutely and everyone else could see it. As Ombudsman Deborah Glass remarks as she greets me inside her Bourke Street office in central Melbourne, can anyone imagine the residents of a luxury apartment block in South Yarra being treated this way?

Eight days before Christmas 2020, the Ombudsman's 200-page report into the detention of public housing residents landed like a brick inside the Victorian Parliament along with its most damning finding: that the tower lockdown unlawfully breached the human rights of people forcibly detained in their homes. Glass's report is methodical and carefully balanced. The Ombudsman's investigation was prompted by a deluge of complaints from inside the tower buildings at the height of the lockdown, and Glass's findings take into account this testimony, the lengthy submissions of DHHS lawyers, and, most importantly, van Diemen's testimony about the judgements she made, advice she provided and decisions she took. Glass accepts van Diemen's evidence that there was a compelling public health reason to confine the tower residents to their apartments. As she tells me, she is not a public health expert; it is not her job to question the veracity of health advice, only to establish what it was. The mistake made by the Andrews government is it didn't follow this advice when it locked down the towers.

If van Diemen had had her way, the residents would have been given thirty-six hours or so to prepare for lockdown. That was the plan forming in her head when she went to bed the night before. And as late as 1 p.m. on the Saturday, that was what she still expected to happen. Then something changed. She told the Ombudsman she didn't know who decided to enforce an immediate lockdown, only that a decision to do so appeared to have been taken by someone early that afternoon. Even though it needed to be her signature on the public health orders, no-one sought her advice on whether a snap intervention was necessary. Had anyone asked her, she would have told them it wasn't. 'It wasn't discussed with me and therefore I didn't advise that for infection control purposes it needed to happen instantaneously,' she said in her evidence.[9] 'I didn't have the whole story and I still don't know what information was put forward pertaining to that decision.'

The decision to implement an immediate lockdown in the nine housing commission towers appears to have been made at a 1.45 p.m. meeting of the Crisis Council of Cabinet, whose members had been handpicked by Premier Andrews. Neither van Diemen nor the Ombudsman know for sure, because the government refused to provide the investigation with the minutes of that meeting, citing Cabinet confidentiality.

The Cabinet decision to detain people in their homes to stop the spread of a virus had no legal force until it was supported by public health orders signed by the chief health officer or their delegates—under the laws enacted at the time, they are the only officials with the launch codes for emergency public health powers. This led to a bizarre episode during which van Diemen found herself in the back of a car, being driven to a press conference to announce an unprecedented lockdown, trying to read on her mobile phone the legal advice and human rights considerations she was lawfully required to contemplate before making such an order. She was emailed the material at 3.46 p.m. Eighteen minutes later, she was standing next to the premier as he announced the tower lockdown.

Throughout the pandemic, Victorians were assured by their premier, health ministers and other senior government officials that decisions taken in response to the emergency were always based on health advice. This was a government that followed the science, they repeatedly told us. The frantic hours before the tower lockdown challenge this notion. In this instance, public health advice was retrofitted to a political decision already made and ready to announce. Journalists were on their way to the press conference before van Diemen had read the final orders. She told the Ombudsman that bringing the lockdown forward instead of giving residents some time to prepare made no difference to the outbreak inside the tower buildings. She also felt that, by the time she was asked to consider the implications of what the government had decided to do, it was too late for her to object.

The Ombudsman says it was the government's failure to seek properly considered advice, particularly on the human rights implications of any proposed public health orders, that rendered the lockdown unlawful. The reason the government took this approach is clear to the tower residents and to the Ombudsman. 'The priority was on security: "We have to stop these people from getting out,"' Glass tells me. 'The contrast between that and every other lockdown, in which people had notice of the intention to do so, could go out and get their groceries, buy their nappies, whatever, was so striking. The question is, why was that? What was it about the towers that was different? There wasn't a public health justification. Where their argument is fundamentally flawed is that was not the advice of the public health expert. That is undeniable. It comes down to the point the residents make: they couldn't be trusted.'

Glass continues: 'If they had not locked down the towers without notice, on the evidence of the public health expert it would not have made a difference to the public health response. It would have made a huge difference to the 3000 people affected and we would not have seen these scenes that bounced around the world. We saw from the complaints we received at the time this sense of shame. How could we do this? How were we doing that to our own people?'

The Victorian Government has never acknowledged that it got this wrong. Its subsequent actions tell us it did. A year after the tower lockdown, there was another COVID outbreak inside the housing commission flats. In August 2021, as Melbourne was entering what would become another protracted lockdown, a family living in a housing commission flat in Flemington tested positive to the Delta variant of COVID-19. There was no crisis meeting of Cabinet, there was no police operation launched in response. Other tower residents weren't locked in their homes. Instead, the infected family was quarantined and health authorities provided additional tests for other people living in the building. In other words, an outbreak in a high-rise public housing building was treated in much the same way as you'd treat such an occurrence in any other apartment block. 'It was a public health response rather than a security response,' Glass says. 'You saw public health teams in place rather than the police.'

What does the tower lockdown tell us more broadly about the Victorian Government's response to the COVID crisis and

Melbourne's experience of the pandemic? In her findings, Deborah Glass makes a salient point about the importance of human rights in a time of crisis. 'We may be tempted, during a crisis, to view human rights as expendable in the pursuit of saving human lives,' she says. 'This thinking can lead to dangerous territory. It is not unlawful to curtail fundamental rights and freedoms when there are compelling reasons for doing so; human rights are inherently and inseparably a consideration of human lives. The government need not apologise for taking necessary and difficult action to keep us all safe—in the face of this pandemic, there is no alternative but to accept the advice of our state's leading infectious-disease expert. But the decision to bring forward the operation to detain 3000 people immediately did not appear to have been based on such advice, and like the virus it sought to contain, risked the health and wellbeing of many people.'

This is not a libertarian argument. The Victorian Ombudsman is an experienced lawyer who previously chaired the Independent Police Complaints Commission of England and Wales, and brought fresh eyes and new vigour to the Hillsborough Stadium disaster investigation in 1989. She has no truck with the views of self-styled freedom fighters who denounce all forms of COVID restrictions. Glass received scores of complaints later in the pandemic about vaccine mandates and declined to investigate them, having judged that it was reasonable to require people to be inoculated against a virus that had inflicted so much death and misery around the world. Glass doesn't hold that human rights are absolute, whether in a public health crisis or otherwise, nor that the government imperative to preserve public health is in conflict with its responsibility to uphold human rights. As she says, these two things are entwined: 'To suggest there is somehow a contradiction between human rights and human lives is to fundamentally misunderstand our entire human rights ethos. To suggest it is one or the other is fundamentally misconceived. Human rights give you a framework within which to make decisions about a crisis like a pandemic.'

The Ombudsman's primary recommendation was for the Victorian Government to apologise for the harm and distress it caused the people it detained without notice in the North Melbourne and Flemington housing towers. The government flatly refused. Richard Wynn, the minister responsible for housing at the time of the lockdown, said the government would not apologise for saving lives—something no-one has asked them to do. Daniel Andrews, when questioned about human rights during the pandemic, retorted: 'It's not about human rights, it's about human life.' It was a pithy line, although Andrews isn't the first political leader to use it. In July 2018, then Philippines president Rodrigo Duterte gave a state-of-the-nation address to the country's congress. At the time, he was being attacked by international human rights groups for the brutal excesses of his war on drugs, a ruthless campaign the United Nations (UN) estimated had resulted in the deaths of 8000 people, mostly through extrajudicial killings by police. Duterte said he was less worried about the rights of drug dealers than the deaths their product caused. He told his critics: 'Your concern is human rights, mine is human lives.'[10]

Daniel Andrews is a long way from Rodrigo Duterte, but there was an authoritarian instinct in his response to the tower outbreak. We saw this same instinct in other public health interventions his government approved. Throughout the first two years of the pandemic, the Victorian Government enforced emergency measures such as a night-time curfew and a 'ring of steel' comprising police barricades around greater Melbourne, and cleared life from suburban and city streets. A blizzard of public health orders regulated nearly every aspect of life, right down to who we listed as an intimate partner, how many people were allowed to stand around the same barbecue, and whether children could go to school, see their friends or kick a footy in the street. As a public health response, it was highly effective in limiting the movement of people and, for a time, the spread of the virus. It also carried significant costs.

The Victorian Government, much like its attitude towards the tower lockdown, is unapologetic for all of this. For the residents of the Alfred Street commission towers, this is what stings the most. 'These people have a lot of heart and soul,' Hava Buday says. 'They can forgive you if you have messed up or done something wrong, but at least say you are sorry. At least say you didn't mean for it to turn out that way. We didn't even get that. It was pretty much a "Fuck you, we did what we had to and you can't do anything about it".'

CHAPTER 2
THE MAN FROM WUHAN

Robin Scott knew something was seriously wrong when, as the taxi carrying him, his wife and two-year-old son wound through the streets of Guangzhou, he saw barely another car on the road. If you have ever been to Guangzhou, you will understand why. A city of twenty million people barely stops to rest, much less sleep. The throbbing commercial, trading and transport heart of southern China, Guangzhou is a sister city to Sydney and shares her love of a good deal and fast times. For nearly forty years, it has been a place where Australian export companies have found new customers and unlocked spectacular fortunes. It is a city that built an entirely new, towering central business district in a matter of a few years, so that China could show a modern, urban face to the world at the 2010 Asian Games. And now its doors were locked tight, its people too scared to venture out. Victoria's assistant treasurer was thankful he and his wife hadn't baulked at the inflated asking price of a one-way Vietnam Airlines flight out of Dodge.

It was 25 January 2020, and Scott says he counted three other cars on the road throughout the entire 30-kilometre trip between the hotel and the airport. As they were driving through the deserted streets, his wife Shaojie Wu—'Tiger' to her Australian friends—checked her Chinese social media feeds for the latest news about the highly contagious pathogen. The city of Wuhan, the epicentre of what was being reported as a novel coronavirus resembling the deadly SARS virus which had plagued southern China in 2002 and 2003, had been thrown into lockdown two days earlier. At 2 a.m., residents in that city received an official notification on their mobile phones telling them that, eight hours later, all public transport would cease, and flights in and out of Guangzhou would be grounded as well. On the same day the text message went out, construction was ordered to begin on a massive new field hospital in Wuhan to treat the critically ill—it was built in ten days. In the province of Henan, the local governor dispatched earth-moving equipment to dig up the roads leading out of Wuhan so that the virus couldn't hitch a ride. By then, however, health officials in Beijing knew it was too late.

For the previous month, people had been turning up at Wuhan hospitals and doctors' offices with mysterious cold-like symptoms and fevers. Since the second week of January, they had started dying of pneumonia and multiple organ failure. Beijing, although limiting its hard quarantine measures to Wuhan, knew the virus had reached other major cities in China. Thailand, South Korea and Japan had recorded cases. Guangzhou registered its first case on 21 January. By the time the Scott family felt the rumble and rush of take-off above Guangzhou Baiyun International Airport, a local epidemic was spreading on the ground below.

After what he saw on the streets of Guangzhou, Scott needed no convincing that Australia, like the rest of the world, was facing the prospect of an economic, social and public health catastrophe. 'I don't like the Chinese Communist Party, but they are not irrational actors,' he says. 'They wouldn't lock down if they didn't think it was a big problem.' He is not an infectious disease expert but, as the former finance and multicultural minister explains, he has a head for maths. Scott told his colleagues, including Premier Daniel Andrews, other ministers and federal parliamentarians, that Australia needed to take the threat seriously and shut its border to China. Instead, they seemed mostly worried about diners saying racist things at Chinese restaurants. 'The human mind is terrible at low-probability, high-consequence risk,' he reflects. 'People thought I was mad, that I had post-traumatic stress or was some sort of germaphobe. No, I was numerate. I knew what an exponential curve looked like.'

At the start of 2020, anyone would have been hard-pressed to pull the attention of Australian governments away from the disaster we were already confronting. Throughout 2019, the red-dirt centre of our dust-dry continent had baked under an interminable sun. The monsoon rains which normally soak the northern part of the country had arrived late, and in their absence, a heat unlike anything previously recorded cooked the nation's interior. Alice Springs, a desert town that sits 600 metres above sea level, recorded temperatures approaching 45 degrees Celsius. On the edge of the Simpson Desert, where dotted lines on a map form the corner of Queensland, the Northern Territory and South Australia, the average temperature for the entire month of December was 42 degrees Celsius. Dr Andrew Watkins, the head of long-range forecasts at the Bureau of Meteorology, told me we had never recorded temperatures that high. All it took was a north wind blowing into Victoria, a strong westerly coming into New South Wales, and the east coast of Australia was primed for destructive fires.

When the fires did come, they set alight our coast, mountains and even areas of rainforest that had never burned in recorded history, scorching 24 million hectares, razing 3000 homes and killing thirty-three people. Holiday-makers were stranded on the sands of coastal towns, and local residents could only prepare to leave and hope they found something other than ash upon their return. On 31 December, when the Wuhan Municipal Health Commission belatedly issued an emergency notice to the WHO relating to a cluster of unexplained pneumonia cases, Victoria was waking to the news that Mallacoota, a popular holiday town in the far east of the state, had been overrun by a firestorm. Up and down the NSW and Victorian coasts, fires were still burning out of control and the army was sent to evacuate stranded holiday-makers. A lab report from Wuhan, for all its troubling portents, seemed a distant concern to a country ablaze.

Brett Sutton should have been on summer holidays at the end of his first year as Victoria's chief health officer. Instead, he was at his desk at the health department's Lonsdale Street offices, having regular phone hook-ups with other public health officials along Australia's east coast to make sure communities blanketed in smoke and ash had the face masks they needed to breathe a little easier. Sutton in late 2018 had stepped into what, in Victoria, had become a precarious job. One of his predecessors, Dr Robert Hall, was sacked after a gastro outbreak at a nursing home, and another, Dr Rosemary Lester, retired after carrying the can for the Victorian Government's slow response to a fire in a coalmine—one of the leading critics of that response was Daniel Andrews, then leader of the Victorian Opposition. When Professor Sutton was appointed, he said he was 'flabbergasted' to get the gig. It is normally a mid-ranked role within Victoria's health department, but in times of public health emergency, it assumes enormous influence over government decisions and extraordinary coercive powers.

Sutton saw the Black Summer fires as further evidence that climate change, rather than any existing or undiscovered pathogen, posed the greatest risk to Victoria's health and wellbeing. Yet, on 2 January 2020, an email he received via ProMED, a global reporting service used by physicians, scientists, government officials and journalists to alert one another about infectious disease outbreaks, caught his attention. 'It talked about a cluster of severe respiratory illness in Hubei Province with links to the Wuhan market,' he recalls. 'It was one of those things that made me think there could be something really significant in this.'

Sharon Lewin, an infectious disease physician and director of Melbourne's Peter Doherty Institute for Infection and Immunity, says she was doing her rounds at the Alfred Hospital on 6 January when one of her patients asked about Wuhan. The patient was Chinese and had been reading on WeChat about a bunch of pneumonia cases that had been linked to a seafood market. Did she know how serious it was? Should he be worried? That night, Professor Lewin searched for news of the outbreak, but the only thing she could find was a small BBC story. Shortly after, she travelled to Thailand, and while there she saw reports that a local case had been recorded. The day she arrived back in Melbourne, as she was driving home from the airport, she rang Jodie McVernon, an Oxford-trained epidemiologist at the Doherty. 'You know, this thing is hotting up,' she told McVernon. 'There are cases outside of China and the predictions are that it is person-to-person spread. I think we should at least get everyone together and find out what people are hearing.' Within a few days, McVernon would start working on modelling for the federal government which would inform one of the most important decisions of the entire pandemic: to close the border to China.

Brendan Murphy was also paying close attention to developments in Wuhan. As Australia's chief medical officer, Professor Murphy was the person responsible under our national biosecurity laws for blowing the whistle on any emerging disease which posed a threat to public health. On 20 January, members of the Commonwealth Department of Health's international surveillance team picked up reports that Dr Zhong Nanshan, China's foremost respiratory disease expert, had declared on state-controlled television that the novel coronavirus at the centre of the Wuhan cases was transmitting between people. Until then, the official line from the Chinese Government had been that it was dealing with an exotic, zoological disease which only passed between animals and people. The likely culprit was thought to be infected bats at the Huanan Seafood Market. A new virus that passes between bats and humans, although a virological fascination, was not cause for alarm. Dr Nanshan's intervention was. He had been dispatched by Beijing to Wuhan from his Guangzhou home to investigate and report on the outbreak. Dr Nanshan, an 86-year-old former president of the Chinese Medical Association and the celebrated public health hero of the SARS epidemic, had travelled close to 1000 kilometres through the night on a high-speed train to find out what was going on in Wuhan.

Professor Murphy called a meeting of the Australian Health Protection Principal Committee (AHPPC). The members of the committee were familiar enough with Dr Nanshan to know he carried the full imprimatur of Beijing. They also knew that what he had said on Chinese television was a game changer: the Wuhan outbreak was on the road to becoming a pandemic. Murphy called Australia's health minister, Greg Hunt, to tell him that he planned to formally list the Wuhan virus as a human coronavirus with pandemic potential, putting Australia on a public health footing to shut its border to China and declare a biosecurity emergency. Hunt says that Murphy and his team, acting ahead of the WHO, recognised in the biological structure of the nascent virus an enormous potential for transmission. 'It was unlikely to be like anything we had seen in our lives,' he says. Neither of them knew the virus was already here.

On 24 January, Professor Rhonda Stuart, Director of Infection Prevention at Monash Health, Victoria's largest health service, received a phone call in her office at the Monash Medical Centre in Clayton, in Melbourne's south-east. A 58-year-old Chinese national had just walked into the centre's emergency department with a fever and a cough. He didn't speak English but his daughter said he'd travelled to Australia from Wuhan six days earlier. As luck would have it, Professor Stuart had not long ago visited the emergency department and walked staff through this exact scenario. They had previously trained to receive Ebola and drug-resistant tuberculosis cases. Now they put into action their newly drawn up plans for the novel coronavirus. The Wuhan man was immediately admitted to the hospital and isolated from other patients. He was given a bed in a negative-pressure room, which is where air from inside the room is pushed out of the hospital through a high-efficiency particulate-absorbing filter, negating the risk of an airborne virus escaping into other parts of the hospital. The nursing staff who attended him wore full protective clothing, including N95 masks which, when fitted properly, shield the wearer's face and nose against tiny aerosol particles. The next day, he was confirmed as Australia's first COVID case.

At the time, Professor Stuart thought she was being overcautious. Only a few days earlier, it wasn't even thought that people passed on the virus. However, as she recalls, you don't take chances with a largely unknown pathogen. 'We managed it as though it could be the worst infection we'd had,' she says. For the next twenty-one days, the man was kept in isolation. He didn't get critically sick; he didn't pass on the virus to anyone, including his family; and he recovered well enough to return to China. Professor Stuart was intrigued by the case but thought it might turn out to be a clinical oddity. 'We'd prepared for Ebola and we'd prepared for SARS and never saw a case,' she says. 'You sort of think, "Oh well, this is one case, we are not going to see many more of these."' Instead, the man from Wuhan was the first of millions of cases in Australia and the start of a rolling public health emergency—over the next two years, the ensuing economic and social upheaval would redefine the relationship between government and citizens, states and the Commonwealth, and individual responsibility and public good, and change how we worked, studied, celebrated, mourned, played and prayed. Although no-one knew it at the time, he was also the start of our way out.

Swabs taken from the man's nose and throat were sent to the Victorian Infectious Diseases Reference Laboratory (VIDRL), a public health laboratory within the Doherty Institute. VIDRL includes a high-security quarantine lab where scientists can safely study the world's deadliest pathogens, and it was there, over the next few days, that a team led by senior medical scientist Julian Druce grew the coronavirus from the man's samples. It was the first time this had been done anywhere in the world and was the first step towards developing antiviral treatments and, potentially, a vaccine. It also revealed, through an electron microscope, a now iconic image to the world: the telltale spiked-ball shape of the novel coronavirus.

Within hours of news getting out about what people at the Doherty had done, the entire infectious disease world wanted to know more. One of the first people to call Sharon Lewin was James Hudson, the Australian representative of Jack Ma, a Chinese businessman and philanthropist whose personal wealth at the time was estimated to be US$25 billion. Ma had heard about the Doherty discovery and offered to give the institute a US$2.15 million grant to develop a vaccine. Another person quick on the phone was Dan Barouch, Director of Boston's Center for Virology and Vaccine Research at the Beth Israel Deaconess Medical Center. Professor Barouch, like Professor Lewin, was one of the world's leading researchers in HIV/AIDs, although he is now best known as the man who made the Johnson & Johnson COVID vaccine. The campaign to make that vaccine began with the phone call to Lewin, and a discussion about whether she could provide him with a live sample of the virus they had grown in the lab.

The pandemic is a very different thing now. If you haven't had COVID-19, someone in your family has. The virus isn't something to be feared anymore, but it remains a constant, unwelcome presence in our lives. Every sniffle, every cough remains a what-if. The daily case numbers no longer stop traffic but still register vaguely, like the forecast for wind direction or high tide. Living with the virus hasn't come easy but we are back to living, released from those interminable months of being confined to our homes, constrained by curfews, and coerced, by threats of fines and appeals to civic responsibility, to follow health edicts pronounced in flat, bureaucratic tones. And mercifully, very few of us have died here compared with most other countries.

To understand where we have ended up, it is important to remember where we thought we were heading. In those early, dystopian months of the pandemic, as the virus overwhelmed First World health systems in Italy, New York and Spain, the federal government commissioned modelling showing that, without the right public health response, up to 150 000 Australians could die.[1] In Victoria, the peak of an unmitigated epidemic was modelled to reach 100 000 cases a day and, potentially, 36 000 deaths. The anxiety that this triggered was most readily seen in supermarket aisles, where panicked families filled trolleys with baked beans, canned tomatoes and pasta, and stripped the shelves of toilet paper. In the parking lot, we argued over car spaces and swore under our breath at those who'd crammed their hatchbacks with fluffy white rolls of SuperSoft. None of this made any sense. Throughout the entire pandemic, the only shortages of toilet paper were caused by people hoarding the stuff. Some were driven by fear of the virus, others by the anticipated loss of control and routine.

Daniel Andrews didn't sugar-coat what was coming. On 10 March 2020, fresh from chairing a three-hour meeting where senior ministers war-gamed the likely shutting of schools, the cancellation of large sporting and cultural events, and forcing people to work from home once the pandemic hit in earnest, the premier stood before television cameras gathered inside the Royal Melbourne Hospital and warned that 'extreme measures' would be required. 'We will need to ask Victorians to do things we have never asked them to do before,' he said. Beside him stood a neat, silver-haired man largely unknown to us. In the months to come, Brett Sutton's face would adorn pillows or dartboards, depending on your view of things. Victoria's health minister, Jenny Mikakos, was also present—she didn't know it then, but within six months, her twenty-year political career would come to an abrupt end. The premier says he clearly remembers that day because the journalists who came to the press conferences were looking intently at him instead of their mobile phones: 'I thought, "Yeah, this is serious, isn't it."'[2]

A striking feature of Australia's initial response was a sudden, unexpected outbreak of political unity. It is easy to forget this, now that the politics of the pandemic have frayed into competing narratives and turned voters against governments. There were times over the past two years when blame-shifting between the states and the Commonwealth—a malaise as prevalent as seasonal flu— or squabbling between neighbouring states over border closures and outbreak responses, was as virulent as the virus itself. This was not the case as Australia emerged from its Black Summer fires into the full glare of the COVID crisis. For a moment in time, as Scott Morrison, a socially conservative, Liberal prime minister from New South Wales, and Daniel Andrews, a Labor premier who refers to Victoria as the progressive capital of Australia, stood on the back porch of the PM's harbourside mansion sipping Scotch and sharing their concerns about what lay ahead, it looked as though the national interest might actually come first.

Australia closed its border to China on 1 February, a week after Robin Scott and his family fled Guangzhou. The urgency of this decision gives an insight into the genuine sense of emergency that had enveloped the most senior figures of the federal government, along with governments around the world. The nominal trigger was that Professor Murphy and the AHPPC had seen evidence that the virus was now passing between people in Beijing. This epidemiological marker surprised no-one. Global case numbers had already outstripped the entire SARS epidemic from seventeen years earlier.

Although COVID wasn't anywhere near as lethal as SARS, a virus that killed one out of five people who breathed it in, it had spread to North America, India, the Middle East and eight European nations. Official case counts had reached double figures in Thailand, Singapore, Japan, South Korea, Taiwan and Australia. Russia, Japan, Pakistan and Italy had already closed their borders to China. Professor Murphy called Greg Hunt on a Sunday morning, while the health minister was watching his son playing cricket, to advise that Australia should follow suit. 'I think it's time,' said the chief medical officer.[3] A meeting of the National Security Committee of Cabinet was called at 2 p.m. that afternoon. By 9 p.m., Australia closed the border to its largest trading partner. Within hours, Donald Trump's White House announced that America had taken the same step.

The WHO, which had yet to declare a pandemic, was opposed to this. It warned that an abrupt disruption of international travel and freight would do more harm than good, particularly at a time when medical supplies needed to be moved quickly around the world. It urged nations to screen for the virus at their borders rather than shut them completely. If that warning reached here, it barely registered. Australia would keep its border closed to China and, eventually, the rest of the world, for the next 750 days. Professor Sharon Lewin says that, if not for that decision, our pandemic experience would have been very different.

In the weeks that followed, as Australia prepared for what was modelled to be a devastating wave of COVID cases, the nation underwent seismic changes. In the space of one week in Melbourne, we went from cramming 86 174 people into the MCG to watch a women's cricket match, to cancelling the Australian Grand Prix and all other large public gatherings, and declaring a state of emergency which remained in place for the next two years.

The morning after Scott Morrison and Daniel Andrews talked on the back porch of Kirribilli House, state, territory and Commonwealth leaders were scheduled to gather at a football stadium in western Sydney for the year's first Council of Australian Governments (COAG) meeting. Established by former prime minister Paul Keating, the forum was as stolid as its acronym suggests. For nearly thirty years, it had wrestled with dry but essential matters at the heart of Australia's federation, such as federal–state financial arrangements and policy demarcations that make the states heavily reliant on Canberra to fund the public services they provide. In recent years, the results of these bouts had been less than spectacular, with the collision of state interests a perennial barrier to meaningful reform. As retired public service mandarin Peter Conran put it in his government-commissioned post-mortem of the forum: 'COAG was a slow, bottom-up framework for intergovernmental cooperation that too often resulted in lowest common denominator outcomes.'[4] The meeting on 13 March 2020 was dominated by the COVID crisis. By the time the state leaders headed to the airport, the forum had ceased to exist. During what had been scheduled as a lunch break attended only by the leaders, Scott Morrison floated an impromptu idea to replace COAG with National Cabinet, a select decision-making body purpose-built to lead Australia through the pandemic.

National Cabinet as a concept promised unprecedented collaboration between the state and federal governments in response to a crisis. It was modelled on the War Cabinet of Robert Menzies, when executive government decision-making was expanded to include direct input from the Opposition. The difference was that, instead of inviting then Opposition leader Anthony Albanese into his Cabinet room, Scott Morrison included state and territory leaders. To inform its deliberations, National Cabinet was given a direct line to the AHPPC, the national public health committee chaired by Professor Murphy which produced consensus advice from the chief health and medical officers of the Commonwealth, states and territories. Under Australia's pandemic plan developed six years earlier, the AHPPC was meant to be the 'key decision maker in a national health emergency'.[5] This meant that, when it came to determining whether businesses should be allowed to stay open or students kept in class, and the isolation and quarantine requirements for anyone sick with the virus or suspected of being a case, every jurisdiction would base its decisions on the same health advice. This in turn would provide a high level of national cohesion and cooperation in our pandemic response. That was the theory, anyway.

The idea of National Cabinet came to Morrison not out of any grand ambition to reform federal–state relations, but a growing concern that, unless something was done, the pandemic would threaten the federation as the last one had 100 years earlier. Its inspiration was an obscure paper written in 1990 by Julian Rait, an eye surgeon and Victorian president of the Australian Medical Association (AMA), when he was doing a summer course in epidemiology at Johns Hopkins University in Baltimore. The paper was a study of the 1919 Spanish flu epidemic in Australia, and the way in which the spread of that deadly virus turned state governments against one another, marginalised the federal government, and undermined public faith in advice that, had it been more closely adhered to, would have saved more lives. Rait's father, a doctor who lived to the remarkable age of 105, endured the pandemic in Hobart as a boy. He recalled accompanying at the age of ten his own father, a city engineer, to Princes Wharf, where corpses were laid out in preparation for burial at sea. Julian Rait's father told him that the government response to the Spanish flu was a 'dog's breakfast', and that the pandemic carried a lesson about how people react to a severe health crisis when governments and conventional medicine lack a single 'voice of truth'. Newspaper journalists and editors who wrote about the pandemic also came in for sharp criticism from Rait's father, who said they 'fanned public reaction with exaggerated reports of cases and deaths along with lurid descriptions of the great plagues of the middle ages'.[6]

The Spanish flu, when compared to COVID-19, was a stone-cold killer. The US Centers for Diseases Control and Prevention estimate that the pandemic caused the deaths of at least fifty million people at a time when the global population was 1.5 billion. In Australia, it caused more than 15 000 deaths, disproportionately killing young, adult men who were unable to stay away from work at the height of the outbreaks. Rait writes in his 1990 paper that the first case was brought to Melbourne by a soldier returning from the battlefields of the Great War in January 1919. Confusion over whether the man had Spanish flu or the previous season's influenza enabled him to travel by train to Sydney. A first-wave epidemic swept across New South Wales between March and May, followed by a larger and deadlier second wave which swamped Sydney and other capital cities in the winter months. Australia, protected from the initial spread of the virus by its isolation and quarantined borders, had tried to prepare for the eventual arrival of the Spanish flu, with the states and the Commonwealth agreeing in November 1918 on a notification system that required states to alert the Commonwealth of any cases they detected. This would enable neighbouring states to close their borders and slow the spread of the virus. Instead, Victoria's failure to promptly confirm and notify the Commonwealth of its first case saw the collapse of the agreement, with all states going it alone via unilateral border closures and differing public health measures.

Some of these measures will be familiar. In Sydney, large public events were cancelled; schools, pubs, theatres, dance halls and churches were shut; and when people left their homes, they had to wear a mask. The social fracturing this caused also rings a bell. As Rait writes:

> There was an unedifying spectacle of some of Australia's most eminent physicians arguing with each other in the popular press over the aetiology, natural history, prevention and treatment of

the disease. With the experts in disarray it was no wonder that people with limited resources to spend on medical care avoided consulting doctors in favour of snake-oil remedies ... Many people rebelled by circumventing the quarantine blockade at state borders or refusing to wear masks. Most people shunned outsiders and visitors from interstate, fearing that they might be a potential source of influenza infection.

Rait's conclusion, borrowed from his father's advice, was that cooperation between state governments and federal health authorities was critical in reducing loss of life in future pandemics.

Rait shared the paper with Hunt, who in turn discussed it with Morrison. On the morning of what would be the final COAG meeting, while Hunt was walking in the bayside woods of Mount Martha, near his electorate office, he and Morrison spoke about the history of the Spanish flu and the pressures that modern Australia would come under if this pandemic was anywhere near as bad. They could also see troubling signs. 'We were looking at what had happened with the federation in that period,' Hunt says. 'The states had basically split. We could see signs that there was a very strong diversity of opinion, where the AMA and different epidemiologists were all putting out views at odds with the chief medical officer. The PM's goal that day was to unify the premiers and the Commonwealth behind a single, national, medical voice which would guide our actions.' This was to be the AHPPC. Morrison knew that if Australia was to respond effectively to the pandemic, he needed a mechanism to bind the states and territories to the same health advice.

Once the final COAG meeting was underway, Professor Murphy addressed the state and territory leaders. He flagged that it was likely, perhaps some weeks down the track, that public health restrictions of a kind not seen since the Spanish flu would be required to slow the spread of the virus. Murphy then left COAG to chair a meeting of the AHPPC, where the overnight developments in China were discussed. In keeping with COAG tradition, the state and territory leaders met on their own for lunch. It was never served. The chief medical officer, at the invitation of the PM, came into the leaders' lunch to address them for a second time. He explained that the situation was now far more urgent and that restrictions were needed in a matter of days. This is the moment when Morrison proposed the idea of National Cabinet. Morrison, a former tourism executive, is not known for his stirring oratory, but according to people in the room, he delivered one of the best speeches of his political career. 'We have a moment in history,' he said. 'We can either fracture or we can unite. History shows that we have to unite.'

From its inception, National Cabinet showed its strengths. On 15 March, Morrison walked out of its inaugural meeting to announce that public gatherings of 500 people or more would be banned, with the exception of schools and workplaces. This might not seem like a big deal now, but at the time it was a public health measure not seen in Australia since the Spanish flu. The prime minister also announced that all overseas arrivals would be required to self-isolate for two weeks. The next day, Daniel Andrews declared a state of emergency and Professor Sutton used his newly enacted emergency powers to give legal force to the National Cabinet directives. Anyone who breached the self-isolation rules faced a fine of up to $20 000. In New South Wales, Minister for Health Brad Hazzard made an order giving force to the same restrictions. By this stage, COVID cases had been detected in all states and territories, and deaths from the virus had been recorded in all mainland states. The state and territory leaders, when they explained the measures, used the same language as the PM. Their shared goal was to slow the rate of infections, to 'flatten the curve' of the coming epidemiological wave, and to give their health systems a chance to cope with the anticipated surge in demand, particularly for intensive care. 'We know that the virus cannot be absolutely stopped, of course not,' Morrison declared. Faced with a fast-spreading virus that had already killed more than

1000 people in Italy and forced that country into national lockdown, Australia was constructing a uniform defence.

Beneath the surface, however, cracks were already starting to emerge. Within the AHPPC, there was disagreement over what restrictions were proportional to the relatively small Australian case numbers and necessary to prevent what might happen if those case numbers continued to grow. The question of whether to close schools and workplaces other than those deemed essential emerged as early fault lines. Professor Murphy and his deputy chief medical officer, Paul Kelly, publicly made the case to keep schools open. They argued that whatever restrictions the states put in place needed to be sustainable through a lengthy outbreak. The notion of keeping kids home from school for months on end was, to them, public health anathema. 'The idea that you can put measures in place for four weeks and suddenly stop them and the virus will be gone is not credible,' Professor Murphy said. Some of the state chief health officers, most notably Victoria's Brett Sutton and Queensland's Jeannette Young, did not accept this. They believed that the virus had already shown that, in the absence of a fast, near-complete lockdown, it would overrun even the best healthcare systems. The disaster that had engulfed Italy and the new one unfolding in New York were cited as tragic lessons on what could happen when countries acted too slowly or not decisively enough when first confronted with an outbreak. Influential public health figures such as Raina MacIntyre, head of biosecurity at the Kirby Institute at the University of New South Wales, called for schools to be shut down immediately. Daniel Andrews had already warned us that 'extreme measures' would be required.

Brett Sutton says there was no 'absolute, unified vision' of how Australia should respond. We were preparing for an influenza pandemic, but the early indications were that COVID-19 was ten to twenty times deadlier than the flu. 'It was a time of enormous flux,' he says. 'Italy was going off, Denmark had just started to pick up, there were all these West European countries that were going from a few cases to hundreds. We knew time was of the essence but no-one had a template to work from.'

Australia and its states were at a point of radical departure from years of pandemic planning. The idea of locking down a city—or, in Australia's case, an entire nation—to stop the spread of an infectious disease had never been contemplated before the COVID crisis. Sharon Lewin, in addition to running the Doherty Institute, leads the Australian Partnership for Preparedness Research on Infectious Disease Emergencies (APPRISE), a network of twenty health and research institutes formed with a federal government grant in 2016 to bolster the nation's preparedness to respond to an infectious disease emergency. APPRISE studied recent outbreaks of deadly pathogens such as MERS (Middle East respiratory syndrome), Ebola and zika virus, and the earlier spread of swine flu and SARS, and it reviewed the Australian Government's management plan for pandemic influenza, its emergency response plan for communicable diseases, and pandemic planning by the states. These plans variously provide for an escalating range of public health measures, including the cancellation of large gatherings and school closures, but it was not until Wuhan that public health and infectious disease experts considered the potential of lockdown. 'This idea of closing everything had never been done before,' Lewin says. 'With Wuhan, it seemed so effective. They did it and a week later, cases came tumbling down. That's why there was this move towards doing it.'

Professor James McCaw, a University of Melbourne mathematician with expertise in infectious disease dynamics, was one of three independent experts invited to join AHPPC. He was involved in our response to swine flu and his research has shaped our pandemic planning for more than a decade. He says that before Wuhan, lockdown would not have been considered a feasible public health response to a viral outbreak: 'If you had asked me in 2019 what would happen if everyone stayed home for three months, I would have told you it's a way of stopping a pandemic. If you had also asked me is this a feasible or palatable response to a pandemic, I would have said no, everyone would laugh you out of the room. It is not that we were surprised that it would work, it's just that no-one believed that it would be something that anyone would be willing to do.' Both Lewin and McCaw are convinced that, in the face of a new virus with significant mortality and no vaccine, a lockdown was absolutely the right thing for Australia to do in March 2020.

Within the AHPPC, there was broad agreement that, to slow the spread of the virus, you needed to stop people from moving between home and work and school and the shops. Within National Cabinet, the Commonwealth and its two biggest states were split over whether people would do this willingly or needed to be compelled. This goes to the heart of the National Cabinet dilemma. Although the new forum was intended to provide national leadership—and perhaps give the prime minister greater personal authority in the pandemic response—most of its decisions could not be enacted by Canberra. The capacity to do things which, until the pandemic, had never been utilised by any Australian Government—closing retail and hospitality outlets, keeping kids home from school en masse, forcing people to work from home instead of the office, limiting the number of people you can have over for a family barbecue or birthday celebration—was grounded in the emergency and public health powers of the states.

In a Westminster system of government, Cabinet decisions are binding on ministers. In this regard, National Cabinet was always a misnomer. From its moment of inception, it lacked agreement from its members to enact its decisions. In the absence of this, it was more an advisory forum than an executive body. This is turn limited the role of prime minister to nominal head of our pandemic response. Had Morrison secured greater solidarity from the states at the start of National Cabinet, perhaps the centrifugal forces which came to bear later in the pandemic could have been kept in check.

Once the virus reached Australia's shores, political affiliation was less important than epidemiology. Victoria and New South Wales were led by governments from different parties, but as the states most exposed to outbreaks because of the size of their populations, service-based economies, and international nature of their capital cities, their interests were more aligned with one another than either was with the Commonwealth. Daniel Andrews and NSW premier Gladys Berejiklian had a good relationship heading into the pandemic and quickly grasped the realpolitik of National Cabinet. They realised that if they joined forces on key issues, they could corner the national response.

In the days after the first National Cabinet meeting, Andrews and Berejiklian became increasingly concerned that Australia was moving too slowly against the virus. Together, they planned an ambush which, if successful, would take the country into its first lockdown and cut it off from the rest of the world. Based in part on the advice they were receiving from their own chief health officers, they wanted to close schools and all non-essential services to slow the rate of infection. They also wanted to close Australia's international border to arrivals from all other countries. They knew these things would be resisted by the prime minister but calculated that, if they acted together at the right time, they would create enough momentum to force changes to the national approach.

Knowledge of the plot was limited to the most senior people in the respective state governments. Andrews and Berejiklian communicated directly, while Andrews's Chief of Staff Lissie Ratcliff and top public servant Chris Eccles liaised with their NSW counterparts Neil Harvey and Tim Reardon. 'It was highly organised,' says a source who knew of the plan. 'Morrison spent a long time trying to play the two off against each other, but Berejiklian and Andrews, at least for the first period, were tight as.' Victoria's Deputy Premier James Merlino says it was a crucial intervention: 'It was the leadership of Victoria and New South Wales, the leadership of Gladys and Dan, that pushed the federal government to close the borders. That action … looking at other parts of the world that were being overrun by this virus and incredible death rates, gave us the time to prepare.'

The two state leaders used a WhatsApp chat group comprising the other state and federal leaders to pressure Morrison to bring forward by forty-eight hours the next scheduled meeting of National Cabinet. As this was happening, other state leaders took matters into their own hands. In the space of five days, Tasmania, the Northern Territory, South Australia, Western Australia and Queensland closed their borders. WA Premier Mark McGowan, a popular leader who would keep his state behind a hard border for the next two years, announced that police would patrol Western Australia's eastern boundaries, and anyone caught crossing in breach of the new border controls would face a $50 000 fine. Where the border decisions of the other state governments were unprecedented since Federation, McGowan's announcement was a classically Western Australian response to a pandemic. In January 1919, when the Spanish flu broke out in Melbourne, WA's acting premier, Hal Colebatch, immediately closed the border. This left his boss, premier Henry Lefroy, stranded on the east coast at a conference of state leaders. Whatever public sympathy there was for Lefroy was dwarfed by the surge in support for Colebatch, who took the former's job three months later. In the current pandemic, Western Australia's hardline border policies climaxed in a magistrate jailing two football supporters for illegally entering the state to watch their team, Melbourne, play in the AFL grand final—the Demons had not won a premiership for fifty-seven years. The pair were fully vaccinated and each returned a negative test before they entered the state on fake drivers' licences, but they received no mercy from the court and spent the next three months inside a maximum-security prison.

The federal government closed Australia's border to international arrivals, other than returning citizens and permanent residents, on 20 March. Two days later, on the morning of the next meeting of National Cabinet, Morrison made what, in any normal time, would have been a show-stopper announcement: a $66 billion economic stimulus package aimed at trying to steer Australia out of a looming recession. He did not announce any new COVID restrictions. Instead, he appealed to people to use common sense and follow the social-distancing rules already in place. This was well short of what Andrews and Berejiklian wanted to hear. Separately but in rapid succession that afternoon, the pair made press statements where they announced that they were taking their own drastic measures to contain the virus. Berejiklian said that, irrespective of what National Cabinet decided later that evening, New South Wales would close all businesses beyond essential services like supermarkets, petrol stations, and freight and logistics companies; she also hinted that schools could soon close. Andrews announced virtually identical measures and went one step further on schools: the school term would end in two days, a week earlier than scheduled, and the premier gave no guarantee that schools would reopen after the holidays. His rhetoric gave that night's National Cabinet meeting little room to move. 'It's clear that if we don't take this step, more Victorians will contract coronavirus, our hospitals will be overwhelmed and more Victorians will die,' Andrews said.

Later that night, the prime minister called a press conference to confirm that, at noon the following day, pubs would close, cinema screens would go dark, restaurant food would only be available in takeaway boxes, and churches would have to limit the number of people they allowed to pray, celebrate or mourn. National Cabinet's position was that schools should remain open—on the available evidence, there was no need to close them. In Victoria, they shut regardless. On the Monday, as shop owners frantically prepared to shift their operations fully online or mothball them altogether,

Melbourne kids went to class for what, for many of them, would be the last time in seventy-seven days. By the end of the week, schoolkids in Queensland, Western Australia and South Australia had joined them. On the night of the National Cabinet meeting, Gladys Berejiklian called Morrison to tell him that, the next day, she would announce that schools would remain open but she would urge parents to keep their kids at home. During a lengthy and at times difficult conversation, the PM urged Berejiklian to reconsider: if New South Wales took the stance she had outlined, it would make the National Cabinet position on schools redundant. Berejiklian explained that parents were already voting with their feet and pulling their kids out of class. Her education advisers were telling her the system couldn't cope if only half the students turned up, and her Cabinet ministers and MPs were all under pressure from constituents for the state to take more decisive action. Her government needed to manage things as best it could.

The nation was now moving quickly to where Victoria had already decided to go. On the evening of 29 March, Morrison walked out of a meeting of National Cabinet and announced that the 'strong advice' for all states was that public gatherings should be banned and people needed to stay at home. In Victoria, the first stay-at-home directions were issued, making it unlawful for anyone to leave their home other than for a handful of specified reasons. Andrews warned that anyone having friends over for a barbecue was breaking the law and could expect police to knock on their door and issue a $1600 fine. On the day Andrews outlined the new 'stage 3' measures, Victoria recorded fifty-six new cases of coronavirus. By then, our first-wave epidemic had already peaked. We would spend the next two months confined by some of the world's most severe COVID restrictions, for a crisis which never arrived.

This episode demonstrated two things which, as the pandemic unfolded, would continue to hold true. The first is that, in a public health crisis, it is the states rather than the Commonwealth that determine the policy response. During World War II, Australia's Labor prime minister John Curtin reshaped the federation—against the fervent opposition of South Australia, Queensland, Victoria and Western Australia—by shifting the power to raise income tax from the states to the Commonwealth. What was intended as a temporary measure to help fund Australia's war effort became a permanent dilution of state power.[7] Throughout the pandemic, however, the Commonwealth relied on state lawmakers to give force to whatever consensus National Cabinet reached. The states were never compelled to do so. The most surprising thing about National Cabinet is how often that consensus prevailed.

The second thing is that, when people feel panicked about a potentially lethal virus, there is little political downside for leaders who favour hard-and-fast restrictions. Every state premier, including Daniel Andrews, emerged from the first-wave epidemic with greater public support than they took in. Mark McGowan's thumping re-election in Western Australia in March 2021, a result which nearly wiped the Coalition parties off the local electoral map, was an emphatic reward for the isolationist policies which kept his state largely COVID-free until the start of 2022. Andrews's dominant role in National Cabinet and surging popularity in Victoria made him, at the time, Australia's pre-eminent Labor leader.

In early May 2020, when case numbers had petered out and the Victorian Government was under pressure to ease restrictions, Andrews's performance received positive reviews from an unlikely source. Jeff Kennett, a former Victorian Liberal premier who, like Andrews, governed with disconcerting authority, praised his successor for sticking to his task. 'He hasn't given in to the bayings of interest groups along the way,' he told me. 'You are ultimately judged by the outcomes, not where you start something like this.' Kennett's judgement is very different now. 'This is a communist state!' he thundered near the end of Victoria's second-wave lockdown. 'If the premier can't lead, get out of the way and let someone else come in and do the job for him.'

Chris MacIsaac describes it as an eerie, uncomfortable quiet. Throughout the panicked days of March 2020, when Australia was subjected to images of breathless COVID patients being treated in the corridors of overwhelmed hospitals in northern Italy, and the dead being carted from New York's Elmhurst Hospital to a refrigerator truck converted into a makeshift morgue, the national response was squarely focused on the intensive-care units of our major city hospitals. Part of this was simple maths. Early studies from China suggested that about one in twenty people who contracted COVID required intensive care, and of those, about half needed the assistance of a mechanical ventilator to breathe.[8] When these ratios were applied to the worst predictions of 100 000 new cases a day in Victoria, it equated to 5000 people needing an ICU bed and about 2300 requiring a ventilator. Victoria began the pandemic with 450 ICU beds. These mismatched numbers were a key consideration that pushed us into lockdown. Yet, at the time when MacIsaac was expecting to be swamped with COVID patients, he saw hardly any. The director of intensive medicine at the Royal Melbourne Hospital isn't complaining, but it felt strange nonetheless, having prepared so extensively for a surge which never came. 'It almost seemed like a phoney war,' he says of those early days. 'We were on stand-by ready to go and had very few patients.'

To prepare for what it thought was coming, the Victorian Government took extraordinary steps to increase the state's ICU capacity. John Brumby, the chair of the Melbourne Convention and Exhibition Centre, confirmed to me that in March 2020, advanced plans were made for the Victorian Government to take over the management of the entire facility and turn it into a 1000-bed intensive-care hospital and morgue on the western edge of the CBD. 'It was just about a done deal,' he said. 'We had builders measuring everything up.' Elsewhere in the city, the government identified empty buildings like the old Peter MacCallum cancer hospital near Parliament House, for conversion into intensive-care spillover facilities. The government announced it was spending $1.3 billion to establish an additional 4500 ICU beds, a figure that dwarfed Australia's entire ICU capacity. That announcement, which seems faintly absurd today, tells us where the government thought the greatest weakness lay in our COVID defences.

Those heady days seem a long time ago to Chris MacIsaac. When we meet at his office inside the intensive-care department in March 2022, it is clear that COVID patients have largely disappeared from the wards. The previous week there were days without a single patient with the virus. At the start of the year, most of those who came in were what MacIsaac calls incidental COVID patients—people who are infected with the virus but need intensive care for unrelated health crises like heart attacks and strokes or critical road trauma. With winter approaching and a more-contagious, less-virulent form of the virus still circulating, the COVID crisis isn't over, but for now, as MacIsaac reflects on the past two years, there is no public health emergency confronting his pandemic-weary staff.

MacIsaac says that, at the start of the first wave, he and other senior physicians at the hospital saw government modelling showing a 'fairly unbelievable' number of admissions for the hospital. He remembers trawling through news and social media reports out of Italy and the United States, reading about hospitals being overwhelmed and ICUs running out of beds and nurses to properly treat people. He knew his staff could respond to a crisis. He saw that first-hand in the aftermath of the Bourke Street tragedy when James Gargasoulas, a 26-year-old man in a drug-induced psychosis, ploughed a maroon Holden Commodore through the city's busiest pedestrian mall. Six people were killed and another twenty-seven were left with horrific leg, spine, internal and head injuries. As the critically injured began arriving in ambulances at the Royal Melbourne Hospital, unrostered staff came into the emergency department and ICU to help out, working late into the night and throughout the coming days. The difference with COVID is that no-one knew how long the crisis would last. 'We knew this event was going to go on, as it has, for weeks, months and years,' says MacIsaac. 'How do you maintain the sustainability of your workforce to respond to that ever-increasing peak in demand?'

Aside from being a senior administrator at the hospital, MacIsaac works as an intensive-care physician. He spends about a third of his working week doing rounds on the wards. He says the hardest conversations he had when planning for the pandemic were about who to treat and who not to treat, if it came to that. 'What we all feared we might get to is some pretty unpleasant triaging decisions,' he tells me. 'Fortunately this never occurred throughout the pandemic, but we were very concerned we may have to make decisions about rationing of healthcare resources, which is not a space that a wealthy country like Australia, with a first-class health system, has faced before. We were worried that we would have to make definitive decisions to deny someone access to intensive care because their chances of survival were low.' Within the hospital, there was a ravenous demand for information about the virus. In the short walk from his office to the wards, MacIsaac would stop to talk to a staff member and realise that, within a few minutes, there were twenty people crowded around, intently following the conversation.

Australia's advantage was that we had time to think about these things. When COVID was unleashed in Wuhan and spread to countries like Italy and Iran, no-one knew what they were dealing with or had a chance to prepare. These were what infectious disease experts call unmitigated epidemics. This is also what the worst-case scenarios in the government-commissioned models were based on. Thanks in part to our geographic isolation and opposite seasons, Australia was never at high risk of an unmitigated pandemic. MacIsaac is convinced we made the right call by heading into lockdown. 'We were so fortunate to benefit from the knowledge of the Northern Hemisphere, to know what kind of response was required,' he says. 'I think quite sensibly, the goal of the pandemic public health response has been to avoid the healthcare system being overwhelmed. Australia and New Zealand were one of the few places that had an opportunity to pursue a lockdown strategy. You would say now, in hindsight, that the virus always surprised us in many ways. History would tell you that you can't control it forever, but I am very grateful we were able to control it for as long as we were.'

Not everyone at the hospital sees it this way. On 25 March, Ben Cowie presented a startling scenario at a meeting of some of the hospital's intensive-care physicians and senior staff. Professor Cowie was as well placed as anyone to know what was coming. He is an infectious disease physician and epidemiologist with appointments at the University of Melbourne, the Royal Melbourne Hospital and the Doherty Institute, where he had led the WHO's global research effort into viral hepatitis. He later joined the Victorian Government's COVID response as a deputy to Professor Sutton. But as he clicked through his presentation slides showing the potential impact of the first-wave epidemic on the Royal Melbourne Hospital, there was scepticism among his audience. According to Professor Cowie, the peak of the wave would crash upon the hospital's ICU wards on 15 June with between 250 and 375 patients in need of intensive care. At the time, the hospital had thirty-two ICU beds.

George Heriot, an infectious disease and general physician, says the modelling felt instinctively wrong. 'You have got to understand that 375 ICU beds at Royal Melbourne is like there is a war in Melbourne,' Dr Heriot says. 'It is so far outside anyone's experience, it is just catastrophic. People were looking at this from a clinical perspective thinking what sort of disease would be required for us to need that sort of ICU capacity. It just seemed fanciful. That would be like smallpox in the Americas.' Dr Heriot remembered similarly dire predictions about the H1N1 virus when it first emerged. 'This has always been the story with major pandemics,' he says. 'Models come out initially with catastrophic predictions and are usually so far wrong that the justification of the modellers—it's important not to underestimate the severity for preparedness—doesn't apply. I don't think you can get away with a ten to 100 times overestimate.' Throughout 2020, the Royal Melbourne Hospital had a total of fifty-two ICU admissions for COVID. During the first-wave epidemic, only one COVID patient required a ventilator. Throughout the first two years of the pandemic, the most COVID patients receiving intensive care at the hospital at any given time was twenty-seven, in October 2021.

Dr Heriot says that, when modelling is routinely wrong by such margins, there is a systemic problem. He says the most likely issue is that researchers, when first confronted with a novel virus, overestimate its severity. The reason for this, which researchers call ascertainment bias, is that when a new disease first emerges, the only patients we know about are those sick enough to see a doctor or go to a hospital. When COVID was tearing through Wuhan, no widespread testing was being done of people with mild or no symptoms. Our initial understanding of the disease was skewed by a necessary and unavoidable focus on the critically ill and dying.

Professor Sharon Lewin rejects this criticism, arguing that while it was true of modelling on the earlier H1N1 crisis, the assumptions about COVID having a 1 per cent infection–fatality ratio, based on data out of China, proved to be right. Dr Heriot says the 1 per cent figure is heavily skewed by the impact of the virus on the elderly. He argues that a better guide to COVID's mortality emerged in Singapore, when the virus spread through the city's densely populated dormitories for immigrant workers. A systematic testing program identified 50 000 cases in the dormitories. Dr Heriot dug through the information about COVID deaths published at the time and found that only two dormitory workers had died from the virus. 'Once it became clear to me that we were talking about a one in 25 000 death ratio for non-immune, unvaccinated working-age adults, this pandemic takes on a very different flavour,' he says. 'If the whole world gets something that kills one in 25 000 people and more amongst the elderly, that is still bad news. It is just very different bad news to the sort of stuff we were talking about.'

The lack of COVID cases, and particularly critically ill COVID patients, throughout the first-wave epidemic speaks to the success of Australia's early response, not its failure. In the same way that Australia was lauded internationally for avoiding recession in the wake of the global financial crisis (GFC) of 2007–08, we proudly took our place among the handful of nations that had avoided significant deaths and disease in the early months of the pandemic. We hadn't just slowed the spread of the virus, we had stopped it in its tracks. Australia was a global exemplar, an exception to the pandemic rule. No longer satisfied with flattening the curve, we became determined to crush it.

James McCaw says this was the point when other infectious disease and public health experts, both inside and outside the government response, started thinking differently about what was possible. 'It became very clear from a scientific point of view, watching what happened in China, that instead of locking in a massive wave that you would have to flatten, if we went into these lockdowns we could absolutely crush the epidemic,' he says. 'That's what happened in Melbourne and it was a very similar story across all of Australia. As traumatic as that period was, it was a success story. We drove the virus away.'

This was the start of our path towards COVID-zero. Melbourne would come to understand what this meant.

CHAPTER 3
WOEFULLY UNPREPARED

Lockdown had its moments. One I remember clearly is Anzac Day. I've been to plenty of dawn services in Melbourne as a newspaper reporter, where you stand quietly in the darkness of the Shrine of Remembrance and, once the sun comes up, you search for an old digger with a new story to tell. In the afternoon, you fall in step with the rest of the city as it makes the short walk down Birrarung Marr to the MCG. The footballers who play in that game will tell you that, while they live for the roar of the 'G, there is nothing quite like the silence of 95 000 people after 'The Last Post'. There was one afternoon when I came across Peter FitzSimons, a prolific author of Australian war history, in the MCG press room. He'd come down from Sydney and, in his typically effusive way, was taking in the scene below, shaking his head at the heaving grandstands. 'We just don't have anything on this scale,' he remarked. Melbourne, in the way we turn up for things, has always been a broad canvas. That's why reducing something like Anzac Day to an online service felt as empty as Melbourne's football stadiums throughout the pandemic.

On 25 April 2020, no crowds were allowed at the Shrine or the MCG. Instead, the RSL encouraged people to get up before dawn and light a candle in front of their house. It sounds trite but, a month into lockdown, it felt good to have a common purpose other than staying indoors. By the time I coaxed my family out onto our driveway, the rest of the street was standing dutifully on their porches or at their front gates, candles and tea lights flickering in the dark. Then, from across the street, we heard the first haunting notes of 'The Last Post'. Little did I know we had a concert trombonist for a neighbour; I'd only ever seen him mowing the lawn. Across Melbourne's suburban expanse, the same observance was made by hundreds of amateur buglers and trumpet players. If you slept through it, you missed the best of Melbourne that day.

In the first lockdown, there was a novelty about getting out of bed ten minutes before your first meeting, and a mischievous pleasure in working an entire day in pyjamas. No-one missed the hours we waste on a freeway or those mornings jammed into a crowded train trying to get to work. Our kids adjusted to the rhythm of Zoom classes and daily walks in the park, and Melbourne's dogs had never been happier. We put teddy bears in our windows, and at our local park someone created a fairy garden. Helen Garner, one of Melbourne's most celebrated chroniclers, wrote: 'A lot of people in isolation confess guiltily to being happy. Resting, cleaning, reading, putting their house in order. I plant lettuces and beetroot.'[1] Everyone else, or so it seemed, had a crack at baking sourdough—if Melbourne's lockdown no. 1 needed an emoji, it would be a slightly malformed loaf. Employers at first fretted about stay-at-home office workers skiving off to watch Netflix, but they soon realised that, when people have little else to do but work, productivity soars.

If you were a business owner unable to trade online or a self-employed person not allowed to work, the experience was very different. If you were one of the thousands of people who lost their job at the start of the pandemic, when the queues outside Centrelink buildings evoked Depression-era images, the months in lockdown were a cruel compounder: not only were you suddenly out of work, you had no way to look for another job.

The remarkable thing about it is we copped it sweet. There were no protests against lockdown during that first wave. Overwhelmingly, the unprecedented restrictions imposed by the Victorian Government, consistent with the approach agreed to by National Cabinet and adopted by the other states and territories, were supported and complied with. If we think about national character, there is a stark contrast between our imagined rebellious selves and how we responded to stultifying restrictions on everyday life. Social researcher Rebecca Huntley observed this from Sydney during the first lockdown. 'Australians like to think of ourselves as iconoclastic rebels,' she tells me. 'There is no evidence from what we actually do that that is the case. That is not a bad thing. The compliance of the Australian community, when they believe in the social good of the thing that requires compliance, is actually really powerful. We see it in response to drought and water restrictions and we see it in response to something like this. When Australians feel there is reason for government to do what it wants, including the significant curtailing of freedom, they are more willing than not to let that happen.'

This is particularly the case in Melbourne. Deputy Lord Mayor Nicholas Reece used to work as a senior adviser for federal and state Labor leaders. A big part of his job was understanding how Melbourne thinks. He points out that Victoria was the first jurisdiction in the world to introduce mandatory seatbelts, in 1970. Despite the immediate impact this had in reducing road deaths, it took Britain another thirteen years to pass similar laws—New Hampshire still doesn't mandate them. In 1990, Victoria became the first state to mandate bicycle helmets. When Reece reflects on Melbourne's social and political culture, it reminds him of a lyric in a Johnny Hodges song, 'Summertime'. 'It has built a city that is very safe, very healthy, very educated and very prosperous,' he says. 'Compared to other cities in the world, Melbourne has become a place where for many people, to quote the old song, "the living is easy". I think there is something in our political culture that means, collectively, Victorians were ready to accept tough safety measures in response to the virus. Some people are quick to be critical of Daniel Andrews but the truth is, most Victorians agreed with those policies because they saw them as an unwelcome but acceptable trade-off to keep them safe.'

The pandemic also exposed fault lines that, in safe, easy-livin' Melbourne, are not always easy to see.

Nick Coatsworth says it was in what should have been good days, just as the first-wave epidemic was receding across the nation, that he became worried about what was happening in Victoria. Dr Coatsworth is a Canberra-based infectious disease physician who, at the start of the pandemic, was invited by chief medical officer Brendan Murphy to join Australia's public health response as one of his deputies. He later became the lantern-jawed face of the vaccine rollout, and a prominent critic of what he saw as a risk-averse culture among Australian public health experts which encouraged our pursuit of COVID-zero and, at a critical time in the pandemic, vaccine hesitancy. Throughout 2020, Dr Coatsworth was a member of the AHPPC group which provided advice to National Cabinet about how best to respond to the COVID crisis. The AHPPC was, in effect, a highly influential public health club. In the first year of the pandemic it met daily. Once or twice a week, Professor Murphy would invite the chief health officer from each state to brief the group on what was happening in their jurisdiction. At the start of the 2020 winter, the information out of Victoria troubled Dr Coatsworth on three counts.

The first was a report compiled by Rear Admiral Jenny Firman, a formal naval medical officer who had advised successive federal governments on the H1N1 influenza pandemic and the Ebola and zika virus outbreaks, into the public health capacity of each state. Her findings, informed by the unvarnished accounts of senior Victorian public health officials and presented to the AHPPC, showed that Victoria was in a parlous state. The contrast with New South Wales, which, despite the mistakes it made in the *Ruby Princess* fiasco, had a capacity to identify and manage COVID outbreaks in the community well beyond Victoria's, was particularly stark.

The second was the difficulty Victoria was having containing what should have been a relatively straightforward workplace outbreak at Cedar Meats, an abattoir in Melbourne's west. Over the course of several weeks in April, four people who worked at the abattoir tested positive to COVD-19. Unexplained delays in the health department notifying the abattoir meant the managers of the meatworks only learned they had a problem twenty-five days after the first positive case was confirmed. By the time the abattoir had been temporarily closed and the outbreak contained, more than 100 people were infected. The people who got sick were mostly the family members of migrant meatworkers and their friends. Health minister Jenny Mikakos, on the advice of Brett Sutton and his public health team, claimed the outbreak response had been handled 'absolutely perfectly'. In a subsequent parliamentary inquiry, Professor Sutton admitted it was anything but.

The third thing concerning Dr Coatsworth was the dearth of information that Victoria, through Sutton and the other senior public health officials who attended AHPPC meetings, was either willing or able to provide about what was going on. The AHPPC should have been well in tune with Melbourne: Professor Murphy had spent much of his career as a hospital administrator at the Austin Hospital in the city's north, and all three of the AHPPC's invited experts were from the Victorian capital. Instead, Australia's second-most-populous state seemed to be withdrawing from the open sharing of information essential to the work of the committee. 'They of all the states needed the wisdom of the group and were the first to retreat,' Dr Coatsworth recalls. 'We didn't think they were hiding things from us. We were worried they just didn't know.'

It is now clear that Dr Coatsworth's three concerns about Victoria were different parts of the same problem. The people working at the sharp end of Victoria's public health response were just as worried as he was. They knew what would happen if the virus got off the chain.

The degradation of public health in Victoria is a thirty-year problem which began with the election of the Jeff Kennett government in 1992, at a time when the state's economy was in deep recession and crippled by $32 billion in public-sector debt. Lindsay Grayson is Professor of Infectious Diseases at the University of Melbourne and one of the state's leading public health experts. He explains that, after the Kennett government corporatised the management of public hospitals with the creation of semi-autonomous health networks, and tied hospital funding directly to acute service provision, the Victorian health department was over time reduced to a bureaucratic husk. It doesn't directly control public hospitals and subsequent Victorian governments haven't invested in public health. Professor Grayson says a shortage of infection-control expertise within the department can be traced back to another Kennett government decision: the closure of the state's specialist infectious disease hospital at Fairfield. Fairfield was the place where anyone with tuberculosis, AIDS, Ebola or other exotic ailments was sent for treatment. It was also a hospital where the principles of quarantine, containment and infection control were drummed into all staff who worked there. The decision to close Fairfield had advantages, including that it dispersed highly capable infectious disease specialists and expensive facilities—such as the negative pressure rooms now in the intensive care department of the Royal Melbourne Hospital—throughout the remaining hospital system. However, Professor Grayson says another service that Fairfield provided—training doctors and nurses in infection control—wasn't replaced by the department.

There are different ways of measuring what Victoria lacked in public health firepower in early 2020 compared with New South Wales but, as a starting point, consider this. At the onset of the pandemic, Victoria's Health Protection Branch—the division of the health department responsible for containing the spread of infectious diseases—employed one infection-control consultant, and she worked part-time. When you are trying to stop the spread of a lethal contagion, you need people who understand infection-control protocols and quarantine principles. Between January and March 2020, when Victoria was preparing for a potentially catastrophic pandemic, the state's entire health department relied on Donna Cameron, an infectious disease nurse who had previously worked as a medical scientist at Fairfield, to provide all the advice it needed about infection control. This jaw-dropping detail, revealed by deputy chief health officer Annaliese van Diemen and confirmed by Cameron in their evidence to a government-commissioned investigation—the Coate inquiry—into the failures of the state's hotel-based quarantine program, is perhaps the most damning insight provided from inside Victoria's public health response into the origins of the second-wave epidemic.

Donna Cameron says that, by the time Victoria's hotel quarantine program was established in late March, she was so overwhelmed with requests about infection control from ambulance drivers, police, firefighters, funeral homes and local councils that she had no capacity to turn her mind to hotels preparing for returned travellers. She says the quarantine program needed its own infection-control expert right from the start but, even if it had tried, the health department would have been hard-pressed to find one. At the time, infection-control nurses working in hospitals were flat out advising their own staff, and Cameron was having to cajole old friends to get other qualified people to help her inside the department. When the virus leaked out of quarantine, Cameron was dismayed. She blames herself but also knows there was nothing more she could have done given everything else she was responsible for at the time. 'When something has gone so horribly wrong, even though I had nothing to do with it, I still felt responsible,' she says. 'I should have made more time, I should have gone there, but our team just didn't have more time to do anything.'

Here is another measure of how depleted our public health resources were at the start of their greatest challenge. The Health Protection Branch, led by Professor Sutton, worked out of the Lonsdale Street headquarters of the department of health. Victoria at the start of the pandemic didn't have local public health units. It didn't have public health officers embedded in the communities they were trying to protect. Instead, it had a total of nine public health officers, all based in the same office. Many of them were on single-year contracts and didn't know whether they would have a job at the end of the financial year—for the umpteenth time, the division had been slated for a departmental restructure. New South Wales, by comparison, had fifteen public health units—that is, teams of people—spread around the state, including eight in metropolitan Sydney. This statewide public health network, first built in response to the AIDs epidemic thirty years ago, had systematically trained and cultivated a strong public health culture. This meant that, by the start of the pandemic, New South Wales could call upon hundreds of people, connected with their communities, who understood the fundamentals of contact tracing, the importance of prompt testing, and the social connections and movements of people within their neighbourhoods. Victoria, in the words of one government minister, had 'staff in Lonsdale Street sending out tweets'.

If you think of it in military terms, New South Wales entered the war with more battalions than Victoria had soldiers, and the soldiers we had were unfamiliar with the terrain. As one original member of Victoria's threadbare public health team explains, when you are so stretched for resources, only the most urgent work gets done. You don't have time to establish the community and professional connections which are vital when responding to a major infectious disease outbreak. When there was a COVID outbreak in the Afghan community in Melbourne's south-east, Professor Sutton reflected on his time in Afghanistan, when he worked with Médecins Sans Frontières to contain cholera and typhoid fever outbreaks, and to address the despairingly high number of deaths in childbirth and rates of preventable diseases. The chief health officer had done commendable work in Afghanistan. Had anyone from his public health team been to nearby Hallam?

About ten years before the pandemic, the Victorian health department employed a group of infection and prevention control experts who could be dispatched to nursing homes confronting influenza outbreaks. At the start of the COVID crisis, when the federal government announced that international arrivals would be temperature-checked at airports, the Victorian health department couldn't spare anyone to do the work. New South Wales dispatched teams of people from local public health units to Sydney's airport and seaport. 'We never had a hope,' a frustrated public health official told me candidly. 'We were overwhelmed from the first case.'

Julian Rait, in explaining to a Victorian parliamentary committee the importance of public health being local, said the strength of the NSW approach is that the local public health teams work closely with general practitioners, community health workers, hospitals, pathology labs, schools, childcare centres and nursing homes in their patch. This meant that, in the event of an outbreak or even a single case, information was quickly shared with everyone who needed to know. Rait contrasted this with what happened in Melbourne in 2020, when GPs were often not told about outbreaks in their neighbourhoods. This happened in Melbourne's north, where a medical practice in Coolaroo which runs a specialist clinic and employs doctors who speak Arabic, Mandarin and Vietnamese were not told about an outbreak at the nearby East Preston Islamic College. It also happened in Melbourne's west, where the health department didn't inform local GPs about an outbreak at another Islamic school, Al-Taqwa College.

Dr Hanna El-Khoury, whose practice in Newport caters to the local Arabic and Lebanese community, recalls his 'bitter experience' in dealing with the department. He says that, in the last week of school before the mid-year holidays, teenage students from Al-Taqwa came to his practice with cold and flu symptoms. When they tested negative for coronavirus, he assumed it was a seasonal flu and told them it was safe to go home to their families. The department had been notified of an outbreak at the school but no-one had thought to tell Dr El-Khoury. Some of the students who'd tested negative subsequently returned positive tests. By that stage, they had already infected other family members and friends. Dr El-Khoury has worked as a doctor in the area for thirty years. He doesn't understand why the health department didn't see him as part of the solution to an emerging health crisis. 'The premier is talking about people not responding to them,' he tells me. 'One way of getting to people could be through their GP.'

In AHPPC meetings, NSW Chief Health Officer Kerry Chant provided granular detail about individual cases and outbreaks. She was obsessive about outbreak management to the point where she refused to go home until every case and their contacts had been called by someone on her public health team. Victoria, by contrast, struggled to provide headline case numbers. Professor Sutton wasn't across the details in the way Dr Chant was, and his deputy, Annaliese van Diemen, was hardworking but overwhelmed. Victoria wasn't holding anything back—they just didn't know. Once the case numbers started to build in Victoria's second wave, Professor Sutton was regularly drawn away from AHPPC meetings to attend daily press conferences with Premier Andrews. The Daily Dans, which often clashed with AHPPC meetings, attracted a bumper audience on social media platforms, and Professor Sutton provided a reassuring presence for them. Nonetheless, Nick Coatsworth wonders if

Victoria would have been better served by Professor Sutton attending all AHPCC meetings. 'It was a media masterstroke but it took out the CHO from the only meeting where he was going to get other advice,' he says.

Public health is elegantly defined by the WHO as 'the art and science of preventing disease, promoting life and promoting health through the organised efforts of society'. In a pandemic, public health officials aren't the ones who intubate critical COVID patients. They are the people whose advice and interventions stop people getting sick in the first place. Victoria's own health minister knew at the start of the COVID crisis that the state's highly centralised and poorly resourced health-protection team was woefully unprepared for what was coming.

On 29 January 2020, five days after the visitor from Wuhan walked into the emergency department of the Monash Medical Centre, Jenny Mikakos lodged a confidential submission with the Expenditure Review Committee (ERC). This Cabinet committee, a powerful group of senior ministers which includes Daniel Andrews, Deputy Premier James Merlino and Treasurer Tim Pallas, oversees a $90 billion budget and decides what the state should spend our money on. By the time Mikakos lodged her submission, an earlier draft had already been shared with senior bureaucrats and political advisers within the health department, Treasury, and the Department of Premier and Cabinet (DPC), as well as the premier's personal staff. Had any of them re-read it as COVID started spreading across Melbourne's suburbs, they would have blanched.

> The current state of our health protection services is placing an unacceptable risk to the whole community. Unlike other states the capacity of Victoria's health protection services are almost entirely based in Melbourne. An emergency physician in Mildura must wait for the six hours it takes an expert, public health physician to drive from Melbourne to consult on the possible human case

of anthrax. We cannot staff regional/local emergency response in addition to state level response to any public health emergency. In its current state the health protection system does not have the necessary capacity or capabilities to prevent, respond and protect against current or emerging threats to the Australian community.

The submission went on to note that the management of public health information, an essential prerequisite for good contact tracing, was ad hoc, supported by old technology and highly centralised. This was a prescient insight into how Victoria later responded to the pandemic, and why that response struggled to keep up with a fast-spreading virus.

Health Protection Service provision in Victoria is currently comprised of a single team of front line professionals working directly from the central office of the DHHS with a small contingent spread across the department's four operational divisions. From the central office, the team follows up communicable diseases and threats from the environment for the whole of Victoria. This includes responding to communicable disease notifications and outbreaks, natural disasters and incidents, and in some cases acting as incident controllers for incidents and emergencies involving food, drinking water, [and] radioactive material. In contrast, NSW and Queensland have decentralised public health structures and services. NSW has 15 public health units, eight of which service metro Sydney. In Queensland 13 public health units operate across the state, four of which service metro Brisbane. These public health units each operate teams responding to communicable disease notifications and outbreaks, natural disasters and incidents at the local level.

Health Protection Service system is our frontline defence against threats from the environment and communicable diseases and it is in disrepair. The government can no longer continue to protect Victorians and is exposing the community to unacceptable risks. We have been doing our best with the resources we have but it is not enough.

The submission was written by Melissa Skilbeck, the health department deputy secretary responsible for regulation, emergency management and health protection. She had written a similar wish two years earlier which never got as far as the ERC. For three years, the former Treasury official had tried to argue the case for more public health resources in Victoria. Yet, when the virus broke out of quarantine hotels, Skilbeck and several members of her team wore the blame and were promptly dumped from the state's COVID response.

The striking thing about the January 2020 submission is that, having identified a glaring deficiency in Victoria's public health defences, it made only a meagre request for additional resources to fix it. Instead of seeking to match the more decentralised, better resourced public health systems of New South Wales and Queensland, it asked for baby steps in that direction to be funded: $17.2 million in 2020–21 and $92 million over four years to hire thirty additional public health staff in regional areas. The submission wasn't written with COVID-19 in mind, and the Victorian Government's subsequent investment in public health dwarfed what Skilbeck and Mikakos had contemplated. Notwithstanding these caveats, the submission reveals how downtrodden public health in Victoria had become. After so many years of neglect, it didn't even know how to ask for what it needed.

Soon enough, it didn't have to. In 2020–21, Victoria had a $9 billion health budget. By the time it was handed down by Tim Pallas in November 2020, the state government had found an additional $2.9 billion for health measures to limit the spread of COVID. This included the creation of six new public health units based in major hospitals in Melbourne and regional centres. Asked for an ounce of prevention, Victoria delivered a pound of cure.

The neglect of public health began under the Kennett government, but responsibility for its continued neglect sits disproportionately on the shoulders of Labor premiers and health ministers who have been in government for all but four years this century. Lindsay Grayson says Victoria's public health malaise is the flip side of our political obsession with waiting lists for elective surgery, delays in emergency departments and ambulance ramping times at hospitals. These are important issues which directly impact people's lives and light up the switchboards of talk-back radio stations. In 2022, they contributed to a change of government in South Australia in March, and as winter approached, they returned as dominant issues in the Victorian health system. Nonetheless, Professor Grayson describes them as the tip of the iceberg. The base, he says, is public health. 'No-one ever talked about smoking cessation or alcohol use or amphetamine use in truck drivers,' he says. 'They weren't on the political agenda.' Creating 1000 new ICU beds and doubling our stock of ventilators, although headline-grabbing measures, are analogous to parking a fleet of new ambulances at the bottom of a cliff.

Daniel Andrews, as a former health minister in the John Brumby government, was politically hardwired to prioritise hospital funding. This ensured that Victoria's response to the pandemic was always going to be strongly focused on ICU capacity and hospital equipment. It also made it difficult for anyone else in Cabinet to question that priority. As one minister told me: 'Dan's baggage as a health minister means he thinks he knows it all. Public health could never get any money.' In March 2020, this is arguably where money was needed most.

COVID-19, like obesity, smoking and alcohol abuse, is a public health problem that was always going to disproportionately infect and kill the poor, poorly educated and socially disadvantaged. An analysis of Victoria's second-wave epidemic by a team of researchers from Deakin University found that if you spoke a language other than English at home, if you rented rather than owned your home, if you were homeless, or if you worked in a job that didn't offer paid leave, you were more likely to be infected with SARS-CoV-2.[2] These are the same people who, due to their social and economic circumstances, are least likely to follow a government directive to stay at home. The neglect of public health is not unique to Victoria, but Professor Grayson says it is more pronounced here than in other mainland states. At the start of our second wave, it was about to cost us dearly.

When a family of four returning from a holiday in Bangladesh flew into Melbourne Airport on 9 May 2020, they were detained by border and Victorian health authorities and bussed to a quarantine hotel in the city. Three days into what they thought would be a two-week stay, the entire family was showing telltale signs of coronavirus infection. The following day, two family members returned positive tests. In keeping with Victoria's quarantine policy, the family was shifted to the Rydges on Swanston, on the northern edge of the city. So far, this was unremarkable. Since renamed, Rydges was a designated 'hot' hotel for returned travellers known to have COVID. Most of its guests had the virus, and everyone was assumed to have it. In the three months during which Victoria's program ran before all international flights were diverted from Melbourne, 274 of 313 guests who checked into the hotel tested positive to the virus.

It is what happened next that changed everything—for this city, for its people, and for a government which, until that point, was considered the national standard-bearer for Australia's management of the COVID crisis. We don't know who the family passed the virus to. It could have been a night manager employed by the hotel; it could have been one of two security guards contracted to work there by the Victorian Government. They all started showing COVID symptoms on 25 May and subsequently tested positive. Despite the best efforts of a $15 million inquiry into the failings of the hotel quarantine program, we don't know the circumstances of how the virus transmitted out of the family's hotel room and into the community. What we can say, with a reasonable degree of certainly, is it had nothing to do with the salacious reports of security guards having sex on duty, or the premier's suggestion that a security guard infected another by offering him a light. However the security guards got the virus, they passed it to their colleagues and took it home to their families and communities. The consequence was a second-wave epidemic which killed 801 people and forced Melbourne into lockdown for another 111 days. The only surprise, considering what we now know, is that it took so long for the virus to get out.

The idea of quarantining returned travellers in city hotels which, thanks to our border closures and public health policies, no longer had any guests, was uncontroversial when it was announced by prime minister Scott Morrison after a meeting of National Cabinet on 27 March 2020. Daniel Andrews, who had taken the plan to National Cabinet and pushed for its adoption by all states, was happy to take credit for it. As Andrews later explained to the board of inquiry chaired by retired judge Jennifer Coate, he went to National Cabinet convinced that the policy until that point, of requiring returned travellers to quarantine at their own homes, placed too much trust in people to do the right thing. In effect, Andrews wanted them forcibly detained by the state for fourteen days. This would also provide jobs for hotel employees who would otherwise have joined the dole queue for the duration of our initial lockdown, and welcome revenue to the hotel owners. It is telling that, when Victoria started organising the scheme, it was the department responsible for jobs, not the health department, which initially took the lead. The health department was supposed to assume responsibility once hotel guests started arriving, but it never entirely did. Put simply, hotel quarantine was doomed from the start.

Given just thirty-six hours to contract hotels and find suitable staff before the first guests were due to be checked in, the bureaucrats who were asked to work non-stop across the weekend approached their task primarily as a logistical challenge. The day before the program was announced, more than 7000 international travellers had arrived at Australian airports. The most pressing concern was finding enough hotel rooms to put people in once the first flight arrived in Melbourne on 29 March. They also needed a workforce to ensure that hotel guests stayed in their rooms. A common thread in the testimony to the Coate inquiry was the absence of consideration given to the primary function of the scheme: how to stop a harmful contagion from getting out through proper infection-control and quarantine principles. The government-commissioned inquiry degenerated into lawyers acting for different government departments trying to blame someone else for what had gone wrong. At the centre of this unedifying duckshove was infection control. Everyone agreed it was essential to an effective quarantine program. No-one accepted it was their job to make sure the right protocols and practices were adhered to.

This is how Jennifer Coate summed it up in her final report in December 2020:

> [I]t was the position of DHHS that it was its role to provide the advice and guidance to DJPR [Department of Jobs, Precincts and Regions] and that DJPR was then responsible for passing it on and managing or overseeing compliance. DHHS took the position that it did not hold or manage the contracts with hotels and did not see it as its role to implement that advice and guidance and ensure it was done to the requisite standard ...
>
> DJPR's position was that although it held the contracts with the hotels, DJPR looked to DHHS for the necessary expertise and guidance in this area. This impasse made its contribution to what became a Gordian knot that developed in the early days of the Hotel Quarantine Program.[3]

It was clear from security guards who cooperated with the inquiry that, while some were provided with training in infection-control protocols and the use of personal protective equipment (PPE), others were not. One guard told the inquiry that on his first day on the job, he was provided with no training or instruction other than to sit on a chair in a hotel corridor and tell any guests who wandered outside their doors to go back inside. He went on to say:

> I didn't have a mask or any PPE. They did have good hand sanitiser at first but after this we were just given hand wash, not proper sanitiser. My friends who were also guards would help the travellers with their luggage and share lifts with them when they arrived from the airport. They didn't have a mask or any other PPE either. We didn't know if any of the travellers had the virus. Our subcontractor told us nothing.[4]

The folly of putting hotel staff without masks in lifts with quarantined guests should have been self-evident, but the security companies and their guards cannot be fairly blamed for this lax approach to infection control. In a two-step abrogation of responsibility, the Victorian Government not only outsourced security within the quarantine program to private firms which normally provide bouncers to pubs and nightclubs and crowd controllers to public events, they outsourced the obligation to train the guards in infection-control protocols. The contracts entered into between security companies and the Department of Jobs, Precincts and Regions stipulated that the companies were responsible for training their own staff to work in the quarantine hotels. They were even required to source face masks and gloves for the guards to wear. The DJPR bureaucrats who drew up these contracts could be forgiven for not knowing any better. The Victorian health department should have known. Having reduced its own infection-control expertise to one part-time nurse, it deferred to private security companies the responsibility for providing casual guards with the public health training in the skills and knowledge they needed to avoid getting infected in a workplace filled with people assumed to have the virus. This happened at a time when six out of every ten COVID cases recorded in Victoria were being imported by returned travellers. What was the point of forcing people to stay in their homes for weeks on end to 'crush the curve' when our most important containment measure was so slapdash?

Nearly 100 witnesses were called over two months of hearings before the Coate inquiry. To understand why the virus leaked out of quarantine, you needed only to hear the testimony of the first. The night before he was due to give evidence, Professor Grayson was sent a document discovered by Arthur Moses, a lawyer representing one of the private security companies. It was headlined 'Operation Soteria', the codename given to the quarantine program, somewhat ironically as things turned out—in Greek mythology, Soteria is the goddess for safety and protection from harm. The document provided a matrix of advice for when PPE needed to be used by security staff in the hotels. The document had been compiled by a Victorian health department bureaucrat with no expertise in infection control. It advised that security guards didn't need to wear masks or gloves when they were in the hotel lobby when a guest was arriving, when they were walking the corridors of the hotel floors, or when they were talking to a guest through an open hotel room door, so long as they maintained a distance of 1.5 metres. This was the advice that was provided to security companies by the health department, and it was all wrong. When Professor Grayson clicked open the document and began reading it, he was shocked. 'I feel sorry for them,' he says of the guards. 'They were put in harm's way. They were trained poorly, if at all, provided with inadequate protective masks and gowns. They had very little oversight to ensure they did the right thing and were blamed when they made a mistake.'

Professor Grayson says the PPE advice provided to security guards reflects a deeper flaw within the now-abandoned hotel quarantine program. An important piece of evidence was provided by Claire Febey, one of the bureaucrats within the DJPR who worked through that crazy weekend to establish the program. When asked about the infection-control protocols inside the hotels, she told the Coate inquiry that, at the start of the program, the health department wanted to preserve its stocks of PPE. This is why people were told they only needed to wear masks when they couldn't keep their distance from hotel guests. Victoria at this stage of the pandemic was building its stockpile of masks, gowns, gloves and face shields and, through its infection-control protocols, trying to preserve PPE. Hospital staff dealing with COVID patients were prioritised. Professor Grayson says the fact hotel staff were not shows a basic misunderstanding of quarantine principles. 'Quarantine assumes everyone is positive until you are found to be negative,' he says. 'Our state, in simple terms, ran it the opposite way. They basically played the odds and when someone was found to be positive the wheels fell off.'

On the morning of 30 June 2020, the Andrews government was plunged into its most serious political crisis since it had come to power. The trigger was an email sent by Professor Sutton to Andrews's Chief of Staff Lissie Ratcliff and forwarded to other people working across the pandemic response in Victoria's emergency management and public health teams. Attached to the email was a genomics report prepared by the Microbiological Diagnostic Unit Public Health Laboratory (MDU PHL).

The MDU PHL, which is located in the Doherty Institute at the University of Melbourne and funded by the Victorian Government, dates back to the reign of Queen Victoria. By the 1880s, the

Victorian gold rush had brought riches and a surging population to Marvellous Melbourne. It had also created a public health hazard, with untreated sewage running in open street channels into the Yarra River and Port Phillip. The resultant outbreaks of typhoid and diphtheria prompted a royal commission, which recommended the creation of the Werribee sewage farm and what was then known as the Public Health Laboratory and Bacteriology Laboratory, to help Melbourne deal with its shit. As soon as Daniel Andrews and his most trusted political advisers read the MDU PHL report, they faced the same task.

The report traced the DNA of every positive COVID sample collected in Victoria to that point of the pandemic. Although the science of genomics is complex, the takeaway was simple enough: nearly every COVID case recorded in Victoria's second-wave epidemic was linked to either the Bangladeshi family at the Rydges hotel or a second breach of quarantine at the Stamford Plaza Melbourne in early June. For Professor Sutton and his public health team, the results showed how close Victoria had come to eliminating the virus from the community a few weeks earlier. 'It was a terrible realisation that what we were facing at that time was out of hotel quarantine, but also that all of that original wild virus that had come in through international arrivals was gone by June and July,' he says. 'It was absolutely a recognition that you can get on top of it and drive it down to nothing.'

For Andrews and his government, the report put Melbourne's outbreaks under a harsh new light. In the twenty-four hours prior to Professor Sutton sending his email, Victoria recorded sixty-four new cases. At that stage of the second wave, only one person had died. As the premier, Chris Eccles, Ratcliff and her deputy Jessie McCrone gathered grim-faced in Ratcliff's office inside no. 1 Treasury Place, they knew that whatever happened next, their government would carry the can for it. Once health minister Jenny Mikakos had joined them, Andrews began to map out a strategy in his most measured voice. Everyone in the room knew what this meant: the premier was furious. 'We were in crisis mode,' one of them recalls. 'This was an absolute bombshell.'

The decisions taken in the hours that followed provide a window into how Daniel Andrews and his government operate. Andrews was not angry because the virus had leaked out of quarantine—that was already widely known. He was angry because his chief health officer, in a naive moment, had circulated damaging information about a politically sensitive outbreak to people outside the premier's trusted inner circle. Andrews knew he had to act quickly and decisively before the genomic results leaked.

Had a casual observer walked into the meeting, they would have been struck by the role played by Chris Eccles. A career public servant who had previously served as then premier Mike Rann's top bureaucrat in South Australia, and NSW premier Barry O'Farrell's director general of premier and cabinet, Eccles had helped steer more than one government out of a tight spot. He also knew what happened when a premier didn't pay sufficient attention to details: his stint in charge of the NSW public service came to an abrupt end in 2014 when O'Farrell inexplicably forgot to mention to an Independent Commission Against Corruption hearing that he'd been gifted a bottle of Grange Hermitage by a businessman. In the hours after Andrews received the genomics report, it was Eccles who advised him to establish an inquiry into the hotel quarantine program. He even offered a recommendation for who should run it. Jennifer Coate, a former Family Court judge, knew her way around government and would bring a 'sensible' level of independence to proceedings, Eccles suggested.

It might seem unusual for a public servant to adopt the role of political adviser in a time of crisis, but by this stage Chris Eccles had become an important confidant to Andrews on both policy and political matters. At the start of the pandemic, Andrews's long-serving consigliore, Gavin Jennings, had resigned as a minister and quit parliament. This followed a cooling of the once strong relationship between the two men most responsible for preparing Labor's return to government in Victoria in 2014. One of the reasons for the breakdown of that relationship was the extent to which Andrews had turned to Eccles, rather than Jennings, for advice. It was Eccles who personally championed one of Andrews's most controversial projects: his government's Belt and Road Initiative agreement with China. Eccles's counsel was also unconstrained by career ambition. He'd originally planned to retire at the end of June 2020 and join his partner in the clifftop beach house they had bought on the NSW South Coast, but he had promised Andrews he'd stay on till the end of the year. Instead, he would join Mikakos and health secretary Kym Peake as high-profile casualties of the Coate inquiry he pushed for on that fateful Tuesday morning.

By mid-afternoon, when Andrews walked into the theatrette near 1 Treasury Place to front the television cameras, he had something to announce that would knock the genomics report off the front page. The concentration of cases in the city's northern and western suburbs—multicultural, working-class neighbourhoods where people are more likely to rely on casual jobs such as security work—had convinced the government it could contain the growing wave of infections by locking down ten select local government areas, rather than the entire city. This meant that about 300 000 people, having only just emerged from lockdown, were ordered back into their homes. For the first time, police checkpoints would be stationed on roads leading in and out of the prescribed suburbs, and motorists would be randomly stopped and questioned about why they were out of their homes. Police would also patrol train stations in case anyone tried to flee by rail. The lockdown was not something the premier and his advisers had dreamed up that day. It had been in planning since the previous week, when case numbers started to climb. The targeting of suburbs with a disproportionate share of migrant families and, in particular, a high concentration of Muslim families, for this heavy-handed police-led response, served as a precursor to what happened at the housing commission towers just five days later.

Andrews said the decision was based on the advice of Brett Sutton and his public health team, and that, if the ten local government areas weren't locked down, all of Melbourne soon would be. He suggested that the problems in hotel quarantine had been dealt with and made it clear who was to blame: 'At least a significant number and potentially more of the outbreaks in the north of the city are attributable via genomic sequencing to staff members in hotel quarantine breaching well-known and well-understood infection-control protocols.' These were the same infection-control protocols no-one in government took responsibility for in the Coate inquiry, the same ill-devised protocols that Professor Grayson says put security guards in harm's way. The failure of security guards to observe infection-control practices reflected the fundamental failing of the entire program, and indeed the Victorian Government, to prioritise these practices in the planning and management of hotel quarantine.

Also in attendance at the presser was Professor Sutton, who described the pandemic as taking a 'heartbreaking turn' and endorsed the restrictions the premier had announced. This show of unity, while necessary to maintain public faith in Victoria's pandemic response, belied the anger that Andrews felt towards his CHO for distributing the genomic report so widely. Throughout the press conference, the pair crossed paths several times on their way to and from the microphone, and Andrews did not look at Sutton once. 'Dan was so furious with him he did not even glance at him,' an insider says. This was Professor Sutton's introduction to 'the freezer', the cold, lonely place where Andrews puts people who disappoint him, cross him or otherwise let him down.

If you lined up the Victorian Government ministers who at differing times had responsibility for the hotel quarantine program—former health minister Jenny Mikakos, Minister for Jobs,

Precincts and Regions Martin Pakula, Minister for Corrections Natalie Hutchins and Attorney-General Jaclyn Symes—none of them would nominate private security guards as their first-choice workforce to keep quarantined guests in their rooms. Instead, when the program was thrown together in a blur of bureaucratic wrangling and furious outsourcing, private security guards were the default choice. They were used because Victoria Police command didn't want their people doing the job and no-one in government wanted the Australian Defence Force (ADF) to do it either. This is the clear picture that emerged over months of tortured claims and counterclaims between Premier Andrews, federal defence minister Linda Reynolds, Victoria's Emergency Management Commissioner Andrew Crisp, previously undisclosed recordings of meetings played to the Coate inquiry, and an exhaustive collection of text and email exchanges between top cops and bureaucrats. When put together, they place Victoria curiously at odds with NSW and Queensland's willingness to use both ADF personnel and police to try to keep infected returned travellers from spreading the virus into their communities.

The reluctance of Graham Ashton, a career cop close to finishing a five-year stint as Victoria Police chief commissioner, to commit hundreds of police officers to sit in hotel corridors is easy enough to understand. That he was able to convince senior figures in the Andrews government that police shouldn't be posted inside the quarantine hotels without ever having to press this point, goes to the unusually cosy relationship between Victorian Labor and Victoria Police. Doug Drummond, a corruption-busting barrister who prosecuted Queensland police chief Terry Lewis and other crooked officers exposed by the Fitzgerald inquiry in the late 1980s, describes Victoria Police as the uniformed branch of the Australian Labor Party. While this might sound hyperbolic, it is telling that when Chris Eccles and the state's senior bureaucrats clicked into a Microsoft Teams meeting an hour after the hotel quarantine program had been announced, Ashton's clear preference that security guards, rather than police, should be posted inside the hotels—albeit related by other people at the meeting—was enough to settle the question.

Andrew Crisp, a former police deputy commissioner who served under Ashton, effectively put the kibosh on ADF personnel being used when he remarked in the same meeting that 'at this stage, we don't see a need for boots on the ground'. Ashton had left the force by the time the Coate inquiry convened, but when called to give evidence, he maintained that security guards should have been suitable for the job. By mid-June, it was clear to everyone that they weren't. After quarantine breaches at both the Rydges and Stamford Plaza hotels had seeded community outbreaks, the Victorian Government knew it had a serious problem and was determined to fix it, even if it meant putting police command offside.

On 24 June, a week before the genomics report was circulated, Jenny Mikakos was considering a plan to replace the security guards with up to 800 police, supported by a team of fifty logistics experts from the ADF. A minimum of three sworn police officers would be stationed during every shift in every hotel. And more than 400 nurses and hospital orderlies would be spread through the hotels to manage any personal contact with guests—or detainees, as they were officially called. An additional eighty health department staff had already been dispatched to the hotels. Although it was a case of shutting a hotel room door after the virus had bolted, this was a considered plan to get private security guards out of hotel quarantine. As Mikakos later told the Coate inquiry, she was 'exasperated and absolutely determined to replace the security guards'.

In the meantime, Crisp formally requested that Canberra send 850 personnel to help out in hotel quarantine. Although this was later presented as unauthorised moonlighting by Crisp, he was acting with the knowledge of senior health department bureaucrats and the health minister, who saw the ADF as an available, interim workforce which could immediately replace security guards while sufficient police resources were being organised. To smooth political sensitivities within Defence, they would be called 'monitoring personnel' instead of security, but they would do the same job. The mistake they all made was to think that such a request could be made without the knowledge of the premier. When Andrews read in the next day's *Herald Sun* that 1000 soldiers were being deployed to help Melbourne battle its COVID crisis, he was livid. Crisp withdrew the request before his ears had stopped ringing.

When seen from Canberra, Victoria's reluctance to make use of ADF resources and other offers of assistance from the federal government in the early months of the pandemic, was baffling. Our second-wave epidemic, which crested at a time when there was no COVID in most other states and only a smattering of cases in New South Wales, isolated Victoria from the rest of the nation and, according to federal Treasury estimates, stripped $1 billion from the economy every week that we remained in lockdown. The Victorian Government and many Victorians were sensitive to criticism from outside the state about how we were handling things. Unless you lived here during that winter, you really can't understand what those months were like. In Sydney and other places in Australia, where people could leave their homes, kids could go to school, and shops and pubs stayed open, the troubles of Melbourne were easily forgotten. It is a rewriting of history, however, to conclude that the federal government saw the difficulties of the Andrews government as an opportunity for partisan politics. That came later. At the start of the second wave, it was in everyone's interest for Victoria to have an effective quarantine system and a well-resourced, competent public health response.

ADF officers were available to Victoria, as they were to every other state, from the start of the hotel quarantine program. Lieutenant General John Frewen, the army officer who commanded the ADF's COVID response, insists that a ready force of 1000 personnel were on stand-by in late March to help Victoria establish its hotel quarantine. Rather than explain why it didn't use them, the Victorian Government denied they were on offer. It took an acute political crisis—triggered by the release of the genomics report—for that to change. On 30 June, Andrews announced that he had asked the prime minister for urgent help. The federal government would provide 500 Commonwealth public servants to bolster Victoria's public health response, 100 people to help coordinate the state's massive testing program, and 200 nurses and medicos from the ADF. Andrews also bought his government precious time to fix the problems in quarantine, with the federal government supporting his request to suspend all international flights into Victoria. When the hotel program was rebooted later in the year, the corridors were guarded by prison officers.

The findings of the Coate inquiry, released four days before Christmas 2020, confirmed that Victoria's hotel quarantine program, in both its design and administration, was a debacle. The overlapping contractual and governance arrangements between the jobs department and the health department meant that, in practice, no-one was in charge. The decision to hire private security guards remains an orphan. As Coate drily put it, it was a decision made without clear articulation that a decision was being made at all. No minister was involved in it and no bureaucrat took responsibility for it.

Health secretary Kym Peake, a rising star in the Victorian Public Service, handpicked to lead the government's health response to the COVID crisis and earmarked to replace Chris Eccles as Victoria's top bureaucrat, quit a month before the report was published. Her testimony to the inquiry revealed how a basic principle of Westminster accountability—that ministers should be involved in any significant decisions affecting their portfolio responsibilities—was only loosely adhered to, when at all, in relation to the hotel quarantine program.

Jenny Mikakos endured an excruciating day in the witness box when she testified that she didn't know that private security guards were working in the hotels until she was briefed on the Rydges outbreak. Footage of an earlier press conference showed she was standing next to jobs minister Martin Pakula when he made this clear. When Daniel Andrews subsequently testified that he held Mikakos accountable for the program, she knew her political career was over. The next day, she resigned as a minister and quit the parliament after serving more than twenty years as an MP.

Chris Eccles appeared to have safely negotiated the Coate inquiry. Instead, he was pulled into the abyss, Gandalf-like, when a belated request by the inquiry for phone records revealed that he had failed to mention a two-minute call he'd had with Graham Ashton at a time when the use of private security guards was front of Ashton's mind. When Andrews publicly said he was shocked to learn this, Eccles decided the time was right to join his partner at the beach.

Victoria was not the only state in Australia where the virus broke out of quarantine. In the twelve months after hotel quarantine was established in all states and territories, there were fourteen recorded breaches. Five of those occurred in New South Wales, four in Victoria and three in Queensland. The Northern Territory, where a disused miner's camp at Howard Springs, half an hour outside Darwin, was developed into a purpose-built quarantine centre, was the only mainland jurisdiction not to record an instance of a guest transmitting the virus to someone working in quarantine. These numbers were compiled by a research team led by Leah Grout from the University of Otago in New Zealand. They found that eight of the quarantine breaches, including the two which seeded Victoria's second-wave epidemic and a later incident in February 2021, when an outbreak was blamed on an asthmatic guest using a nebuliser, led to lockdowns. The figures show that over the twelve months in question, more than 250 000 returned travellers were quarantined in Australia, more than half in New South Wales. This included 3400 people who had the virus. This means that once in every 250 cases, the virus leaked out.[5]

It is possible that, had we used police officers or soldiers instead of private security guards inside Melbourne's quarantine hotels, we would have had fewer outbreaks. It seems more likely, considering what we now know about the virus and how it spreads, that had police or ADF personnel been stationed inside the hotels armed with the same infection-control advice that the health department provided to security companies, we just would have had cops and Defence personnel taking the virus home to their families instead of nightclub bouncers. As Donna Cameron reflects, 'If they are not trained properly in the first place, no-one is going to get it right.'

Even if they were, the hotel quarantine program might still have run into trouble. In the first half of 2020, the WHO, Australia, Europe and the United States were all slow to accept and adjust to what nearly every virologist now understands: that the virus transmits not only through touch and close proximity but also through the air, in tiny particles that can hang in a poorly ventilated room and infect anyone who breathes them in. In the early months of the pandemic, we couldn't stop our doctors and nurses getting sick, despite them being highly trained, well equipped and proficient in the use of PPE. Yet, whenever there was an outbreak in hotel quarantine, we blamed security guards or, subsequently, a chronic asthmatic who needed a nebuliser to breathe more easily, for doing the wrong thing. The security guards were told they didn't need to wear masks all the time, and the only ones they were given were loose-fitting surgical masks which help to protect other people if the wearer is sick but not the wearer from infection.

Victoria's biggest problem wasn't that COVID escaped from quarantine but what that meant for all of us. Whether fair or not, the genomics report sheeted the entire second-wave epidemic directly to the Victorian Government. It also convinced Brett Sutton that elimination of the virus was possible. The only way for Daniel Andrews to politically recover was to take us back down to zero.

CHAPTER 4
AN UNCONSCIONABLE DELAY

On the day we went into stage 4 lockdown, my wife panic-bought a duck. That sentence will only make sense to you if you lived through Melbourne's COVID winters of 2020 and 2021, when every announcement of new restrictions sent waves of anxiety coursing through the suburbs and triggered fresh bouts of hoarding at supermarkets and bottle shops. Each time this happened, Premier Daniel Andrews would tell us this was unnecessary, that supermarkets would stay open and food wouldn't run out, that there was no need to have a year's worth of toilet paper stuffed in the garage. He was right, of course. But even if you are willing to place your faith in what political leaders say, it is unnerving to walk into a supermarket and see the aisles stripped bare of pasta, rice, canned food and meat.

The day in August 2020 that Andrews announced Melbourne was moving to the state's toughest setting for COVID restrictions—basically, the rules we had been living under for the previous month plus a curfew to keep us indoors at night, and what became known as the 5-kilometre rule, which prevented us from leaving our local neighbourhoods—shoppers with gaping trolleys lined up outside Costco outlets and Dan Murphy's booze barns to ensure that whatever happened next, they wouldn't go hungry or have to endure it sober. That afternoon, my wife drove to our local Coles and discovered the place had already been raided by an Atkins Diet horde. In the meat section, there wasn't a packet of mince or chicken thighs to be found, and the exasperated staff explained there wasn't any more out the back. With a sense of rising panic, she scanned the barren shelves and saw that one of the few items left was a frozen duck. She'd never bought a duck before and neither of us had any clue how to cook one, but in that moment, such practicalities were overwhelmed by a hunter-gatherer instinct to bring home meat to feed the kids. For the next five months, the duck sat in our freezer as a rock-hard reminder that, in a pandemic, the only thing that spreads quicker than a respiratory virus is fear. It wasn't until New Year's Eve that we finally thawed it out, stuck it on the Weber, and cremated without ceremony a forsaken bird and a wretched 2020.

The witching hour for announcements was between 3 p.m. and 5 p.m. Whenever the premier's office sent through an alert for an afternoon press conference, the city knew it wasn't good news. There was a rhythm to those days that became drearily familiar: a speculative story published in the morning's paper, a drip-feed of off-the-record confirmation throughout the morning, a tip-off that an announcement was coming, a hastily scheduled meeting of senior ministers, and finally, the afternoon press conference, with the premier flanked by the health minister and Professor Sutton, always with a slightly new story to tell but the same result: we were heading into lockdown.

At first, there was a genuine reluctance within the Andrews government to reimpose stay-at-home orders after the first wave. In June 2020, as case numbers bubbled up from breaches in hotel quarantine, the concern within the AHPPC, Australia's peak COVID advisory group, was that Victoria was moving too slowly to contain outbreaks.

Throw forward to the middle of the following year and it wasn't even a debate anymore. In July 2021, Andrews declared he had 'no option' but to return the city to lockdown. 'You only get one chance to go hard and go fast,' he said. The following month, as Melbourne lurched into its sixth and final lockdown, the premier's conviction was absolute. 'There are no alternatives to lockdown,' he said. 'If you wait it will spread and once it spreads you can never even hope to run alongside it, let alone get out in front of it and bring it back down to zero. This is now settled.' That was 5 August 2021. The entire state of Victoria recorded eight new cases of coronavirus that day. What was supposed to be a seven-day lockdown was finally lifted on 22 October, some eleven weeks later.

How did we arrive at such a place? Before we get into it, let's remember the Doherty maxim: COVID-19 is a story of a bad virus, not bad guys. The greatest challenge to the Victorian public health response came from the virus, in particular the capacity of SARS-CoV-2 to mutate into variants which were more infectious, more virulent and sometimes both. That the virus mutated was not a surprise to anyone familiar with the evolution of infectious diseases or, indeed, within the Victorian Government. The government's cautious approach throughout the pandemic sought to make allowances for the likelihood that the virus would change both in how it passed between people, and the risk it posed to their good health and lives. Despite these allowances, the evolution of the virus from its wild Wuhan form to the Beta strain which emerged in South Africa, Delta and the game-changing Omicron, reduced our public health defences to an epidemiological Maginot Line.

In this, we were not alone. The much-vaunted NSW public health system, having managed outbreaks throughout the 2020 winter without resort to lockdown, was eventually overrun by the Delta outbreak of 2021, though not before it seeded cases into Victoria. It was the emergence of Delta, a more virulent and infectious strain which drove devastating outbreaks in India and the United Kingdom, that helped convince National Cabinet, in July 2021, to change its formal positions on lockdowns from a measure of last resort to something that 'would likely be required to control epidemic growth' until we reached sufficient vaccination levels.[1] On this basis, Daniel Andrews could rightfully say, when he announced on 5 August 2021 that Melbourne was returning to lockdown, that his government's actions were consistent with National Cabinet policy and the consensus advice of the AHPPC.

Whether this was the right thing to do is another matter. The paradox of Victoria's second-wave epidemic is that it forced the state government to confront its long-term neglect of public health and, in doing so, construct Australia's best contact-tracing and case-management system. It also rendered the government either unwilling or unable to trust this system to contain outbreaks without resort to lockdown. There is little doubt that, when you are trying to contain the outbreak of a highly transmissible infectious disease, lockdowns make the job easier. Data compiled by Victoria's health department show that, when the city was not in lockdown, every COVID case generated on average 100 contacts. In lockdown, the average number of contacts per case is reduced to five. These figures illustrate why fast, precautionary lockdowns became the default position in all states, other than New South Wales, as the pandemic dragged into its second year. In Melbourne there was something else at play. The trauma of our long COVID winter of 2020, an epidemic which ostensibly began with the government's mismanagement of quarantine but can be traced to decades of underinvestment in public health, meant the Andrews government, even if it thought it could control an outbreak without lockdown, had no appetite to try. 'We were absolutely risk-averse because we recognised what Victoria, uniquely in Australia, had been through [in] 2020,' says Jeroen Weimar, an operations manager who led Victoria's pandemic response after the second wave. 'That was a cathartic experience where you just weren't inclined to run the risk of letting it get out of control again.' Once bitten by the pandemic, Victoria was twice shy in how it responded to future outbreaks. This approach, while understandable, imposed a disproportionate burden on the city and its people.

Chris Eccles was at his home in Guerilla Bay, a clifftop house which takes in breathtaking views of the South Pacific, when he received the call from Daniel Andrews's Chief of Staff Lissie Ratcliff. It was Saturday 11 July 2020 and Eccles, having intended to spend a weekend at the coastal property he and his wife were preparing to retire to, had been marooned by a snap decision by the NSW Government to close its border to Victoria, where the second-wave epidemic was starting to turn deadly. Case numbers were rising by about 200 a day, large outbreaks were linked to the housing commission towers and Al-Taqwa College, and the first cases had been confirmed inside St Basil's Homes for the Aged. St Basil's, a residential aged-care facility in the northern suburb of Fawkner and owned by the Greek Orthodox Church, would provide the setting for the deadliest episode in Melbourne's pandemic. The stage 3 restrictions announced by Andrews a week earlier had already confined five million people living in greater Melbourne and neighbouring Mitchell Shire to their homes, but it was clear that the state's public health team, although significantly added to since the start of the pandemic, was overwhelmed.

As each new case was reported, contact tracers spent hours on the phone talking to them to work out where they had been and who they had seen while they were potentially infectious. Their contacts needed to be quarantined and interviewed so that the people they had mixed with could in turn monitor themselves for symptoms. This process, a laborious and time-intensive approach that, prior to the pandemic, had never been attempted during an outbreak of this scale, couldn't keep up with the virus, which was being passed between predominantly young people from large, migrant families, in many cases before they had so much as a sniffle to suggest they might be infected. Part of the problem was that contact tracers working from the DHHS office or their own homes had little insight into where people went, what they did, and how the virus was spreading in suburbs like Coolaroo, in the city's north, and Tarneit and Truganina, flat expanses of affordable housing estates to the city's west. In contrast to New South Wales, Victoria's health department didn't have local public health units embedded in these communities and few established links with local doctors, schools, nursing homes and childcare centres.

An already difficult job was not helped by the reporting system they were using to record cases. PHESS, the Public Health Event Surveillance System, was introduced by Ted Baillieu's government in 2012 to provide an electronic database in which to store details of infectious diseases detected within the community. Prior to the emergence of COVID, there was a list of more than seventy conditions, including infectious diseases like measles, tuberculosis, meningococcal disease and legionellosis, which doctors and pathology laboratories were required by law to report to the health department. PHESS was designed for data to be entered electronically but, from the first year of its operation, information was entered manually.[2] This practice, which everyone had grown accustomed to, continued through the early months of the pandemic. PHESS is a good system for what it was designed to do, namely keep a record of instances of certain diseases, along with basic details about the cases; a variant of the same system supported New South Wales's contact tracing throughout the COVID crisis. The shortcoming of the system, at least in Victoria, is that contact tracers were unable to upload the information they gained from case interviews directly into PHESS. Instead, they had to type out notes of their interviews, print them off, make copies, and fax or scan them to other people in the department, who would then paste the information into the system as an attachment. This cumbersome method meant that information needed by contact tracers to identify links between different cases and the likely source of outbreaks, was in the system but not in a searchable form. Every time someone typed in the data, they introduced the risk of human error: misspelling a street name or surname, or entering the wrong postcode. The delays this caused in contact tracing were compounded by delays in pathology, which the health department had no direct control over.

None of this meant that Victoria's contact-tracing and case-management system couldn't have worked but, as the rising case numbers swamped the people making the phone calls, entering the data and ordering tests, it was clear that it wasn't. In the wake of the genomics report which linked the entire second-wave epidemic to hotel quarantine, Eccles and Andrews deployed one of their most trusted public servants from within DPC, Kate Houghton, to the health department to help manage the fallout. She reported back that, for all the failings of hotel quarantine, contact tracing was a much bigger problem. When Ratcliff called Eccles in Guerilla Bay, she told him that the premier, having accepted until now the assurances of the public health team that they had the situation under control, was convinced that serious changes were needed.

Eccles knew that, as a first step, he needed his best people at the centre of Victoria's pandemic response. He handpicked from his own executive team Jeremi Moule, a communications professional who had worked with Eccles in South Australia and quickly earned the trust of Andrews, and Sandy Pitcher, his best public administrator. Under what became known as the COVID-19 Public Health Incident Management Team, Moule was appointed as the state's first deputy secretary of public health, a seven-day-a-week job he split with Nicola Quinn, a colleague from DPC. Pitcher was put in charge of all case, contact and outbreak work alongside Euan Wallace, an experienced clinician and expert in health governance. Jeroen Weimar, a senior bureaucrat responsible for the state's road and rail networks, was put in charge of testing. They worked with Kym Peake, the health department secretary who, under this new, bulging public health bureaucracy, was made DHHS state controller. By the end of the year, Moule would replace Eccles as the new secretary of DPC, Pitcher and Wallace would be given their own departments to run, and Weimar would take charge of the entire response.

This bureaucratic surge force, although evidence of the singular focus Daniel Andrews now had on public health, is only part of the story of how our pandemic defences were rebuilt. An equally significant change was cultural. The Victorian Government, having previously resisted offers of assistance from Canberra, the ADF and the private sector, now accepted it needed help. Alan Finkel, Australia's chief scientist, was embedded within Victoria's COVID response. Commodore Mark Hill (since promoted to rear admiral) was deployed into DHHS headquarters along with an additional 183 ADF personnel. Another 200 casual staff were sourced from labour-hire companies Health Direct, Helloworld and Stella, and Commonwealth public servants were mobilised in Melbourne. On the day of Ratcliff's phone call to Chris Eccles, 452 people were working in case, contact and outbreak management in Victoria. By the end of the month, that number had more than doubled.

It was on 15 July 2020, a typically clear, cold winter's day in Canberra, when the second-most-senior officer in the Navy, Rear Admiral Mark Hammond, asked Mark Hill whether he was able to deploy to Melbourne at short notice. That same night, commodore Hill flew into a deserted Essendon Airport as the only passenger aboard an RAAF King Air. Hill is a warfare officer, not a public health expert. He has seen active duty in Iraq, Afghanistan and East Timor, and at the start of 2020 was the commander of ADF joint taskforce 633, Australia's military deployment across the Middle East and Afghanistan. When the commodore walked into the DHHS offices at 50 Lonsdale Street the next morning, he found an organisation overwhelmed by the scale of the outbreak, its people exhausted but stoically sticking to their tasks. As an organisation, Victoria's health department was under siege from journalists, epidemiologists and political opponents of the Andrews government. Hill says his first job was to figure out the command arrangements. 'I had some difficulty at the time really trying to nail down responsibilities and accountabilities in that organisation,' he says. 'They might have been readily apparent to others but they weren't apparent to me initially.' Over the next few days, he realised that the most pressing problem, other than the virus, was a lack of timely and reliable data within the COVID response. He arranged for ADF personnel to shift to the front line of the public health crisis: data entry.

Jeroen Weimar's shift from running Public Transport Victoria and VicRoads to overseeing Victoria's COVID testing program might seem a strange career progression, but the pandemic was not the first or worst crisis he had confronted. On 7 July 2005, Weimar was sitting in a Starbucks cafe on Buckingham Palace Road when he received a text message identifying an electrical fault in the London Underground rail network. At the time, Weimar was the head of transport, policing and enforcement for Transport for London, the government authority responsible for the day-to-day operations of the city's public transport networks and main roads. The control room for the London Underground was only 100 metres down the road from where he was having coffee with a colleague. By the time they reached it, it was clear they weren't dealing with an electrical fault. Three terrorists wearing backpacks filled with homemade bombs had detonated massive explosions on separate trains at the height of the morning commute, killing thirty-nine people. A short time later, another blast detonated by a fourth suicide bomber ripped through a double-decker bus, killing a further thirteen people. Weimar says that managing the aftermath of that horrific event taught him the importance of fast, reliable and well-communicated information in a crisis. This is what Victoria's early response to the pandemic sorely lacked but what it started to gain in the winter of 2020.

Sandy Pitcher and Euan Wallace, the departmental executives in charge of an army of contact tracers, now had the people they needed. A more difficult challenge, Pitcher explains, was how to fix a system groaning under the weight of information it was not designed to manage. 'We had a system that was doing the job it was built to do. We just didn't have a fit-for-purpose system for that part of contact tracing,' she says. Pitcher and Wallace, bringing fresh eyes to a problem that had plagued our public health response since the start of the pandemic, saw there were choke points in the system. One was the enormous amount of negative test results being loaded into the PHESS database. Between 1 July and the end of August 2020, an average of 23 720 people in Victoria were tested every day for SARS-CoV-2. At the peak of the second-wave epidemic, 687 of those tested positive. Since the start of the pandemic, the health department had entered every negative test into the system as well as the positives. This told them the rate of positive cases, which can be a helpful guide to how fast the virus is spreading. The issue was that a mountain of negative test results, which all had to be entered manually, was delaying the entry of data which mattered far more. In the month of July, only half the people who tested positive to COVID-19 were notified within the first twenty-four hours, and some of them had to wait five days. 'There was no way to prioritise the queue,' Pitcher explains. 'The positives didn't get in ahead of the negatives; they just waited in line.'

With the virus now starting to spread through residential aged-care centres, the delays were becoming deadly. Wallace and Pitcher decided that, to unclog the system, they had to jettison the reporting of negative tests. In effect, the doctor and the bureaucrat performed bypass surgery on a stricken system. By then, they both knew its heart also needed to be replaced.

In the early months of the pandemic, the Victorian health department was approached by Salesforce, a US tech company based in Silicon Valley, about an information-management system it had adapted to support contact tracing on a mass scale. The system was a customer relationship management (CRM) platform, a kind of social network used by businesses to better understand and respond to their customer base. When applied to contact tracing, it takes data gathered from case interviews and uses it to provide an interactive map of outbreaks showing connections between people, places and times. By the time of Victoria's second wave, the Salesforce platform was being used by South Australia, Western Australia and New Zealand, as well as thirty-five American states. For reasons the company couldn't understand, its sales reps had never been able to pique the interest of anyone working for the Victorian Government, despite multiple approaches. That changed under Victoria's new-look COVID response. Wallace and Pitcher, encouraged by Dr Finkel, engaged with Salesforce and ditched PHESS for the new CRM platform. Changing IT systems at a large company or a government department is fraught at the best of times. Hill says that doing it in the middle of an epidemic was like installing a new combat system in the midst of a gunfight. Six weeks later, the Salesforce platform was carrying our contact tracing.

The elevation of Wallace to a senior position within the public health response ushered in more changes. Wallace had spent years researching and practising gynaecology and obstetrics at city hospitals and Monash University. Over that time, he had developed a wide network of friends and contacts across academia and health. Some of them happened to be the state's best hospital-based infectious disease experts, whom he now asked, and in some cases cajoled, to get involved. They included Paul Johnson from Austin Health, Michelle Giles from the Alfred and Monash hospitals, and Rhonda Stuart from Monash Health, who all came to work at the department. The other person Victoria wanted was Professor Allen Cheng, an infectious disease epidemiologist from Alfred Health who was considered the wisest head on the AHPPC—when infectious disease people get together, he's almost always considered the smartest in the room. Several approaches made to Cheng failed, but he finally agreed, and when he walked into the health department's Lonsdale Street office, the impact was immediate.

Professor Cheng clearly remembers his first day as Victoria's deputy chief health officer. It was 23 July, a Thursday, which meant that Brett Sutton was on his regular day off. This put Cheng, a career researcher and clinician who had never worked in government, in charge of the state's entire public health response. It was both daunting and exciting. Professor Cheng could see he was surrounded by some of the brightest, most capable and ambitious people in government; fellow infectious disease experts like Johnson and Stuart, whom he had known for years; and a room full of weary people who were grateful that, not before time, reinforcements had arrived. 'There was a sense that it is all hands on deck and anybody who could help was needed,' Cheng says.

A few hours earlier, for the first time in any jurisdiction in Australia, it had become mandatory for everyone in Melbourne to wear a mask whenever they ventured outside their home. Professor Cheng thought this would help, but at this stage no-one really knew what impact the new rules would have. The virus was being spread predominantly by young people, who were unlikely to get seriously ill from COVID and were unwittingly infecting their families. Having seen up close the limits of the state's capacity to contact-trace new cases and isolate people when case numbers were running as they were, Professor Cheng believed that more dramatic restrictions were required to provide an epidemiological circuit-breaker. This was also the view held by the rest of the AHPPC and Professor Murphy, who saw in Victoria a reluctance to move to a hard, New Zealand–style lockdown. Only one day earlier, Professor Sutton had publicly made the case to keep restrictions where they were. 'To go to a particular model of lockdown that worked for one country at one point in time is not the solution,' he said at that morning's Daily Dan. 'It may well be that it's an awful impost on the economy and on people's lives with no material benefit.'

Professor Cheng saw it in simpler terms. What mattered now, more than anything else, was getting the case numbers down, and he didn't think this would happen with the restrictions Victoria had in place. 'What I thought very early on is whatever solutions we might come up with to fix the capacity of contact tracing or the turnaround time for tests … would probably break if we had twice the number of cases,' he says. 'And all the problems we had would probably be fixed if we had 100 cases a day instead of 500 cases a day. That really said we needed to do something to get those cases down to give ourselves a fighting chance. The thinking was, "If we are going to have to lock down, how hard can we lock down to make it as short as possible?" Every trade-off that you'd make to leave something open would lengthen how long it would take. That was the equation.'

Professor Cheng was convinced that all of Victoria needed to be locked down and Melbourne needed to move to stage 4 restrictions. This was the idea he took to Daniel Andrews, at the end of his first day in charge, on a Zoom call. 'It was a pretty intimidating moment I have to say,' he says. 'To be fair, I am not sure I was the first person to think it. But I talked to the directions team and said, "Look, I think we are going to have to at least start thinking about this." I spoke to the secretary, I spoke to all the people I knew above me. Then we had a meeting with the premier that night.' Andrews's response, as recalled by Professor Cheng in an ABC Radio interview, was blunt: 'That's a billion-dollar-a-week decision. Are you really sure about that?' Professor Cheng was sure. He spent the next few days refining what the new public health orders would need to be and how they would operate. On 2 August, Daniel Andrews announced that Melbourne would move to stage 4 restrictions and the rest of the state would be subject to stay-at-home orders. Victoria was declared a state of disaster.

Rhonda Stuart describes her first day with the department as a weird experience. It had been more than thirty years since she graduated from medical school, and throughout that time, she had only ever worked in hospitals. She understood how people worked in hospitals, how they thought and how to navigate the politics. She understood none of that at the DHHS. 'To get called into a department where you don't know any of the people, you don't know any of the structures and you certainly don't know the politics, was quite daunting,' she says. 'To be honest, it was a bit of a mess.'

Paul Johnson, part of the last generation of epidemiologists and infection disease specialists to train at Fairfield Hospital, came to the surge team from the Austin Hospital, where as director of research he had led a thirty-year-hunt for the Buruli ulcer, a (likely) mosquito-borne bacterial infection notoriously known as the flesh-eating virus. Mark Hill was keen to instil a 'daily battle rhythm' in the fight against COVID, and Johnson was an enthusiastic convert, urging his contact tracers to 'Go fast! Stop COVID! Report to base!' After a while, it occurred to Professor Johnson that they were approaching things the wrong way. Instead of the best infectious disease clinicians taking up residence inside the health department headquarters, why not shift the public health response back into the major hospitals, where it could be supported by their own pathology services, testing facilities and, if and when a vaccine became available, mass vaccination centres? This was already being done to a large extent by Barwon Health in Geelong, which had acted quickly to bring an outbreak in the Western Districts town of Colac under control.

Once the second wave started to subside, Johnson returned to the Austin—taking a relieved Annaliese van Diemen with him—and established the North-East Public Health Unit. Professor Stuart went back to the Monash Medical Centre to set up a South-East Public Health Unit. Finn Romanes, one of the department's most experienced public health physicians, also left Lonsdale Street to establish a Western Public Health Unit at Sunshine Hospital. The map of greater Melbourne with its five million people was carved up and divided between the three public health units, which each accepted responsibility for, and autonomy in, managing outbreaks, testing and, eventually, vaccinations on their patch. Weimar describes the creation of local public health units as the most important reform to Victoria's health system throughout the pandemic years. 'Colac was our wake-up call that we needed a localised response, that these local outbreaks could not be managed from a centralised team at Lonsdale Street, no matter how many resources you threw at it,' he says. 'You need the information on the ground and, crucially, you need relationships of trust. When the local abattoir becomes a major outbreak, if nobody understands or has a connection to the community of itinerant labour-hire workers who are working there ... you sure as hell aren't going to start creating trust when half of them are lying sick in their beds and the other half are terrified about losing their jobs.'

A year later, when Victoria's COVID response was mopping up the tail of another outbreak, Professor Stuart took me inside the 'War Room' at the Monash Medical Centre, the nerve centre of the South-East Public Health Unit. There isn't much to it: just a ground-floor, windowless space where contact tracers sit at rows of desks, talking on the phone to people who are infected with COVID, as well as the people nominated as their close contacts and the people those contacts might have come into contact with. Most of the people here don't have extensive experience in health care, but you don't need a nursing or medical degree to be a good contact tracer. Mostly, you need to be a good listener with an intuitive understanding of what it is you are listening for.

I met Richard Flanagan, a 57-year-old community health nurse who joined the unit at the start of the year, and who quickly became one of its gun interviewers. Flanagan explained that the art of contract tracing is quickly earning people's trust and then holding it through what can sometimes be a four- or five-hour conversation. It is not a normal thing for people you don't know to share with you personal and sometimes intimate details about where they have been and who they have seen, especially when they have been seeing someone they shouldn't. Flanagan has heard confessions of illicit affairs, criminal activity and flagrant breaches of COVID restrictions. He is not there to pass judgement, though, only to put information into a system that helps map the spread of the virus. 'You have to not be rushing,' he told me. 'You are requiring their patience and you have to be sensitive to them. If you lose their cooperation, you are not going to get the information you need. So it is about maintaining a relationship. It is about getting it right, rather than getting it quick.'

Current Victorian Health Minister Martin Foley says the decentralisation of public health will be an enduring change from the pandemic. He sees local public health units becoming a permanent feature of the state's health system, with their future roles going well beyond infectious diseases. Foley hopes they can help bridge a deeper, more entrenched divide within public health. 'Health care moving outside the four walls of hospitals into the community and homes,' he explains. 'If you are rich and white and in the south-east and eastern suburbs, your chances of having got through this pandemic were a whole lot better than if you weren't. The capacity of local public health units to deal with those structural inequalities will be built considerably.'

At the end of his three-month deployment in 2020, commodore Hill wrote a series of observations in his journal. When read nearly two years later, they open a window into what it was like on the inside of Victoria's public health response at its most difficult time. 'Everyone in Victoria has an opinion about DHHS—few of them good,' he writes. 'Everyone is an expert on contact tracing—it sounds easy but it is difficult. Everyone including other jurisdictions is very keen to give advice.' His notes go on: 'Every system is good until it's stressed, as would probably be the case in NSW. Victoria has improved in leaps and bounds over the last three months.'

The notes also offer a commentary on the white noise of competing expert opinions that surrounded Victoria's second-wave response:

> I didn't know there were so many epidemiologists. Regardless of restrictions they all have a different opinion about how Victoria should handle COVID. Like doctor shopping, if you look long enough you'll find an opinion you want to hear. There is no 'right answer'. Victoria is doing better than most in my opinion.

At the peak of the second-wave epidemic, Hill travelled to Sydney with Sandy Pitcher, Euan Wallace and Alan Finkel, at the request of Scott Morrison, to observe and learn from the NSW public health response. Hill says that, as good as the NSW approach was, it was very similar to what Victoria was already doing. 'Any Australian jurisdiction would have been challenged by the scale of the outbreak that Victoria was dealing with,' he says. We would find that out soon enough.

It is harder to come out of lockdown than it is to go in. This was never more true than in the Melbourne winter of 2020. For three and a half months, the city was held in a state of lonely and cold isolation. We put on a brave face. There were attempts to rekindle the spirit of lockdown no. 1, when we understood that Australia was responding to a global crisis and it seemed as though everyone was in it together. In reality, this was a sad, slow grind disconnected from the lives and understanding of people in other states.

For the previous twenty years, Melbourne had been Australia's boom town, a story of uninterrupted economic growth, surging population, low unemployment, and cultural and social vibrancy.

Before the pandemic, greater Melbourne had just nudged past five million people and was forecast to overtake Sydney as Australia's most-populous city. Not everyone was comfortable with how fast Melbourne was growing but it was a measure of the city's success that so many people wanted to come here: to live, to study and just to have fun. Where the economy of Western Australia is built on digging stuff out of the ground and selling it overseas, our two largest export industries are education and tourism. Put another way, our primary business is bringing people here, in massive numbers, through temporary migration schemes. At least, it was before the pandemic. Between 1 July 2020 and 30 June 2021, nearly 90 000 people abandoned Melbourne to return overseas or move to another state.[3] This is the greatest exodus since the 1990s recession. Before the COVID crisis, one of the fastest-growing parts of Melbourne was its city centre, where up to one million people walked through the downtown area on an average workday. In the depths of lockdown, that figure dropped to 50 000. Streets usually teeming with people were all but deserted. The city just stopped. And with it, so did the livelihoods of anyone who owned or worked in restaurants, bars, retail shops, drycleaners, and any other service industry that depends on being in the same room as another person.

Deputy Lord Mayor Nicholas Reece recalls that, when he travelled to Canberra between lockdowns and explained to a local government conference what Melbourne was going through, delegates from other cities confessed to having no idea that it had been so bad. After he'd finished his presentation, the mayor of Wagga Wagga offered him a hug. Reece realised that Melbourne's pandemic disaster, unlike the fires that tore through east-coast communities the previous summer, was largely hidden from view. In other cities, where life throughout 2020 resumed largely uninterrupted after the first lockdown, Melbourne's ongoing restrictions were a distant, amorphous concern to people living elsewhere. Haunting images of shuttered businesses and empty trams ghosting through abandoned city streets captured what we were going through but meant little to those who weren't experiencing it. 'I don't think people's hearts were touched in the same way as they are when you see a flood or a bushfire or some other terrible, natural event,' Reece says. 'Most Australians have had some experience of natural disaster, so they reflect on that and connect at an emotional level when they see other Australians in other parts of the country going through the same thing. With the pandemic, we were on our own. There just wasn't that empathy there. I think that had a psychologically scarring effect on the city.'

Every morning, the premier would present a daily count of case numbers and deaths. For 120 days straight he fronted the cameras, often for more than an hour at a time, promising to stay on his feet until every question was asked, if not necessarily answered. The conferences were broadcast live on television and streamed on social media platforms to a daily audience which, at its peak, rivalled the number of people who used to walk through the city. At 6 p.m. every night, the television news would faithfully recount the same information, with sombre-faced broadcasters standing in front of vibrant graphic displays. These bookends to our lockdown days reinforced the idea that the fortunes of the city were entirely dependent on the latest epidemiological data. Our mood rose if case numbers fell, then plummeted with any new spike in infections. Looking back now, after the Omicron strain has introduced Bolivian-style inflation to the currencies of the pandemic, you might wonder what the fuss was all about. If you look at a graph of Victoria or Australia's pandemic case numbers from January 2020, everything that happened before the Omicron waves of late 2021 and early 2022 barely registers as a blip. In statistical terms, the mountain we thought we were climbing back in 2020 looks like a bump in an otherwise smooth road. It wasn't.

In Victoria's second wave, 801 people died with COVID-19. Of those, 655 died in aged care. Not only did the virus break out of quarantine, it spread into the one place we most needed to protect.

People of advanced age dying in their beds from a respiratory infection is not always a tragedy. At the end of July 2021, the average age of people who died with COVID-19 in Australia was eighty-seven,[4] which is four years older than our average life expectancy. The most common cause of death in COVID patients was pneumonia, and three-quarters of those who died had a pre-existing chronic condition, most commonly dementia. Before the pandemic, aged-care and palliative-care nurses called pneumonia the 'old person's friend'. When my father, having reached an advanced stage of dementia, died from pneumonia a few years ago, I understood why. It was sad and confronting, but in the end we were grateful for him to be spared what was coming next. The tragedy of Melbourne's second wave is that, unlike my dad, people at the end of long lives died separated from the people who mattered most to them. Some in their final days were denied basic care. They died from neglect as well as the virus, in chaotic circumstances which, for a dementia patient, would have been torturous.

It was bad, although probably inevitable, that the virus got out of quarantine. It was worse, although not unexpected, that it spread into residential aged care. What happened next was shameful, and the worst of it happened at St Basil's Homes for the Aged. There, we saw everything that is wrong with aged care in Australia and deficient with public health in Victoria.

St Basil's is an aged-care facility owned and managed by the Greek Orthodox Church, which, since 1996, has provided care to Greek migrants nearing the end of their lives. It was built on 3 hectares of grassland in Fawkner on the edge of Merri Creek, a waterway that snakes from the lush Yarra Valley down through Melbourne's northern suburbs. It was in these suburbs that, in the years after World War II and the civil war in Greece, so many from the Greek diaspora found work and affordable housing in blue-collar areas like Brunswick, Preston and Coburg. St Basil's has a hostel for residents who can mostly care for themselves, a nursing home and a dedicated dementia ward. At the start of Victoria's second-wave epidemic, St Basil's had 117 residents. By its end, forty-five had died. It remains Australia's deadliest COVID outbreak.

Aged care in Australia is predominantly regulated and funded by the federal government. St Basil's received money from the Commonwealth Department of Health, and its standards and practices were overseen by the federal aged-care watchdog, the Aged Care Quality and Safety Commission (ACQSC). According to a July 2019 reassessment by the ACQSC, it was a well-run facility.[5] The ACQSC also believed St Basil's was prepared for the pandemic. On 30 June 2020, an infection-prevention and control-outreach team from the Victorian health department visited the facility and raised no serious concerns about its COVID precautions.[6] Dr Ian Norton, a global expert in emergency medical responses who was asked by the Coroners Court of Victoria to review the outbreak as an independent witness, found that St Basil's was as prepared as most residential aged-care facilities were in Victoria.[7] According to Dr Norton, it is the federal and Victorian governments that were not adequately prepared. At the time of the St Basil's outbreak, the federal government didn't have a dedicated, national COVID-19 plan for residential aged care, and there was no recommendation for people who worked in nursing homes to wear masks. More pertinently for St Basil's, the Victorian and federal health departments, in a slew of conflicting documents and online resources provided to nursing homes, created confusion about where help would come from in the event of an outbreak. The DHHS documents suggested that the state health department would be the primary response agency. In reality, this was never going to happen. Instead, it was the responsibility of the federal health department, although the St Basil's management would have done well to know this.

On 29 June, the federal health department published on its website a document titled 'First 24 Hours: Managing COVID-19 in a Residential Aged Care Facility'. It sets out the immediate steps a nursing home should take in response to an outbreak, including contacting both federal and state health authorities as soon as they learn of a COVID case. Once the federal health department is notified, it appoints a case manager as a single point of contact to manage the outbreak and arranges for everyone at the facility to be tested for the virus. Recognising the importance of a speedy initial response, its guidelines advise that testing should be done within four to six hours of a confirmed case. Had the St Basil's management seen the document and followed its recommended steps, the disaster which followed might have been averted. Dr Norton found no evidence the document was seen by anyone at St Basil's prior to the outbreak. A link to the document was included in a health department newsletter distributed on 3 July, and the federal aged care minister, Richard Colbeck, also included it in a letter he sent to aged-care providers on 7 July. The ACQSC first wrote to nursing homes bringing the document to their attention on 22 July. By that time, St Basil's was already deep in crisis.

The outbreak began when a personal care assistant (PCA) came to work with the virus. She says she didn't know she had it and wasn't showing any COVID-19 symptoms. It is now clear she shouldn't have been at work anyway. She lived in one of the ten local government areas ordered into lockdown by the Victorian Government on 30 June. Prior to the 'postcode lockdown', the government launched a testing blitz of people living in the northern and western suburbs. On 5 July, after the care worker finished a shift at St Basil's, she went to a nearby drive-through testing clinic, which is where you sit in your car, roll down the window, and a nurse sticks a series of swabs in your mouth and up your nose. Normally, you would only get tested if you have reason to believe you might have come into contact with the virus. For this reason, you shouldn't go to work—especially not in a residential aged-care facility—between the time you are tested and when you receive your results. The care worker did go to work, however, on the advice of a registered nurse she spoke to at St Basil's. The nurse told a coroner's inquest that this was consistent with the nursing home's COVID policy. The PCA worked two full shifts at St Basil's on 6 and 7 July, and she was back at work the next day when her husband texted her to say that a family member had tested positive. She went home immediately and, the following day, her own COVID test came back positive. By then, the virus had sunk its hooks into St Basil's. At the end, ninety-four residents and ninety-four staff had been infected.

Aged care in Australia is a basket case. The final report of the Royal Commission into Aged Care Quality and Safety, published in March 2021 after more than two years of public hearings, submissions and deliberations, ran to more than 1000 pages and identified systemic problems of inadequate funding, enormously varied standards of care, poor governance and an absence of leadership across the sector. Private and not-for-profit residential aged-care facilities rely heavily on the labour of PCAs. These are the people who wash and clothe residents, feed them and give them their medication, and provide whatever stimulation they receive between family visits. PCAs are overwhelmingly women and first-generation migrants. It requires a six-month TAFE course to become a qualified PCA, and the work is low-paid and highly casualised. At the time of the St Basil's outbreak, the average starting wage for an aged-care worker was just under $22 an hour.

Whatever mistakes were made by the PCA at St Basil's, she isn't to blame for what happened there. Neither is the nurse who told her to come to work. In 2021, after federal and state health authorities and aged-care regulators and providers had the benefit of learning from all the mistakes made at the Newmarch nursing home in western Sydney and St Basil's in northern Melbourne, outbreaks continued in residential aged care. The story of St Basil's isn't that someone let the virus in; it's the dysfunctional response of nearly everyone involved—the management of the home, the state and federal health departments, the contractors brought in to fix the problem, and the regulators who failed to see it coming—once it became clear that a potentially lethal situation was rapidly unfolding.

When Vicky Kos, the manager of St Basil's, got off the phone from talking to the COVID-positive PCA on the morning of 9 July, she immediately rang the Victorian DHHS to let them know they had a positive case. If she had followed the federal government guidelines issued a week earlier, she would have also informed the federal health department, other residents, their families and her own staff. Some St Basil's workers say they weren't informed until 13 July that one of their colleagues had tested positive. In the absence of this information, they kept working, oblivious to the risk they posed to the old, frail people in their care. The Victorian health department, once notified of the COVID case at St Basil's, did not make contact with the facility for another three days, and it didn't think to tell its federal counterparts until 14 July, a full week after the infectious staff member worked her last shift.

Bizarrely, neither did the ACQSC. By coincidence, the aged-care watchdog found out about the St Basil's outbreak on 10 July but didn't pass on this critical information to the federal health department. It assumed the DHHS already had. It was only after the federal health department was informed that testing of staff was arranged. The testing took place on 15 July and the results were returned on 17 July, eight days after the PCA returned her positive test. Those results revealed that eleven staff and sixteen residents were already infected with the virus.

Dr Ian Norton managed the WHO's Global Emergency Medical Team for six years and has also directed AUSMAT, the Australian Medical Assistance Teams. In July and August 2020, when Victoria's second wave crashed over forty nursing homes, he was seconded by the federal government to be the lead clinician in the newly established Victorian Aged Care Response Centre jointly funded by the state and the Commonwealth. In his report to Victorian Coroner John Cain, he describes the eight-day gap between the first case and comprehensive testing at St Basil's as the 'root cause' of the failure to contain the outbreak. From this unconscionable delay, everything else flows. As he explains in his report, everyone who visits St Basil's before 17 July, whether they are from the Victorian Government, the federal government or the regulator, is comfortable with how the aged-care facility and its staff are responding to the outbreak. The staff have a good supply of PPE and a good system in place when taking it on and off. The parts of the nursing home infected with COVID are quarantined from those that aren't. Some staff are at home with the virus but there is still a continuity of care. Once the Victorian and federal health departments see the test results and decide to intervene, everything changes, to the detriment of the St Basil's residents and their families.

Dr Norton's report challenges the prevailing narrative about St Basil's—that the deaths of forty-five people were caused by a rogue operator which didn't follow the COVID rules. On the day that Dr Norton was scheduled to testify before the coroner, his independence and expertise were challenged by the three parties which stood to lose the most from his evidence: the federal health department, the Victorian health department, and the lawyer representing a group of St Basil's family members who, at the time, were pursuing the facility, and by extension the deep pockets of the Greek Orthodox Church, for damages. Their submissions persuaded John Cain not to call Dr Norton as a witness or treat his report as part of the evidentiary brief. Despite this, the Norton report remains on the court file. It is the story of St Basil's, related by one of Australia's foremost experts in clinical emergency management, that powerful interests don't want told.

* * *

When University of Sydney Professor Lyn Gilbert and Professor Alan Lilly from the Australian Catholic University were asked by the federal government to conduct an investigation into St Basil's, the disconnect between federal and state authorities, and the failure of St Basil's management to communicate to the families of residents what was going on, were sadly familiar. Only months earlier, as the St Basil's crisis was unfolding, they were gathering witness testimony and other evidence about the bureaucratic and administrative failings at Newmarch House, a residential aged-care facility in western Sydney run by Anglicare, the welfare arm of the Anglican Church. As with St Basil's, an infected staff member triggered a deadly COVID outbreak at Newmarch. By the time it was brought under control, nineteen residents had died. As with St Basil's, the outbreak also triggered a bitter dispute between federal and state health authorities about what should be done. In the meantime, calls and emails to the nursing home from family members desperate for information about their loved ones went unanswered, and some replacement aged-care workers provided by private contractors didn't turn up to their shifts because they were worried about getting sick.

One of the mistakes made in the Newmarch response was the failure to listen to doctors on the ground instead of bureaucrats in Canberra. Rather than follow the advice of the doctor from the local public health unit who wanted to treat infected residents in the nursing home, the Newmarch management sided with the ACQSC's medical adviser and transferred all infected patients to hospital. Professors Gilbert and Lilly noted:

> For frail elderly people, admission to an acute hospital, where most staff have limited experience of their complex care needs, can be extremely distressing. Caring for residents in an aged care home, during an infectious disease outbreak, was also the preferred option of public health authorities.[8]

The report concluded this is also what most residents would have wanted, if they were given a choice.

The denial of individual agency, even to people who no longer wanted medical interventions to prolong their lives, is a recurring theme in Australia's pandemic response and was manifest in Victoria. 'Did we learn anything from the Newmarch in Sydney?' a frustrated family member of a St Basil's resident asked professors Gilbert and Lilly during the St Basil's review. 'We were just literally going from a mistake to a bigger mistake.'[9]

At St Basil's, the tipping point came in the form of a two-page letter written by Brett Sutton on 21 July 2020. By that stage, Victoria's health department was aware of fifty-eight confirmed cases, including forty residents. Professor Sutton declared the outbreak a 'significant risk to public health' and a danger to the lives of residents and staff, and ordered that all staff who worked shifts between 1 July and 15 July should quarantine at home for two weeks. Professor Sutton said that, as a consequence of this, St Basil's would need a replacement workforce to continue to operate: 'The department is working with the Commonwealth Department of Health and the Aged Care Quality and Safety Commission to support this. This course of action has been taken in other aged care settings with widespread transmission among staff.'

On the same day that Professor Sutton wrote his letter, doctors working on the front line of the outbreak warned during a meeting with federal and state health officials of the potentially catastrophic consequences of furloughing all staff. The coroner's inquest was told that Dr Sandra Brown, the manager of a Northern Health residential inreach team treating St Basil's residents, had expressed strong concerns. Dr Zi Yi Low, a geriatric medicine specialist who had private patients at St Basil's, warned it was a shocking idea and that, when the same thing had been done at Estia in Heidelberg West, another residential aged-care facility, residents had gone without medicine, meals and basic care. In an email sent the previous day,

Dr Low wrote: 'If St Basil's goes down this path this is a facility with triple the size of Estia Heidelberg—this will be disastrous.' Dr Rabin Sinappu, a senior geriatrician, told the meeting it was essential to have continuity of care.

Professor Sutton's decision, based on the advice of Finn Romanes, was built on the assumption that the federal government, through its contractors, would be able to provide a suitably skilled and experienced replacement workforce, and that the management of St Basil's would give the surge workforce whatever help it needed to make sure that residents were cared for. Neither of those things happened. Aspen Medical, a Canberra-based company contracted by the federal government to provide health services throughout the pandemic, had already indicated that it would struggle to find staff at such short notice. With the help of Victorian health authorities, it cobbled together an inexperienced staff of about thirty people to do the work of a regular, full-time staff of about 100 people. In the meantime, senior federal government officials were already discussing the possibility of shifting St Basil's residents to private hospitals. Brendan Murphy, by then the Commonwealth's health secretary, was so concerned about St Basil's that he told his chief nurse, Professor Alison McMillan, to inspect the nursing home and report back. 'At this juncture we merely observe that a number of senior Commonwealth public servants in Canberra, none of whom had set foot in St Basil's, were making decisions on 21 July 2020 about the residents in the teeth of very clear warnings from doctors who were caring from the same residents,' Peter Rozen noted at the opening of the coroner's inquest.

When the replacement workforce did take over at St Basil's, the outcome was worse than even the most dire warnings from the local doctors. The surge workforce was led by a senior manager and experienced registered nurse borrowed from Fronditha, another Greek community aged-care provider, and a team of nurses who had less than two years' experience—and in some cases, no experience in aged care. The senior manager, Heleni Bagiartakis, thought she would be acting as a liaison between the federal government and St Basil's management. Instead, St Basil's management abandoned their own residents, leaving Bagiartakis and an inadequate staff in charge with instructions not to contact management about any issues relating to clinical care. The days that followed were nightmarish. 'We literally went from crisis to crisis,' Bagiartakis told the inquest. 'It was clear that the new staff were not coping with what they had to do. From the second day, and on subsequent days, a number of staff refused to attend. They simply did not turn up.' Those who worked did what they could to help residents eat and drink, change their clothes, bathe them and pick those who fell up off the floor. Some residents went without food. Others developed horrific bedsores. Others became critically dehydrated. And by this time, they had started to die from the virus.

Kirsten Congerton, a Victorian health department nurse who volunteered to do a night shift inside St Basil's at the peak of the crisis, emailed colleagues at 4 a.m. to explain what she witnessed:

> St Basil's was horrific. I cried several times on-site and I'm pretty tough. We had one person pass away, we expect two or three more overnight. They have written many residents off as palliative … The place is a mess. It is not stable or improving … We had to manage the staff, none were capable of standing up as a leader and were in no condition psychologically to do so. Lucy and I did our best to help them survive the night, but we had to call it at 2am. Pca's [personal care assistants] in tears, RN [registered nurse] in over their heads and obviously frightened.

For family members stuck outside St Basil's, the situation was even worse. Since March, visitors had been excluded from the facility for all but a brief two-week respite between lockdowns. Some of them now couldn't find out whether their mother or father was dead or alive. The replacement staff had no opportunity to get to know the residents, and even if they did, they didn't have time to attend to them beyond the most basic care. The pandemic and Victoria's resort to hard lockdown meant that, at the very time that St Basil's residents needed the support and intervention of their families, a bureaucratic curtain descended between mothers and fathers and their sons and daughters.

On 26 July 2020, Christine Golding sidestepped security and found her way across the St Basil's grounds to the outside window of her mother's room in the hostel. Efraxia Tsaaniidis was seventy-nine years old and had lived at St Basil's for nearly ten years; she had migrated to Australia from Greece in 1966. The federal government had already started to evacuate residents to hospitals. That Sunday, the most critical cases were wheeled out of the nursing home on hospital beds and gurneys, attended by paramedics in full hazmat suits. Over the next five days, the entire facility was emptied. When Christine Golding reached her mother's window, she pulled off the dusty flyscreen and tapped on the thick double-glazed glass. A nurse heard the tapping and opened the blinds. Golding was devastated at what she saw. 'Mum's eyes had a hollow look, she appeared malnourished and couldn't speak,' she said in her statement to the coroner. 'She looked completely helpless and hopeless.'

Two weeks later, a doctor from the Peninsula Private Hospital called Golding to say that her mother was dying and she should come quick. She rushed to the hospital and dressed in full PPE. Her mother was sedated with morphine and could not speak. Efraxia Tsaaniidis died the next day. Golding told the coroner:

> It was extraordinarily sad. Worse was the anger and sadness I felt. The neglect that my mother suffered at St Basil's during the

period 22 July to 27 July 2020 was inhumane, cruel and degrading. I want the true story to be told and documented. Australians deserve to know why our aged care COVID-19 preparedness was so poor, why it spectacularly failed my mother and contributed to her premature death.[10]

On the same day that Christine Golding tapped on her mother's window, Branka Lyons and Robert McDougall had a conversation Lyons will never forget. Lyons's father was a resident at St Basil's. McDougall had worked in aged care since 2014. When he saw a story on the television news about the unfolding disaster at St Basil's, he clicked onto an online employment agency, took a job inside the COVID response and drove from his Gippsland home to his first shift. As soon as he walked into St Basil's, he knew what had to happen. 'I've asked them … please shut this place down,' he told Lyons. 'It's the worst I have ever seen in my life.'

CHAPTER 5
THE LONELY RUN

GABRIELLE'S ESCAPE WAS running. In the depths of a Melbourne winter, when everything else had stopped in its tracks, there was something about running through the streets of her neighbourhood, the rhythm of her breath and the purpose of her gait, that made her feel as though she was getting somewhere, even if she always finished in the same place she started. She had run since she was a girl. Now that she was twenty-three, it felt as though running was the only thing in her life that still made sense.

Under Victoria's state-of-disaster decree, she was allowed outside for one hour a day to exercise. She set goals for how many kilometres she could cover in that hour, in a week, a month. Sometimes she didn't feel like running at all. As the lockdown wore on, she felt listless and irritable. There were mornings when it took all her energy to get out of bed, other mornings when she'd stare at the wall for several hours, at a loss about what to do next. Eventually, though, she always ran, harder and further, as if to show her own body who was in control. She didn't know that her heart had slowed. She didn't realise her blood pressure was dangerously low. She didn't know that to protect her health, she needed to run less and eat a lot more.

Even if she had known, she probably couldn't have done anything about it. Once anorexia gets into its stride, it can be diabolical to stop.

The winter of 2020 should have been a good time in Gabrielle's life. In July that year, she handed in the final assessment of her law degree at Monash University. Having spent five years at uni, she was excited about the idea of leaving behind the lecture theatres and tutorial rooms and starting a career. She'd done internships with not-for-profits in Indonesia and New York, and she had a placement lined up at an intellectual property firm in the city and a part-time job with the Victorian Supreme Court. Anyone smart enough to get into law school, let alone complete a law degree, knows how insanely competitive the job market is for law graduates, and Gabrielle thought the stint with a Melbourne firm would round off her CV nicely. And if she couldn't find a job straight away, she had a bit of money saved with which to travel back to Indonesia. 'I went into 2020 feeling really optimistic,' she says. 'I wanted to get out into the real world.' Instead, Melbourne went into lockdown, the work placement at the law firm was cancelled, our borders stayed shut, and Gabrielle found herself marooned in the bedroom she'd slept in since she was little, in her parents' house in suburban Glen Iris, knowing there was nothing she could do about it. It was a strange, frightening, discombobulating experience—she felt both trapped and completely unmoored.

Gabrielle first developed anorexia in 2014, although no-one formally diagnosed it at the time. Another way of putting it is that, in 2014, something or several things happened in Gabrielle's life to trigger anorexia. Christine Morgan, CEO of the National Mental Health Commission, was formerly the national suicide prevention adviser to prime minister Morrison, and she also used to run the Butterfly Foundation, a national charity for people with eating disorders. She explains that, although we have a long way to go in understanding eating orders, a consensus is emerging that some people inherit genetic markers which make them more vulnerable to disordered eating. These markers, which Morgan likens to switches in the brain, can be tripped by psychological factors such as obsessing about body image, environmental factors such as stress and anxiety, or simply not eating enough. Once such a switch is tripped, something happens to our neural pathways, the circuit board which operates our brain. The way we think about food becomes distorted. Starvation, both a cause and a symptom of eating disorders, becomes the goal in anorexia. This is why it is so difficult to treat.

Once people are diagnosed with depression or bipolar disorder, they usually want to get better. Anorexics often don't. It is, in the words of Morgan, 'a perfect storm between mental wellbeing and physical wellbeing', where the sufferer knows they have to eat but can't silence the voice in their head telling them not to. For anorexics, starving yourself is success. This is part of the reason why eating disorders have the highest mortality rate of any mental illness. Anorexia can lead to depression and suicide, but in the meantime it destroys your body. It can make your hair become brittle and cause a fine down to grow over your skin, like lanugo on a premature baby. To preserve the body, the heart slows. Other vital organs, like the kidneys, are at risk of failure. And the more starved you become, the louder anorexia is in your head. This is why Gabrielle kept running through Melbourne's lockdown, even though she was not eating enough to replace the energy she was expending. If she had been listening to her body, she would have known that something was terribly wrong, but in those wretched months of being stuck at home, another voice had taken over.

'I feel like society doesn't really understand eating disorders all that well,' Gabrielle says. 'A lot of the rhetoric I get is "Why don't you just eat more?" It is so obvious what the problem is. I think that eating disorders, for a lot of people, are a coping mechanism. When you are struggling with something, you need to reinforce that sense of control. That's what happened in the pandemic. I felt like I had nothing. I couldn't do all these things and I needed to have something that I could do, that I could control … I had this problem that was simmering beneath the surface for ten years. The pandemic made it insufferable.'

Professor Susan Sawyer is the Director of the Royal Children's Hospital's Centre for Adolescent Health and Professor of Adolescent Health at the University of Melbourne. I ask her whether, when we closed down schools and community sport, and ended music lessons and locked up art studios, and told people to go home and not come out until the pandemic had passed, we were really thinking about the impact this would have on the young. 'I don't think people were,' she says. 'We threw money at breadwinners, we threw money at industries, we threw money at employers, but did we throw serious money at schools to help them pivot towards online learning in ways that are more meaningful? Keeping your granny safe isn't really a message that is going to cut through for every young person. There was a complete failure to think about the communication required. How do we speak directly to young people about what this pandemic means?'

Professor Sawyer is sitting on the patio of a 1960s house, where gumnuts from an enormous eucalyptus seeded years before the house was built are peppering the tin roof in the afternoon wind. She observes that being stuck at home wasn't all bad for all young people. It was, for some kids and their families, a chance to slow the frenetic pace of things, to declutter organised activities from young lives and give them some time and space to breathe. If you went to a school that had the resources to support meaningful online teaching, if you lived in a home where you had your own space and good wi-fi and parents who could support you, there was something to be said for a simpler life, at least for a while. If you were a kid who struggled with the anxiety of meeting people or navigating schoolyard politics, you were probably happier studying at home. For other young people, being stuck at home was a form of grinding mental torture. One of the complexities of talking about the way the pandemic affected young people is that the story varies so wildly between families and households, circumstance and fortune.

One measure of Victoria's response to the pandemic is the number of children who stopped eating during the lockdowns. Professor Sawyer saw this at the Royal Children's Hospital in a surge of seriously ill kids who had starved themselves to the point where they needed to be admitted into the hospital's specialist eating disorder ward, and in a marked increase in demand for the family-based therapy her centre offers. If you graphed the number of patients on Professor Sawyer's books against the introduction of harsh restrictions to reduce the spread of COVID, they would appear as very similar waves in both 2020 and 2021. The difference is that, for most young people, recovering from a bout of COVID is a doddle compared to dealing with an eating disorder.

We kept being told that we were in this together, but for young people, the equation of the pandemic was very different to that for adults in the middle to late stages of their lives. The direct threat posed by the virus to the health of young people is minuscule. As at 5 April 2022, 1.2 million people in Australia under the age of twenty had been infected with COVID-19 and twenty-seven had died.[1] That is a mortality rate of 0.002 per cent, or one death for every 50 000 cases. At the same time, the impact of lockdown was more potent for young people and the losses greater. To understand why, you need to step back into the Converse sneakers of your twenty-something self and remember what it was to be young. 'At birth and in the first years of our life, our brains are biologically primed to connect with caring adults and for speech, for sight and hearing,' Professor Sawyer says. 'Adolescents are biologically primed to socially engage with their peers. Connection to family matters at all stages of life but in adolescence, we are biologically primed to step outside of the family. We learn from making mistakes. We learn by doing.

We learn by experiencing. The fact that young people have missed out on two years of experiential learning is a real challenge.' Gabrielle puts it more bluntly: 'I know that a lot of people in our twenties really feel like we have been robbed of our youth.'

Beginning towards the end of Melbourne's second-wave lockdown, and continuing well into 2021, psychologists who specialise in treating adolescents with eating disorders experienced such a demand for their services, some stopped taking new clients. A survey of 1000 people aged between sixteen and twenty-four, conducted in February 2022 for *The Age* and *The Sydney Morning Herald* newspapers by social research company Resolve, found that during the first two years of the pandemic, three-quarters of respondents experienced anxiety, two-thirds experienced depression and thirty-six per cent personally experienced an eating disorder.[2] It may seem curious to link eating disorders and lockdown. What does the imposition of COVID restrictions have to do with dysmorphic body image? The best way of answering this question is to return to something that Gabrielle said. For her, anorexia was primarily about control. When you are a young person who has been told you can't go to school, can't go to work, can't see your friends, can't travel and can only leave home for one hour a day, anorexia is a desperate, self-destructive assertion of control over one of the few things you still can control: the food you put in your mouth.

Christine Morgan says that restricting people with a genetic vulnerability to eating disorders is like throwing kerosene on a fire. 'It is just the worst environment for you,' she says. Is there a more graphic illustration of the severe impact that lockdown had on some young people than the image of bright, motivated individuals, in what should be the best years of their lives, refusing food until their heartbeat slows to the point where their bodies are at risk of collapse?

* * *

The frustrating thing for people who work in adolescent health is how predictable this was. In mid-May 2020, as Australia was emerging from its first lockdown, the country's best-known advocate for youth mental health, Orygen Executive Director Patrick McGorry, released modelling showing that by the middle of 2023, an additional 82 000 Victorians between the ages of twelve and twenty-five would experience mental health disorders because of the pandemic. The modelling wasn't predicated on Melbourne spending two years in and out of lockdown—on the day that McGorry stood next to Martin Foley, the Victorian minister responsible for mental health, to release the report, COVID hadn't yet broken out of quarantine and the first-wave restrictions were starting to ease. Yet already, it was clear to researchers like McGorry that young people would disproportionately feel the brunt of the pandemic because of the jobs they do in retail, tourism and hospitality—sectors hit hard by our initial public health response—and the disruption to school and university life.

In November 2020, as Melbourne was celebrating a run of 'doughnut days'—the colloquialism for days on which the state recorded no new cases of COVID-19—a research team from the University of Sydney's Brain and Mind Centre released a study with another sobering set of predictions. According to the research, the three years between March 2020 and March 2023 would see a 31 per cent increase in suicides, a 30 per cent rise in hospitalisations caused by self-harm, and a 28 per cent increase in mental-health-related presentations to emergency departments. The predictions for Australians aged between fifteen and twenty-four were even more alarming: a 36 per cent increase in suicides, a 33 per cent increase in self-harm admissions, and a 31 per cent increase in people walking into emergency wards because of their mental health.

These predictions, like some of the early modelling forecasting catastrophic casualties from COVID, have not been realised. The greatest difference between what researchers feared would happen and what Australia experienced is that the labour market, supported by a $120-billion wage subsidy introduced by the federal government at the start of the pandemic, and other federal and state government economic assistance, shuddered but did not collapse during the COVID crisis. Although national unemployment nominally spiked at 15 per cent in April 2020, it peaked in real terms at 7.4 per cent by July, with youth unemployment topping at 14.5 per cent. The Brain and Mind Centre research team, like the federal Treasury, assumed the employment trough dug by the pandemic would be twice as deep and that it would take much longer for Australia to climb out of it.[3] Instead, national unemployment dipped under 4 per cent in May 2022, its lowest level since the GFC, and was tipped to fall further. The team has since updated its work, taking into account Australia's rapid economic recovery. The revised findings, although less alarming than the earlier ones, are still sobering. The latest report projects that, because of the pandemic, between March 2020 and March 2026 an additional forty-three Victorians aged between fifteen and twenty-five will kill themselves, 829 will be hospitalised through self-harm, and 1786 will present to an emergency department because of mental health.[4] The paper analyses how these impacts can be mitigated through better awareness, education, job creation and mental health services.

At the time of writing, there has been no recorded increase in suicides generally or youth suicides specifically in Victoria. Beneath this headline statistic, however, there is a concerning trend in the number of people presenting to emergency departments with self-inflicted injuries. The Monash University Accident Research Centre gathers statistics on transport accidents, home accidents, DIY mishaps, farmyard injuries, cycling accidents and emergency department admissions. Throughout Melbourne's lockdown months, the city's big emergency rooms were unusually quiet. The combination of a night-time curfew and closed pubs meant our emergency doctors and nurses were spared the normal mayhem that greets them on a Saturday-night shift. Yet, the four months of our 2020 COVID winter show a disturbing pattern. Between July and October 2020, 3372 people presented at Melbourne emergency departments with self-harm injuries, an increase of 13 per cent from the corresponding four months in 2019.[5] Throughout the rest of 2020, presentations for self-harm were down from the previous year. Although the data does not reveal why people were deliberately harming themselves during the winter lockdown, the increase was predominantly driven by girls and young women between the ages of fifteen and twenty-four. Researchers also saw a surge of online contact with Kids Helpline, a national counselling service for children and young adults, at the start of the first- and second-wave lockdowns.[6]

James Merlino took over from Martin Foley during the second-wave epidemic as the Victorian Minister for Mental Health and is also the state's Education Minister. He predicts that we will be dealing with the consequences of the pandemic for young people for a long time. The most encouraging sign is that some of these impacts are already receding. Although the rise in eating disorders remains an acute problem, mental health presentations to emergency departments have again fallen below 2019 levels. In the third term of the 2021 school year, a survey of Victorian school principals found that 62 per cent reported concerns about student mental health and wellbeing—by term two in 2022, that figure had fallen to 17 per cent. 'Knowing it was going to have a mental health impact on our kids in particular was incredibly difficult,' says Merlino, but he adds: 'I would support those decisions again because they had to be done.'

Professor McGorry believes that, like the systemic problems that plagued aged care nationally, and the chronic underfunding which hollowed out Victoria's public health capacity long before the pandemic arrived, the COVID crisis and our resort to lockdown exacerbated existing problems in our approach to mental health. He is not critical of the Victorian Government, which established a royal commission into the state's mental health system and, in McGorry's assessment, has done as much as any government to prioritise mental health. On the eve of the pandemic, the royal commission reported that Victoria's mental health system had 'catastrophically failed to meet expectations and was woefully underprepared for current and future challenges'; the Andrews government has vowed to overhaul the entire system. McGorry also does not question the sincerity of then prime minister Scott Morrison, who called McGorry late in 2020 to express concern about the impact of the pandemic on young people, and asked plainly: 'What do I do?' McGorry's suggestion, which Morrison took up, was for additional funds to train and kit out workers from headspace, a national youth mental health foundation, so they could safely visit people in their homes while COVID restrictions were in force. However, while McGorry believes that Victoria's public health leadership was genuinely concerned about what lockdowns were doing to young people, he says 'they didn't do anything meaningful about it. Everything they did was focused on COVID. I kept telling James Merlino and Martin Foley that this is having a serious effect. There was no pushback. I just think governments got overwhelmed'. The most important thing that governments can do now, McGorry says, is to provide money to train people to help address what is expected to be a long mental health tail of the pandemic, especially in Victoria. He says that headspace and Orygen have lengthy waiting lists for their services in Melbourne's western and northern suburbs where, for socioeconomic reasons, young people were hit hardest by lockdown.

Susan Sawyer, like McGorry, does not question the public health measures taken to slow the spread of the virus. 'None of us had experienced a pandemic like this,' she says. 'We really didn't know what these impacts were.' She also points out that every state reported a surge in eating disorders, including those lightly touched by lockdown policies. Still, she says one thing we could have seen coming in Victoria was the role that social media would play, once we stopped young people from being able to see their friends, in amplifying the anxiety and unhappiness that feeds mental disorders like anorexia. Social media is difficult enough to navigate in normal times. In lockdown, it offers a social lifeline but there is no face-to-face contact to balance your online interactions. The genius of social media algorithms is the way they curate content to reinforce what people are already thinking. It doesn't take long for anorexics on Twitter or Instagram to find their way to 'pro-ana' hashtags and sites where anorexic people try to convince one another that skeletal is sexy, and that the doctors, dietitians and psychologists telling them to eat don't know what they are talking about. 'These are online communities of really disturbed people,' Sawyer says. 'When you are feeling socially isolated, when you are feeling lonely, when you are feeling bored, you will just get sucked into this vortex of unhealthy ideation.'

Isolated, lonely, bored. In the Resolve survey, 84 per cent of respondents said they felt bored during COVID, 84 per cent were uncertain about their future, 31 per cent said they were more worried about things, and 80 per cent felt less in control. You might have felt the same way, but the survey showed that people aged twenty-five and over reported poor mental health during the pandemic at half the rate as people between the ages of sixteen and twenty-five. Young Victorians were significantly more affected than respondents from other states. The survey also asked a series of questions to tease out whether the anxiety and uncertainty experienced by young people were driven by the pandemic or the state's policy response. Resolve founder Jim Reed says the results are clear: 'The medicine has been worse than the disease for young people.'[7]

What are the long-term impacts likely to be for the coronials, the generation of adolescents whose lives were brought to a halt by the pandemic? We don't know yet, but studies about people who came of age during the GFC present a worrying picture. A survey by the Washington-based Pew Research Center found that, eight years after international credit markets collapsed and triggered a global recession, an alarming number of young people in Europe and America were neither in work nor studying.[8]

Disordered eating, like so many fault lines uncovered by the pandemic, was a serious problem before COVID-19. Louisa Hoey, a clinical psychologist who has been treating people with anorexia, bulimia and binge-eating disorders for nearly twenty years, says that we entered the pandemic with a loaded gun pointed at our young—Melbourne's lockdowns merely pulled the trigger. Every year, Mission Australia conducts a survey of Australian youths. In the eight years before the pandemic, the three greatest issues of concern nominated by young people were stress, mental health and body image. Even as the pandemic raged and the daily death toll was recited on the nightly news, young people were more concerned about how their bodies measured up than they were about COVID-19.[9]

Dr Hoey offers cognitive behavioural therapy at a private practice in Kew, one of Melbourne's most affluent suburbs. She says that her typical client is a high-achieving girl in her late teens or early twenties, a perfectionist and socially anxious. The girl's parents are professionally successful and she feels intense pressure not to let them down. And she cannot escape the omnipresent reinforcement, whether through social or traditional media or what friends and family say, of how she is supposed to look. 'We have got a pre-existing problem where we are telling people that your worth is defined by your shape and how you control it,' Hoey says. 'It is crazy and unfair because the ideal is so narrow.'

Governments are alive to the problem. In 2019 the Australian Government introduced a new Medicare scheme for eating disorders which provides forty subsidised sessions with a psychologist and twenty with a dietitian. The problem is, there aren't anywhere near enough qualified psychologists who want to do this work. At the end of the second wave, Hoey was so overwhelmed by people trying to see her that she started a waiting list for new patients. It was the first time in her two decades of practice she had been unable to see people straight away. Knowing what she does about the importance of early intervention to effectively treat eating disorders, it was a heartbreaking decision.

As Melbourne's lockdown started to lift, Gabrielle finally sought help. She was given a referral to see Dr Hoey in October 2020—she waited another three months to have her first session. The sessions with Dr Hoey encouraged Gabrielle to confront her relationship with food and exercise, and on the day that she agrees to meet me at a park near her parents' house, she is in a good place. Anorexics are never entirely cured but she has muted the voice in her head which, during that awful winter of 2020, kept telling her to run more and eat less. She is maintaining her weight, has started a full-time job as a lawyer, and is preparing to move out of home into a share house with friends. She still likes to run but is content to keep it to a few kilometres, at a gentle cadence, when she feels like she has the energy for it; sometimes she takes the dog for a walk instead. Her family and friends tell her the old Gabrielle is back, that there is a lightness to her that went missing for a while. But there is still a part of her that is angry. She is now twenty-five, and she knows she will never get back those missing years. She wonders if, at some point in the pandemic, we forgot what life is about.

In 2021, Gabrielle's grandfather became unwell and had to be hospitalised. The restrictions in place at the time meant he couldn't have visitors, not even his wife. 'What is the point of keeping these people alive if they can't see their loved one?' asks Gabrielle. 'We all place so much value on the length of our lives rather than the quality of them and what we are living for. I do understand why they did it but I don't think they considered how hard it would be.'

Michelle Lim describes the worst of her lockdown experience as a malaise. She wasn't depressed—having worked as a clinical psychologist for twenty years, she has treated enough depressed people to know—but she felt trapped in a *Groundhog Day* script of working in the same room, walking the same streets, and desperately yearning for something spontaneous or unexpected to happen. 'I felt like Bill Murray,' she laughs. 'Every day was the same bloody day.' As Australia's leading researcher on loneliness, Dr Lim also knew that if she was feeling this way, people all over Melbourne would be struggling with the protracted social isolation we had to endure to reduce the spread of COVID. Lim says the impacts of previous pandemics on physical and mental health were extensively studied and well known. The world's response to COVID was something else. She likens it to a social experiment, conducted on a mass scale, where the results won't be known for years to come. She says that studies done so far on loneliness in the pandemic suggest that duration of lockdown had a bigger impact than severity of lockdown. If this holds true, Melbourne will be ground zero for the future study of loneliness, a creeping public health crisis that US Surgeon General Vivek Murthy brackets with smoking and obesity.

Loneliness isn't the same thing as being alone. As Susan Sawyer told me, plenty of people enjoyed solitude during the pandemic. There are also people who can feel terribly lonely in a crowded room. Murthy, in a book on loneliness published in the early months of 2020, defines it as a subjective feeling of lacking the social connections that people need. 'It can feel like being stranded, abandoned, or cut off from the people with whom you belong, even if you're surrounded by other people,' he writes. 'What's missing when you're lonely is the feeling of closeness, trust and the affection of genuine friends, loved ones and community.'[10]

A white paper on loneliness in Australia, authored by Lim, estimates that loneliness affected one in four people before COVID.[11] Since the onset of the pandemic, that number is likely to have doubled. Lim says that, as a public health issue, loneliness is under-researched, poorly understood and not well treated. 'We see loneliness as a soft issue, something that only happens to people who are weak, when we know it is no different to feeling hungry or thirsty,' she says. 'Mental health services treat it like it is a consequence of mental ill health when, in fact, loneliness is an antecedent to poorer health.'

The international research on this is arresting. Lonely people are 29 per cent more likely to have coronary heart disease, 32 per cent more likely to have a stroke, and 26 per cent more likely to die prematurely.[12] Vivek Murthy in his book cites research showing that the direct health impacts of loneliness equate to smoking fifteen cigarettes a day. Perhaps the most surprising data on loneliness, compiled over several years by Swinburne University, the Australian Psychological Society and VicHealth, and quoted in Lim's white paper, is the demographic breakdown of who suffers loneliness. Australia's two loneliest demographics are older adults approaching retirement age and adolescents aged between eighteen and twenty-five. The thing these two groups have in common is they are transitioning out of or into the workforce. It is the impact of loneliness on the young that most troubles Lim.

The stay-at-home orders of the Victorian Government forced people already susceptible to high levels of loneliness to isolate from their peers and socially withdraw. They could stay in contact with others online but were denied the opportunity to sit with someone, read their facial expressions and body language, and build a relationship through the gradual, cumulative interactions we have with people we are getting to know. The skills needed to nurture friendship, intimacy and sex were put on a shelf for the best part of two years. If you think about how important this stuff is when you are young, how central it is to being young, it is difficult to imagine a government policy better designed to mess with the heads of young people than lockdown. 'I think the ramifications and the social disruption to people is going to be immense,' Lim says. 'The only way we will know how detrimental it will be is to track them over time and compare them with different cohorts.'

If governments want to understand what loneliness means, they don't need to look far. One of the loneliest jobs during the pandemic was that of parliamentarian. They couldn't visit their constituents, and in Victoria, the cancellation of parliamentary sitting days and the online migration of committee work separated MPs from their colleagues. Some parliamentarians shut their offices and worked entirely from home. If they had families, it was nice for a while: they were there for birthdays and family occasions sometimes missed because of work, and were present for every family dinner. If they didn't have a family, life was reduced to an endless series of Zoom meetings and phone calls and briefing papers, and not much else.

For Victorian Senator Raff Ciccone, the hardest time was Friday night through to Sunday morning, which he called 'the danger zone'. In January 2020, Ciccone separated from his partner of ten years. He wasn't blindsided by the separation, but he wasn't prepared for it either. If it had happened at another time, he would have done what most people do to cope: spend time with family, reconnect with old friends, bury themselves in work. On work days, Ciccone, who joined the Senate the year before the pandemic hit, was buried in the needs of constituents desperate to get home from overseas or save their businesses, but on the weekends he was more alone than he'd ever been in his adult life. He'd do the washing in the morning and plan a trip to the supermarket in the afternoon and make sure he had a couple of long phone calls lined up for after dinner. In lockdown, he wasn't allowed to see his family or drop by a friend's place. 'I looked forward to going to work on a Sunday night because I thought, at least I'll be able to go to an office Monday to Friday,' he says. 'On the weekends it was a bit harder to justify going to the office ... There was a lot of time for reflection and you start to process that shock of what had happened. There were regular phone calls to friends and Zoom meetings and chat groups but you still miss that interaction, that face-to-face, being able to grieve or at least talk to someone in person about how you are feeling.

It is always hard to open up too much. You don't want to be seen as a weak person.'

When 2021 arrived, it felt harder than the first year of the pandemic. 'From the third lockdown onwards is when it really started to test people,' says Ciccone. 'I just felt there are only so many times you can stand up and get beaten. It wasn't a criticism of government but it was just like, "How often do we keep having to keep doing this? Is there a light at the end of the tunnel?" Every time we saw that light it disappeared. Just when you thought we had turned a corner, there was something else.' Throughout this time, Ciccone never sought help for how he was feeling. Lonely people often don't.

Andrew Giles started thinking about loneliness well before the pandemic. The federal Labor MP can nominate the date because it is one seared into the memory of parliamentarians around the world. On 16 June 2016, Jo Cox was murdered outside a public library in Birstall, West Yorkshire. Cox was a 41-year-old mother of two and former humanitarian aid worker who, the previous year, had been elected to the House of Commons. She was shot and stabbed to death by a white supremacist in what the sentencing judge described as a terrorist attack. Cox was the same age as Giles, her kids were similar in age to his, and their politics were closely aligned. He kept thinking about her senseless death, started reading about her life, and discovered that one of the issues she was most passionate about was loneliness. Before she died, she had established a cross-party commission of inquiry into how to reduce loneliness. Giles was inspired to establish a bipartisan parliamentary group of Australian MPs to try to put loneliness onto the nation's political agenda.

'I thought, "These are things that people talk about, that are big things in their lives, that we are not having as part of our political conversation,"' says Giles. 'I wondered if it was a bit like mental health twenty years ago. When I looked at what was going on in the UK, I thought about what was happening in Australia and why the conversation was so under-developed. The obvious inference you would draw from lockdowns is that people became more lonely. We have a big dataset that says it was a huge issue before the pandemic and the data says it basically got twice as bad. The next question is how enduring is that twice as bad going to be?'

In 2018, Duncan Maskell moved to Melbourne from the University of Cambridge with his wife Sarah to take over the running of Australia's top-ranked university. By the time he became Vice-Chancellor of the University of Melbourne, Australia's universities had become highly dependent on fees paid by international students and were financially broadsided by the decision to close our international border to anyone who wasn't a permanent Australian resident. The fiscal hit was made worse by the federal government's refusal to extend its JobKeeper wage subsidy to academic staff at public universities. A study commissioned by the National Tertiary Education Union calculated that, between the start of the pandemic and September 2021, 400 000 people lost their jobs in tertiary education.[13] Maskell was also concerned about what that response was doing to the young, smart people who should be in lecture halls or the Baillieu Library or stretched out on the university lawn, but who instead were stuck inside their parents' homes, shared flats or student dormitories, cut off from their peers. He believed that, while the public health goal of limiting sickness and death from the virus was self-evident, there were difficult questions Melbourne needed to address.

In September 2020, two weeks after the Andrews government released its plan for Victoria's slow exit out of winter lockdown, Maskell gave voice to an idea which had become politically taboo. In an interview with me done as part of a series in which prominent Melburnians were invited to offer constructive ideas about Victoria's way forward, he raised one of the thorniest issues of the pandemic.

'We have to look at this as an overall picture,' he said. 'My personal view is there should be some form of sensible, public health, QALY-based analysis done and tough calls made. It boils down to a basic but very hard moral philosophy: what is the value of a 90-year-old's life versus the value of the continuing livelihood and happiness of a 25-year-old?'[14]

Quality-adjusted life year is a unit of measurement widely used by health economists that assumes a life nearer its expected end has a different value than a life closer to its start. It is used by hospitals to help determine the benefits and relative costs of treatments and to allocate finite resources. Any time it is raised with reference to the pandemic, it provokes accusations of seeking to economically rationalise the deaths of the elderly. This is a simplistic argument. Maskell wasn't arguing that old people weren't worth saving from the virus. Prior to his career as a university administrator, he spent his working life researching salmonella and golden staph in animals—the same nasty bugs which cause serious disease in hospitals and aged-care centres. His point was that policymakers need to weigh the imperative to prevent deaths from COVID-19 against the risk of downstream consequences to other people from those same public-health interventions.

'The question everyone is skirting around here is what is the appetite in any country for disease and mortality associated with this virus?' said Maskell. 'Every answer to that question is valid in one way or another. If you were to say, "We have no appetite whatsoever for any deaths from this virus," that is a perfectly reasonable position to take, but you have to take that position knowing the consequences. If that decision stops people dying now from the virus, what are the economic consequences of that for people and how will that play out in terms of future mortality? It would be crazy if, hypothetically, we stop 100 people [dying] from the virus but over the next two years, 200 people died from [the effects of] poverty and mental health.'

In short, Maskell was encouraging governments, including the Andrews government, to think more broadly about the implications of their pandemic responses. In other countries, political leaders were already doing this. In the same month that Maskell's comments were published, French President Emmanuel Macron and British Prime Minister Boris Johnson both made it clear that hard lockdowns were a measure of last resort. 'We must adapt to the evolution of the virus, slow down its circulation as much as possible,' Macron said. 'But we must do it by allowing us to continue living: educating our children, taking care of other patients, treating other health matters, and having an economic and social life.'[15] The British PM, addressing his nation in the face of rising case numbers, warned about the implications of another national lockdown: 'It would mean renewed loneliness and confinement for the elderly and vulnerable, and ultimately it would threaten once again the education of our children. We must do all we can to avoid going down that road again.'[16]

This did not keep France or England out of lockdown. Both nations enforced nationwide shutdowns in early winter 2020 and again in 2021, as Delta became the dominant variant throughout Europe. European countries didn't have the choice that we did. From the early months of the pandemic, the virus took root in their communities in such a way that elimination was never a possibility, much less seriously contemplated. If it was possible, would they have tolerated the harsh social restrictions that we did, for months on end, to stop anyone from getting infected? When Giuseppe Conte, Italy's prime minister through the first year of the pandemic, began easing his country's first national lockdown in April 2020, more than 100 000 people were still infected with the virus, yet he was criticised for moving too slowly.

In Australia, a different view had taken hold among our political leaders and public health officials. By the start of winter in 2021, there had been 926 registered deaths from COVID in Australia.[17]

If you take away the toll from Victoria's second wave, this left 125 registered deaths from COVID, throughout the rest of Australia, in the first year and a half of the pandemic. These remarkable numbers, although almost certainly an underestimate of Australia's true death toll from COVID, set us apart from nearly every comparable nation and encouraged a sense of Australian exceptionalism. Just as we dodged recession in the wake of the GFC, were we now a miracle country where no-one needed to die from the virus? Jeannette Young, Queensland's former long-serving chief health officer and now its governor, appeared to think so. In September 2021, she was asked by a journalist what number of deaths she would be comfortable with to reopen her state's border. Dr Young was aghast at the question: 'Comfortable with? I'm a doctor. None. Can you please remember who I am? I stand up here every day but ultimately I went into medicine to save lives. I am not comfortable with any deaths that are preventable.'

The absurdity of this position is now clear. By 6 December 2021, when Queensland Premier Annastacia Palaszczuk announced that, in a week's time, her state's border would reopen to interstate travellers, Queensland had recorded seven COVID deaths. Palaszczuk, having previously shown little sympathy towards people trying to get into Queensland from other states to visit loved ones, declared Christmas reunions her new priority. 'It's been nearly two years, tragically we've lost seven lives, but the results have been really unprecedented compared to the rest of the world,' she said. Within four months of this statement, nearly 800 people died with COVID in Queensland. There was little public criticism of the decision to open the border—current Chief Health Officer Dr John Gerrard maintains it was the right thing to do.

Much changed in the pandemic in the three months between Dr Young's comments and the decision to open Queensland's border. The emergence of the Omicron strain, a variant of concern shown to be more infectious but less virulent than previous strains, made

COVID-zero more difficult to sustain. And nearly 80 per cent of Queenslanders were vaccinated against the virus, giving them strong protection against serious illness and death. Yet, how is it that seven deaths are a tragedy when 800 deaths are an acceptable cost of Queensland rejoining the federation and the world?

Young Australians have every right to look askance at the gen X leaders who decided the course of our pandemic response. Before the first case of COVID-19 had emerged, the prospects of young people ever being able to afford to buy a home in markets supercharged by decades of tax breaks for property investors, were already bleak, especially when they considered the higher-education debts they were likely to lug into the start of their careers. As a further insult, the federal government announced at the beginning of the pandemic that it would double the fees for some of the most popular university degrees. In the last federal budget handed down before the pandemic, Australia's gross debt was forecast to peak at $578 billion. In May 2022, then federal treasurer Josh Frydenberg announced that gross debt would now peak at $1.2 trillion in 2025. Although Australia's debt levels are still low by international standards, we are leaving the next generation a steep mountain to climb. For all this, the most perverse intergenerational transaction of the pandemic was the compulsion to make young people suspend their lives so that the lives of the already very old might be extended. The young were given no say and little choice in the matter, but then neither were the old. We decided that old people should be isolated from their loved ones, and in some cases kept in miserable circumstances, for their own sake. If we had talked to the elderly about what this would mean for them, let alone what it might do to our young, would they have supported this?

There were two things that kept Merle Mitchell alive: her family and her community. She died at the age of eighty-seven, in the depths of Melbourne's sixth and final lockdown, after nearly two years of being denied vital connection to both. It was late on a Sunday that Mitchell's daughter Sally got a call from the nursing home to say Merle didn't have long to live. Sally called her brother Rick, who drove down from Ballarat, and the pair went to their mother's bedside. Merle Mitchell died the next day. Rick says the people who run the Waverley Valley Aged Care Centre were fantastic in those final hours. 'We weren't allowed to visit at that stage,' he says. 'They said, "Come whenever you want, stay as long as you want, come back as often as you want."'

Merle had been ready to go for a while. As she'd explained in typically matter-of-fact testimony to the aged-care royal commission a year earlier, lockdown had reduced her life to a series of pointless days in the confines of her room, staring at a brick wall. Her first thought every morning was 'Damn, I've woken up'.[18]

Merle Mitchell and her husband Eric built a house in Gray Street, Springvale in the 1960s and raised their family in the suburban heart of multicultural Melbourne. Eric was the last mayor of Springvale before the Kennett government amalgamated the local councils. For twenty years, Merle ran the Springvale Community Aid and Advice Bureau, a community organisation which advocated for and coordinated social services for local families. She was president of the Victorian and Australian councils of social services, worked for the Refugee Council of Australia, and served on more than twenty Commonwealth and state advisory boards. Melbourne broadcaster Jon Faine first met Merle Mitchell when he was a law student and described in her obituary how her career 'bridged the unfathomable gap between prime ministers, premiers, ministers and bureaucrats on the one hand, and the most disadvantaged in our community on the other'.[19] One of the politicians Mitchell knew was Daniel Andrews, her local member of parliament. You couldn't be a Labor politician in those parts and not know Merle.

Merle left her Springvale home and moved into care with Eric in 2015 after a fall and much cajoling from her kids. Eric Mitchell died the following year and Merle had been at Waverley Valley ever since, never feeling it was her home but resigned to the fact she would never leave. 'I'm here until I die, so I've got to make the best of it and that's what I try to do,' she told the commission. 'Which is not to say that I'm not being cared for, but I am sure if you really asked most people here, they would all say they would rather be dead rather than living here. If they're honest, that is.'

Honesty isn't a strong suit when we talk about aged care, COVID and death. In June 2020, at the start of Victoria's second wave, 184 000 people were living in permanent residential care. The average age on entry was eighty-two-and-a-half years for men and eighty-five for women. Aged-care residents live, on average, for thirty months after they go into care. For most of them, the only thing that makes aged care bearable is regular visits from family and friends. To protect them from COVID, we took that away.

Eric Mitchell had polio as a child and by the time he went into care, he was experiencing the exhaustion of post-polio syndrome. Before he died he'd had two respiratory infections and asked not to be treated if he got sick again. Rick Mitchell describes his father's death, when it came a short time later, as 'beautiful'. Merle was left to grieve. 'I think the staff in aged-care facilities just don't know how to cope with people who are grieving,' she told the royal commission. 'For example, there was one time I tried to get the physiotherapy manager to say the word "death" and "dying". I was unsuccessful.' Merle didn't like euphemisms.

In 2020, COVID was a deadly disease for people in residential care. For every three residents infected with the virus, one died. Rick says that, at the start of the pandemic, Merle understood and accepted the public health rationale for locking down nursing homes, but as the months of lockdown stretched out, she became frustrated at being cut off from people. She needed a wheelchair to move around but before the pandemic, she had struck up a friendship with a local maxi-cab driver who would pick her up from the home and take her to see people in the community. Sometimes she would be out till 10 p.m., much to the consternation of the Waverley Valley staff. That all stopped with COVID. 'She was stuck in her room, watching the news to find out what was going on and not having that personal contact,' Rick says. 'She was cut off from individuals because people couldn't come and visit her, and she was cut off from a community that had been such a significant part of her life. She found that extremely frustrating and that isolation certainly wasn't good for her mental health.'

For people in aged care in Victoria, the first lockdown of 2020 bled into the second with only a short reprieve between. Visits were limited to family and only then in sterile, impersonal surrounds, where mothers and fathers were separated from their children and grandchildren by windows or perspex screens. At Waverley Valley, visits were limited to half an hour. 'In some ways it was more stressful than not going,' Rick says. 'The physical barriers to communication were extreme. There was no touching. It was like being in a prison.' Rick Mitchell isn't critical of the Waverley Valley management or the public health orders they were following. 'It's that balance between community welfare and individual welfare,' he says. 'I don't know what we could have done better.' He also knows from first-hand experience with his mum and dad that even a well-run nursing home needs family to be involved in the care of those residents. He wonders whether, if the Victorian Government and other states had embraced rapid antigen tests when they first became available in 2020, it might have transformed the capacity of aged-care facilities to protect residents from infection and keep them connected to family. He still remembers the howls of another resident, who had dementia and took comfort in seeing her son at the same time every day.

She had no comprehension of why her son was no longer coming to see her. How can anyone explain this to a confused person who suddenly finds themself alone at the end of their life?

On the same day that Merle Mitchell testified to the royal commission, the daughter of an aged-care resident in another home also gave evidence. She explained that her 82-year-old dad had been diagnosed with motor neurone disease in 2016. Before COVID, he would take long walks with his daughter around the local streets and a park. Her last happy memory of him was on one of those walks. 'We stopped and walked and stopped and walked,' she says. 'And it was just beautiful. And he'd stop and look at the trees and just wander and then he'd just keep going. He was actually pulling me along that day. I will never forget it.' When COVID came, the walks stopped. Instead, father and daughter had to meet in a room, separated by glass, unable to touch. Later, the rules changed and they could walk around the nursing home's garden, but they were still forbidden from holding hands. She didn't touch her father again before he died. She told the commission:

> I believe that I could have taken dad by the hand and walked him around. Even if I was wearing a glove, we could have still had a relationship. I felt as though I was no longer trusted to care for him even though I had been only weeks and months before. I lost this connection with my father and I felt as though he had become the nursing home's property. I believe that during this time, love was not the biggest priority but enforcing the system was. I felt that all that had been promised when Dad entered the nursing home had changed. All the wonderful leisure and freedom aspects such as coming on visits to my home and being able to take Dad shopping and for walks had all gone suddenly overnight because of the virus.[20]

Waverley Valley hadn't recorded a COVID case throughout the entire pandemic on the day that Merle Mitchell testified to the royal commission. Paul Bolster, one of the counsel assisting, asked her what lockdown meant to her. She replied:

> Well, it means that I'm in my own room. The only time I can go out of this room is when I've got a physio session, and that happens four times a week. Otherwise, from the time I wake up to the time I go to sleep, I'm sitting in my own room in my one chair.

To extend her life, we made it barely worth living.

CHAPTER 6
DEMENTOR'S KISS

It's the end of summer 2022 and the University of Melbourne for the first time in two years is showing signs of life. The sun is out for O-week activities and so are the university clubs, spruiking the benefits of membership to students who since early 2020 have only known college life as remote lectures, Zoom tutorials and the dry bones of the academic syllabus. A queue snakes out of the cafe beneath the Glyn Davis Building, young people are milling about in University Plaza, and although he is a little distorted by the PA speakers, Justin Timberlake has never sounded so good. The pandemic has confirmed what many university administrators had already cottoned on to: that most courses can be taught and studied entirely online. The idea of university on demand, like an academic streaming service, has obvious appeal to a generation of students accustomed to all their content—be it music, TV, or lectures in macroeconomics—being accessible whenever they feel like paying attention. For universities, it has opened enrolments to students living interstate and around the world. The pandemic has also taught us that, although degrees can be completed in this way, it is not what universities are there for. A university is supposed to be a community. A campus without students is like a pub without beer. This week, the local publicans are delighted to see a new harvest of first years slouched around tables and propped up at bars.

I'm at the University of Melbourne to meet Zeb Jamrozik, an infectious disease ethicist who throughout the pandemic became increasingly concerned that the Victorian Government's repeated resort to lockdown contravened basic principles of public health. In the aftermath of the second-wave epidemic, he was so alarmed at what he was seeing and hearing that he took a job with the health department, advising the hotel quarantine program so as to address from the inside what he describes as Victoria's 'more egregious policy responses'. In this job, he served as both a public health expert and an unofficial watchdog, using his position to provide guidance and attempt to guard against abuses of power. 'I don't know how effective I have been,' he muses. With the quarantine program at an end, he has returned to his clinical work as a hospital physician and research into global public health which, so far, has taken him to Monash University, Oxford University and the WHO in Geneva.

Anyone familiar with public health research in Australia wouldn't be surprised to learn that Jamrozik is passionate about the subject. His late father, Konrad Jamrozik, a former professor of public health at the University of Western Australia, head of the School of Population and Health Clinical Practice at the University of Adelaide, and chair of primary care epidemiology at London's Imperial College, dedicated forty years of his life to establishing the links between smoking and terminal disease, and lobbying governments to introduce tobacco controls. His mother, Criena Fitzgerald, is a public health historian. Jamrozik says some of the things we did in Victoria to limit the number of infections and associated deaths from COVID hadn't been tried before, and it will take years of research to determine what the long-term effects are. His principal criticism is that our public health response was myopic—that by adopting a singular focus on stopping the spread of the virus, we became inured to other harm we were causing.

Australia and Victoria's responses to the COVID crisis did not unfold in an ethical vacuum. There are well-established principles in public health which are meant to guide government decisions. In April 2021, the National Health and Medical Research Council published an ethical framework for decision-making in a pandemic. Written with government officials in mind, the framework stipulates that, even when facing a crisis like a pandemic, public health decisions need to respect the dignity of people and communities, and affirm self-determination and individual choice. An ethical pandemic response should be transparent, accountable and proportionate to the public health risk. 'When people talk about effectiveness, they are often talking narrowly about reducing the number of cases or hospitalisations,' says Jamrozik. 'What matters ethically in public health is the overall value of health and wellbeing. The real question is: how do we promote that in the longer term for all different health and wellbeing issues?' Reducing sickness and death from an infectious virus is important. So, too, are keeping kids at school, people at work, and people at the end of their lives connected to loved ones.

These well-accepted principles are embedded in the laws which, before the passage through parliament of pandemic-specific legislation at the end of 2021, gave Victoria's chief health officer emergency powers to respond to a public health risk. It was part of the CHO's statutory obligations to ensure that any public health orders they issued were couched in these principles. The Victorian laws set out the precautionary principle, which recognises that the speed with which decision-makers need to respond to a public health emergency may require governments to act in the absence of complete certainty that what they are doing will work. 'If a public health risk poses a serious threat, lack of full scientific certainty should not be used as a reason for postponing measures to prevent or control the public health risk,' the Victorian laws read.[1]

Mike Ryan, an Irish epidemiologist who worked on the front line of Ebola outbreaks before coming to global prominence as the Executive Director of WHO's Health Emergencies Programme, made this point early in the pandemic. 'If you need to be right before you move, you will never win,' he said. 'Perfection is the enemy of the good when it comes to emergency management. Speed trumps perfection. The problem we have in society at the moment is everyone is afraid of making a mistake, everyone is afraid of the consequence of error. The greatest error is not to move. The greatest error is to be paralysed by the fear of failure.'[2] This is essential wisdom to keep in mind when judging, with the benefit of considerable hindsight, advice provided by public health officials and decisions taken by government ministers when the world was still working out how the virus spread, who it infected, what worked to stop it and what didn't. The precautionary principle was regularly cited by Professor Sutton when he was explaining some of his more contentious public health orders.

The precautionary principle does not provide carte blanche for a government to do anything it deems necessary to stop the spread SARS-CoV-2. Jamrozik says a balancing principle of proportionality requires decision-makers, when choosing between a range of public health measures, to go with the least-restrictive alternative. 'If you have two public health policies which can achieve a similar benefit and one of them involves a lot more restriction on freedom, most people in public health agree that the higher end of liberty restrictions, like mandates, should be a last resort,' he says. The Victorian laws require the chief health officer to also follow this maxim when issuing public health orders, but Jamrozik argues that Victoria, when it set itself on a path to COVID-zero, abandoned proportionality. Once you decide you cannot tolerate a single infection in the community, draconian measures become easier to justify. In Victoria, this led to a form of public-health zealotry that resulted in the banning of activities that carried no practical risk: walking on the beach, sitting in a park, washing your car on the street, accompanying your L-plate son or daughter on a drive, or, dare we say it, playing golf. It also resulted in police issuing nearly 45 000 fines to people between the start of the pandemic and September 2021, for breaching public health restrictions.

The public health rationale for policing such innocuous activities, as explained by Professor Sutton, was to give people fewer reasons to leave home. If you outlaw nearly everything that can be done beyond someone's front door, why would they bother to walk through it? There is a certain logic to this, although it is not really about science, as Sutton explained one Saturday night during our first-wave lockdown, in an unusually unguarded radio interview on Melbourne station 3AW. 'There is no science here Sally,' he said to Sally Cockburn, a medico well known to Melbourne listeners via her sex therapist alter ego, Dr Feelgood. 'I understand that people think, "Look, if I play golf I would do it right and I wouldn't put up a new mate every week in the car and be in close contact and I wouldn't go round in close contact with a bunch of other people on the course." That is a rational, law-abiding person. But I have to think about what it would mean to allow it across the board for all of the people who would comply with that and who wouldn't comply with that.'

The idea that the chief health officer, or indeed the Victorian Government, must step in and protect us from our lesser selves reveals the paternalism at the heart of our pandemic response. Would Victoria have stuck to such a dogmatic approach if the second wave hadn't been seeded by a quarantine breach and there was no political imperative for the government to clean up its own mess? Jamrozik is doubtful. 'There is a parallel between the Victorian Government wanting to go to zero to hide their own errors and the Chinese Government wanting to go to zero because they were embarrassed that this virus had emerged just as China is positioning itself as a major new world power,' he says.

* * *

COVID-zero put Melbourne on a knife's edge. When a single case or a small outbreak is enough to prolong lockdown for an entire city, it elevates community anxiety and fear about the virus and anger towards anyone seen to have done the wrong thing. Citizens were encouraged to spy on their neighbours, dob in their friends, and to be hyper-vigilant regarding anyone illegally celebrating birthdays or visiting their parents. We didn't need much encouragement: a police assistance line for Victorians to report breaches of COVID restrictions was swamped with calls. These circumstances made it difficult for anyone to question the state's restrictions without being accused of seeking to undermine the public health response, or being wilfully reckless to the fate of older Victorians and others most at risk of getting critically sick and dying of COVID-19.

The Australian Health Practitioner Regulation Agency, the organisation responsible for accrediting medical and allied health professionals, issued a warning to its members against criticising public health restrictions, noting that any practitioner who made comments or shared social media posts that contradicted the best available scientific evidence, might be found in breach of their professional responsibilities. 'It became verboten to say, "We have got to accept some deaths among the old and frail," as we do in every influenza season,' Jamrozik says. 'That became a very simplistic response to anyone who tried to push back against the idea of hard, fast, early lockdown: "Do you want old people to die?"'

It was within this climate, less than a week after Sutton circulated the genomics report and shortly before Melbourne entered its protracted winter lockdown of 2020, that the Andrews government placed 3000 housing commission tower residents under home detention. Peter Godfrey-Smith, Professor of History and Philosophy of Science at Sydney University, and a former professor of philosophy at Harvard, describes this episode as 'one of the worst COVID-related abuses of power in western democracies'.[3] Jamrozik, who was also appalled by what happened at the housing commission towers, returns to his central point about proportionality: 'Why did those cases warrant such extreme intervention? If you are imposing more liberty restriction, more harm, more overpolicing on poor and marginalised people than on the wealthy, then that is grossly inequitable.'

In a 2021 essay on what he calls the 'COVID heterodoxy', Professor Godfrey-Smith examines the way in which precautionary thinking was applied throughout the pandemic. He points out that, when weighing the potential impacts of increased infections, worst-case scenarios are rightly considered by governments and public health authorities. These are the kinds of assumptions that produced mathematical models showing that 150 000 people could die in an unmitigated epidemic in Australia. Professor Godfrey-Smith questions why, when looking at the potentially harmful impacts of those restrictions, worst-case scenarios are rarely, if ever, weighed. Instead, we tend to make optimistic assumptions about businesses being able to recover, young people being resilient, and older people being able to endure the isolation and loneliness of being cut off from their families, so long as they remain COVID-free.

Godfrey-Smith does not oppose lockdowns in all circumstances. He was sceptical but accepted the rationale for them in March 2020, when all Australian jurisdictions supported severely restricting our social interactions to enable our health systems, and particularly the intensive-care departments of our major hospitals, to prepare for what we thought was coming. He believes that protracted lockdowns of the kind Melbourne languished in do more harm than good. The difficulty, he says, is that where the harm associated with thousands of COVID patients needing critical care or dying is easy to measure, the harm associated with disruption to schooling and work, and the loss of 'foundational' liberties like being able to visit friends and family, is not. Moreover, it is likely that the full impact of these things will only emerge in years to come, after those responsible for making the decisions have retired from politics or public life. He writes:

It is simply an error to consider worst-case scenarios on one side and not the other. An uncharitable interpretation of the situation is that the scenarios that drove policy have been not worst-case scenarios overall, but worst-case scenarios that the people making decisions today might be blamed for. High death rates in 2020–21 are in that category. Bad outcomes years in the future, filtered through other causes, are not.

Professor Godfrey-Smith is not a libertarian. He explains that part of his motivation for writing the essay was to explore from a centre-left perspective an issue which has tended to be hijacked by anti-vaxxers, spruikers of ivermectin, and people for whom surgical face masks became a symbol of government oppression. Another motivation was the incredulous questions he kept getting emailed to him by friends from America who couldn't understand why Australia, a country which prior to the Omicron wave had recorded so few COVID cases and deaths by global standards, was enforcing harsh public health restrictions so late in the pandemic.

When I spoke to Professor Godfrey-Smith about his essay, Melbourne had just emerged from a torrid week in September 2021 when an unlikely alliance of out-of-work construction workers, hard-right political agitators, and people dislocated and disaffected by the pandemic response, staged a series of volatile and occasionally violent protests across the city. That was the first time that Victoria Police used paramilitary munitions, including non-lethal projectiles fired from assault rifles, to contain a mass protest. In his essay, Godfrey-Smith warns of an unintended consequence of the more mundane police duties we regularly saw throughout the pandemic:

> It is bad to have a situation where the police are routinely spending a lot of their time harassing people for trivial things—gathering, meeting friends at home, going on walks together, and so on. We don't want a lot of police action directed at those non-crimes.

This should be extremely rare, but it is now becoming increasingly common, and is changing the relationship between population and their police forces.

Victoria Police Chief Commissioner Shane Patton agrees that some of the duties police were asked to perform in lockdown, such as stopping people from fighting over rolls of toilet paper in supermarkets, were 'bizarre'. But he says police had to take seriously their responsibility to enforce Victoria's public health orders. Police officers lived through our lockdowns as well as enforcing them. When they weren't on duty, there was no place for them to have a drink with colleagues or blow off steam. When at work, there was always the chance they'd run into someone who refused to wear a mask or go home and, when challenged about it, would recite sections of the Constitution or UN doctrines in their defence, all the while filming the whole confrontation on their phones. Patton told police to treat everyone they came across the same way they'd expect their own family members to be treated, but as lockdowns wore on and people's tolerance waned, it wasn't always easy to follow this advice.

Speaking to me early in 2022, Patton argues that the work police did during our two years of lockdowns was as important as anything his officers are likely to do in the rest of their careers. 'There had to be a consequence,' he says. 'If there was no consequence, there would have been very little adherence. We went out of our way to say, "This is the real job." There was no bigger show in town than what we were doing. That was the most important work that we could be doing because it was about saving lives.'

David Nabarro, one of the WHO's special envoys on COVID-19, would prefer not to talk about lockdowns. As he explains from Geneva, the politics of the pandemic have become so polarised that it is difficult for public health experts to comment about lockdowns without their words being coopted by protagonists at the extremes of the debate. Dr Nabarro discovered this in October 2020, as Melbourne was exiting its winter lockdown and the UK Government was under pressure to enforce a new one in England. In an interview with the conservative *Spectator* magazine, Nabarro noted that the WHO considered lockdowns a measure of last resort and appealed to governments around the world to stop using them as a primary means of controlling the virus. Within the space of those few remarks, Dr Nabarro became the unwilling poster child for an anti-lockdown movement that had coalesced around the Great Barrington Declaration, a petition signed by scientists and medical practitioners calling for lighter, more focused public health restrictions to protect those most vulnerable to the virus, while allowing the young and otherwise healthy to return to normal life.

This wasn't where Nabarro wanted to be or the debate he wanted us to have. He wanted us to be talking about what he calls the 'middle path', a public health response built on the fundamentals of good contact tracing and case management, and sensible, personal precautions against viral spread such as washing your hands, keeping your distance and wearing a mask. 'We just couldn't understand why so many countries were seesawing between what was sometimes called freedom and lockdown,' he says. 'That is not the way. You keep your number of cases down by having really good surveillance and detection and isolation. I just thought the narrative was wrong. Why on earth are people always going on about lockdown as though that is the best thing a government can do when, in my judgement, it was a failure of narrative and a failure of policy?'

Dr Nabarro is not anti-lockdown. His position and, indeed, the WHO's position since the start of the pandemic, is that whole-of-population restrictions can serve an important, specific purpose: buying a country or jurisdiction time to build its hospital and public health capacity to deal with a wave of infections. Nabarro says this is the only time lockdowns are justified. The reason for this is the catastrophic impact that lockdowns can have, particularly in countries where poverty and social inequities are already serious problems. An important caveat here is that, when Nabarro talks about the potential consequences of lockdown, he is not thinking about wealthy countries like Australia. When he warns of the harm caused by keeping kids home from school, he is informed by his experience in having worked in famine-stricken countries in East Africa and developing nations plagued by malaria, where, for many children, a day at school offers the only chance to get a square meal. The reason he appealed to governments to stop resorting to lockdowns is that he could see the impact such harsh restrictions were having on global poverty, Pacific economies which rely heavily on tourism, and smallholder farmers. The consequences of lockdown for most Australian families, although very real, are on a different scale.

At a more fundamental level, Nabarro's reflections and the WHO's position on lockdown raise important questions about the Victorian Government's approach and, to a lesser extent, the reflexive resort to lockdown by South Australia, Queensland and Western Australia when faced with outbreaks. When the first WHO investigative team returned from China in February 2020, it reported that SARS-CoV-2 virus was highly infectious and potentially deadly. If left unchecked, case numbers would double every two to three days and the mortality rate, depending on the quality of a nation's health system, would range between 1 per cent and 10 per cent. As dire as this sounded, the WHO team also had good news. They believed the virus was primarily spread by droplets and that transmission, so long as governments and public health authorities acted quickly, could be reduced by tried and proven means: reducing social contact and the standard principles of infection control. The additional risk of airborne spread, if the WHO had accepted it earlier, would not have changed this assessment. In simple terms, the WHO advocated a standard public health response to a novel but familiar disease.

No-one within the organisation believed Western democracies should replicate China's hardline approach in Wuhan. No-one thought that such tactics would be tolerated by people in Europe, America and Australia.

'All we were saying to everyone was: "Public health matters here,"' Nabarro recalls. 'That means putting in place these alert, detect and respond strategies which, for us, was test, trace and isolate. And something went wrong. We watched this virus start to come into Europe in March 2020 and we were hearing people say, "We want to delay the peak." People started to talk about herd immunity or population immunity. It was as though the playbook for flu was coming out, rather than what one might need for a droplet-borne coronavirus that comes in spikes and surges. There was a kind of disconnect, right from early on.'

China demonstrated, albeit in brutal fashion, that lockdowns, when rigidly enforced and adhered to, can stop the transmission of coronavirus. Nabarro could see the short-term benefits of this approach but worried about what it would do, in the longer term, to the willingness of people to comply with and support public health measures, particularly if harsh restrictions were imposed for too long. By April 2020, it was already clear that the virus had spread globally and would be with us for years to come. A shock-and-awe public health response might contain an initial outbreak, but what would it mean for the inevitable future waves of infection? 'The virus is the problem and people are the solution,' Nabarro says, adding that 'whichever approach you use you have got to have people onside with you. Where it goes wrong is when people can't make sense of it, get angry and feel they are being pushed around. You can lose the trust of people very quickly. It will get your numbers down but everyone knows it will have enormous impacts on the living of people in the informal economy, it will lead to a disturbance of all essential services and supply chains. There is a huge cost to this 100 per cent lockdown approach.'

This is why, just as the WHO didn't advocate the use of lockdowns as a primary means of controlling the virus, it didn't support the idea of COVID-zero. It didn't think it was feasible to eliminate all local transmission of the virus, nor was it necessary to try. 'Just as we didn't like 100 per cent lockdown because of its destructive nature, we also didn't like zero COVID, because the implications of zero COVID are taking you towards very high levels of restrictions on what people can do and where they can do it. Our line was stick with the basic public health principles.' Nabarro adds a further caveat here. Jurisdictions like Western Australia, Queensland, Tasmania and South Australia all showed that it was possible, in an island nation, to eliminate the spread of the virus for a time. If anyone stood a chance of maintaining COVID-zero, it was countries like Australia, New Zealand and Taiwan. Victoria's failure to do so, despite Melbourne spending more than eight months in lockdown, returns us to Dr Nabarro's central point: in a pandemic, you are only as good as your public health ground game.

How did the Victorian Government come to decide that a single COVID case was one too many? It's a complicated story, but perhaps the best place to start is the day that Jason Thompson, an Associate Professor with the University of Melbourne's School of Design, received a call from a senior bureaucrat in Victoria's health department. Thompson is not an infectious disease expert or an epidemiologist. He is an expert in computational modelling who, prior to the pandemic, helped Victoria's Traffic Accident Commission save a bundle of money by better understanding the intersection between human behaviour and insurance claims for personal injuries. This might sound a bit wonky, but what sets Thompson apart from other number-crunchers is that he understands people and why they do things. He has a background in clinical psychology and uses this to develop agent-based models which, when applied to a complex problem like a pandemic, can help governments predict what the likely impact of certain policies will be well into the future.

The difference between agent-based models and the more common susceptible–exposed–infectious–recovered (SEIR) models that epidemiologists from the Doherty Institute and the Burnet Institute, and also Neil Ferguson from London's Imperial College, were using at the time is that in agent-based models, the datapoints are pretend people, not specks on a mathematical graph. They have motivations, they interact with one another and their behaviour is subject to change. Agent-based models are models of exchange. Normally, you might use them to model the transfer of property in a real estate market or power in an energy market. In this case, the virus was the unit of exchange. A mathematical quirk and limitation of SEIR models is that, when you graph the downward slope out of an epidemic, you never quite get to zero cases. Even when the likelihood of a case is infinitesimally small, it is never zero. In an agent-based model, anything fewer than one is treated as zero. Jason Thompson, working crazy hours in the spare bedroom of his Castlemaine house, built an agent-based model showing how Victoria could get to fewer than one case of COVID-19—in other words, how we could get to COVID-zero.

Thompson wasn't convinced that it would work, and his collaborator at the University of Melbourne, epidemiologist Tony Blakely, was even more sceptical, at least at first. 'I thought they were mad initially,' he says. Blakely is a New Zealand–born epidemiologist who came to Melbourne from the University of Otago in Wellington shortly before the pandemic. He explains that, when countries like Australia and New Zealand were first planning for COVID-19, we were all thinking about it in the same terms as influenza. 'We wouldn't normally think about eliminating it,' he says. 'That was the starting position for all the people that were inside the beltway; it just wasn't on their radar. Elimination was for smallpox and maybe polio, not something you'd think about with a pandemic virus.' The idea of eliminating COVID first started gaining traction in New Zealand through the work of two of Blakely's former colleagues in Wellington: public health physician Nick Wilson and epidemiologist Michael Wilson. The more Blakely looked at their work and the model Thompson had developed, the more he came around to the idea that Victoria, if it had the right restrictions in place, could replicate these theoretical outcomes in real life. People living in Melbourne would need to demonstrate a forbearance beyond what the bravest public health expert would normally expect, and Victoria would need a dose of good luck—something it hadn't experienced much of so far. But if the alternative was bouncing in and out of lockdown and being isolated from other states until a vaccine developed, Blakely figured it was at least worth trying.

Blakely started publicly pushing the idea of COVID-zero. The idea met stiff resistance from Professor Paul Kelly, who had taken over from Brendan Murphy as Australia's chief medical officer, but it resonated with Brett Sutton, who didn't see why Victoria shouldn't aim for what other Australian jurisdictions, New Zealand and Taiwan had already achieved. On 9 July 2020, the day Melbourne went into stage 3 lockdown, Blakely wrote a punchy article in *Pursuit*, the University of Melbourne's in-house magazine, titled: 'Victoria—Are You up for Elimination?' It put the case for a COVID-zero strategy, arguing that until Victoria eliminated local transmission of the virus, it would remain a pariah state. 'Is going for gold and having a crack at eliminating the virus in Victoria worth it? I argue "yes",' he wrote. Four days later, Brett Sutton, during an interview on ABC Radio, suggested he too was up for elimination—so long as it was possible. 'To be on a seesaw where you are locking down and easing up will be almost intolerable, I think,' he told broadcaster Raf Epstein. 'So we need something that is sustainable. That might be elimination, if we have got any feasibility of getting there, or it might be a suppression that doesn't involve really significant constraints on behaviour.'

On 17 July, a research team led by Blakely and Thompson published a more-considered article in the *Medical Journal of Australia* advocating for COVID-zero to be adopted as the state's public health strategy. The paper argued that, through a combination of harsh restrictions, the use of masks, improved quarantine measures and a change in luck, Victoria could eliminate all local transmission of COVID until a vaccine was developed. It included important caveats about the uncertainty of being able to sustain COVID-zero settings and the social pain that any prolonged lockdown would cause but reasoned that these were risks worth taking to enable Victoria, like other states, to live relatively freely within Australia's closed borders. The most important piece in this public health picture was not the current wave of infections or the inevitability of a future wave, but rather the good times that could be had in-between, even as the pandemic raged in other parts of the world. 'We argue that Melbourne and Victoria should not waste the opportunity this lock-down presents,' the paper argued, continuing:

> There is the risk of failure … but we argue that it would be a bigger failure to not enhance the probability of elimination by augmenting the current lock-down now. Our work and those of others who have independently considered the alternatives consistently demonstrates that elimination is possible, and if achieved optimal for health and long-term for the economy.

Shortly after the paper was published, Thompson got the call from the health department. Thompson and Blakely's team was given two weeks to construct a model to get Victoria down to zero while still allowing for the provision of essential goods and services. It was a crazy time frame. Thompson wrote the code himself, working closely with Rod McClure, Dean of Medicine at the University of New England, to build about 200 variables into the model. The Victorian public health team and the Andrews government could then tweak and manipulate the model according to what restrictions they were and weren't willing to impose, and how long they were prepared to impose them. Blakely continued to be a prominent voice in an elimination campaign which now included ABC science commentator Norman Swan, Brett Sutton, Victoria's deputy chief health officer Allen Cheng, and a group of senior ministers within Victoria's Crisis Council of Cabinet. They all understood that, to give Victoria a chance of eliminating the virus—loosely defined as recording no COVID cases for twenty-eight days, or two life cycles of the virus—they would need to keep Melbourne in lockdown considerably longer than the original six weeks that Daniel Andrews had flagged. The lockdown would also have to remain tight: the harder they went now, the greater their chance of pulling it off. Once it became clear what Victoria was contemplating, the response from Canberra was cool. Nick Coatsworth, the deputy chief medical officer, wrote on the federal health department's website that elimination, as a public health goal, was unrealistic and dangerous.

As he reflects back on what we can now see was a critical turning point in Victoria's response to the pandemic, Brett Sutton says one of the recurring issues public health and infectious disease experts confronted throughout the pandemic was the difficulty in overturning orthodoxy. Just as no-one had contemplated before Wuhan the idea of locking healthy people in their homes to prevent the spread of a virus, there was slow acceptance that many of the public health assumptions everyone had been taught about responding to an influenza pandemic didn't apply to COVID-19. One of these assumptions was that harsh restrictions would only ever have to be imposed for a maximum of six weeks to contain an outbreak. Sutton says that, from the earliest, crudest modelling of the likely spread of COVID in the United Kingdom by Neil Ferguson's research team, in March 2020, Australia faced only bad choices. 'It was a horrific realisation to see what the alternatives were. One was tens of thousands of cases a day and tens of thousands of people hospitalised.

The other was you flatten the curve and just keep it trickling along under ICU and health service capacity and you stretch it out for more than twelve months. Neither of them were tolerable options.'

One of Sutton's greatest regrets about the second wave is that he allowed cases to build before the city went into lockdown. He says that, instead of issuing stay-at-home orders for people living in ten local government areas in Melbourne's northern and western suburbs, he should have put all of Melbourne and perhaps country Victoria into stage 3 restrictions much earlier. 'If I had acted earlier in June just with a trickle of numbers, it wouldn't have got to that peak and we may never have needed stage 4,' he says. He learned that Melbourne's reliance on people travelling across the city to do essential work—like caring for people in nursing homes, butchering meat and transporting food to supermarkets—meant that keeping COVID at bay was an all-or-nothing gambit. Sutton says the federal government eventually backed the new elimination strategy—so long as no-one called it that. 'It would be called aggressive suppression,' he says. 'I didn't care what we called it as long as we were doing what needed to be done to get there.' Allen Cheng, like Sutton, fully backed elimination. 'What is the alternative?' he asks.

Jason Thompson estimates he hardly slept and lost about 10 kilograms in the space of those two weeks. During the day, he would consult with Blakely, Cheng and Kate Haughton, a Department of Premier and Cabinet bureaucrat who had the ear of the premier, about what variables they should include or take out. During the night, he would write code. He spoke regularly with other modellers from the Doherty Institute, the Burnet Institute and within the Victorian health department about what he was trying to do. As the model took shape, he assumed the public would only support what they were asking them to do for up to sixty days. Beyond that, the compliance so crucial to the success of any restrictions would collapse. The dilemma was that there was no way to bring Melbourne down to zero within this time frame unless you stopped everyone, including essential workers, from leaving their home. The lockdown would have to be longer than had been imagined. All involved knew that if the Victorian Government went with this plan, it would carry significant social and political costs.

It was only on 6 September, when Daniel Andrews announced Victoria's roadmap out of lockdown, that Thompson realised they had decided to go for it. He was on the Midland Highway, driving between his Castlemaine home and Bendigo, when the premier's voice came on the radio and confirmed the details. 'That's gutsy,' he thought. He also knew it would cause a lot of anger in the community. For all the premier's talk of a COVID-normal Christmas, the bottom line was that we were staying in lockdown at least until the end of October, and there was no guarantee it would then lift. Regional Victoria was given some measure of relief but greater Melbourne almost none. Kids would be studying from home and parents would be working from home and most shops would be closed until we had zero cases.

'It was pretty radical,' Thompson says. Andrews didn't say Victoria was pursuing an elimination strategy but he didn't need to. Melbourne's roadmap out of restrictions led to only two places: COVID-zero or nowhere.

The day the Victorian roadmap was announced, it felt as though all remaining happiness had been sucked out of the city by a Dementor's kiss. We'd been in lockdown for two months, the numbers had dropped below fifty new cases a day, kids had missed two terms of school, and business owners felt as though the government either didn't understand what it felt like to have your life's work fall apart in front of you or simply didn't care. September in Melbourne is normally about football finals, school holidays, spring festivals and a lightening of the city's mood. We wouldn't have any of that. Australian business, especially big business, is normally reticent to openly criticise government, but on the morning of Andrews's announcement, the Business Council of Australia's Jennifer Westacott appeared on ABC TV to make an impassioned plea: 'This is not about statistics, this is about people's lives,' she said. 'This is about the businesses they built all their lives. It is about that sense of hope versus despair.'[4] Shortly after the announcement, restaurant manager Ben Logan put it more bluntly: 'People are done. People are finished.'

Ben Logan, a father of two from the Mornington Peninsula, had become an unlikely talisman for the cooks, kitchenhands, bartenders, waitstaff, sommeliers and maître d's of Melbourne who, for all but a few weeks since the start of the pandemic, had been unable to work. He'd grown up in what he calls a family of dysfunctional lawyers, performed as an opera singer in Europe for a time and, when the pandemic hit, was managing one of the city's best-known eateries, Di Stasio Citta, owned by celebrated restaurateur Ronnie Di Stasio. When Melbourne first went into lockdown in March 2020, Logan had seen chefs openly weeping in the kitchen. He'd begun writing posts on his LinkedIn account which chronicled the mood and malaise of a hospitality industry that felt abandoned by government decision-makers. The roadmap out of the second wave was especially bleak for hospitality. Before people could again start eating inside restaurants and cafes, all of Victoria would need to record no new cases for a two-week stretch. The target date for this milestone was 23 November, another eleven weeks away. By the time Andrews released his roadmap, Logan had built a following of more than 100 000 regular readers. Within Melbourne's large hospitality sector, despair had turned into a simmering anger. 'I had never been political,' Logan says. 'When the second wave came we just thought, "This is an unmitigated disaster." It is about lives, no question, but it is about so many other things. Small business didn't feel they got any sort of a voice on that.'

The national political consensus that backed Australia's first-wave lockdown and, for the most part, Victoria's decision to lock down a second time, started to fracture. Prime minister Scott Morrison and the two most senior Victorian members of his Cabinet, treasurer Josh Frydenberg and health minister Greg Hunt, issued a joint statement which pinned Melbourne's predicament squarely on the state government. It called the decision to extend lockdown as 'hard and crushing news', and what happens when you can't contain outbreaks.

> The proposed roadmap will come at a further economic cost. While this needs to be weighed up against mitigating the risk of further community outbreak, it is also true that the continued restrictions will have further impact on the Victorian and national economy, in further job losses and loss of livelihoods, as well as impacting on mental health. Of course the Federal Government would like to see restrictions in Victoria lifted as soon as it is safe to do so, but at the end of the day these are decisions solely for the Victorian Government to determine and the roadmap released today is a Victorian Government plan.

Martin Foley, who at the time had recently replaced Jenny Mikakos as Victorian health minister, remains furious at the intervention, particularly by Frydenberg and Hunt. 'The visceral attack that those two launched on us when we told them precisely what we were doing and why, just showed they put crass politics above public health,' he says. 'The weaponisation of public health by those people, against all the states but particularly the Labor states, poisoned the well of cooperation.'

Daniel Andrews saw Canberra's response as a betrayal. The Victorian premier knew that, once the contents of the genomics report became public, his government would be blamed for the failings in quarantine and, more broadly, the systemic weakness in Victorian public health which had allowed the virus to seed into the community and spread. He also knew that, at this moment of the pandemic, Victoria faced a devil's choice. Extending the lockdown through to the end of October would be deeply unpopular and, for some people, devastating. But unless Victoria joined the other states in eliminating the virus, it would be frozen out of the federation by interstate border closures until a vaccine arrived. It was in the national interest, as well as Victoria's interest, for the state to rejoin the rest of the country. Victoria's problem was as much the success of the other states in keeping COVID at bay as its own difficulties in containing the virus. New South Wales, Australia's largest state, didn't eliminate local transmission in 2020, but it controlled—without resorting to lockdowns—all the outbreaks it experienced between the end of the first wave and just before Christmas, when the virus broke loose on Sydney's northern beaches. Between the end of May and New Year's Eve, New South Wales recorded just five deaths from COVID. Elsewhere in Australia, no deaths and hardly any cases were recorded between the end of the first wave and the end of 2020.

Infectious disease expert Sharon Lewin says Victoria's only choice was plain. 'There is no way Victoria could have let COVID run at that time,' she says. 'We had no vaccine, so the mortality would have been quite significant, and we would have been cut off not just from the rest of the world but the rest of the country. Because the rest of the country had no COVID, that had to be the goal. As painful as it was for everyone, I personally think it was the right thing to do.' On the day he announced Victoria's roadmap, Andrews presented it as the only way out. 'You can't argue with this sort of data,' he said of the modelling. 'You can't argue with the science. You can't do anything but follow the best health advice.'

The science, however, was anything but settled. Professor James McCaw, through most of the pandemic, has supported the response of the Victorian Government and its public health team. The roadmap was his first divergence from this. He lived in Melbourne throughout the lockdown months and could see the city was desperate for relief. He was also concerned that, according to his team's analysis of the data, a continuation of the lockdown might not do what the Victorian Government hoped. 'The roadmap that was articulated was presented as something that was very inflexible and wouldn't be responsive to the future epidemiological situation,' he says. 'I was concerned that we had a roadmap that required the infection to be driven to incredibly low levels before there was a lessening of restrictions. The roadmap was putting us in a position where we would end up with restrictions that were not commensurate and not necessary for the safe operating of our society.'

Aside from the work he did for the AHPPC, which at that point was meeting every day, McCaw spoke regularly to Brett Sutton and Allen Cheng. After the roadmap was announced, he provided a weekly update to Sutton about the probability of Victoria reaching the threshold of case numbers it had set as the target to lift lockdown. Most weeks, the state had no better than a 50-50 chance of success. McCaw and fellow AHPPC member Jodie McVernon publicly warned of this in October 2020. They pointed out that other jurisdictions, such as Hong Kong, had safely managed second-wave epidemics without resort to harsh lockdowns. 'Lockdowns have served us well,' they wrote. 'Australia has avoided catastrophe. But it is not lockdown or bust. We have other alternatives.'[5]

For what felt like the first time in a long time during the pandemic, Victoria caught a break. On 26 October, the state recorded no new cases of COVID-19, our first doughnut day since 8 June. Our fourteen-day rolling average of cases, a metric the Andrews government had cleverly introduced to encourage Melburnians to collectively count our steps, like a COVID Fitbit, was below the target contained in the roadmap. We were coming out of lockdown. Daniel Andrews said it was a day on which Victorians should be proud of what they had achieved, and he planned to celebrate it in style. 'I don't know that I'll be drinking a beer tonight, I might be going higher up the shelf,' he said. Melbourne claimed to have achieved something no other city in the world had. Readers of *The Age* newspaper dubbed the premier a hero of the pandemic. Businesses parked their frustrations, finally able to see some blue sky. A state that only weeks earlier was being derided as a COVID laggard was now being heralded as an exemplar. James McCaw says he couldn't have been happier that Victoria had defied the odds.

Sharon Lewin, reflecting at the time, said the story of Melbourne's second wave was globally significant: 'It shows this virus can be overcome with public health measures but you need strong leadership, bolstered public health capabilities—which we didn't have at the beginning of the outbreak—and really strong community engagement.' She also added a word of caution. Although it was clear that lockdowns worked, it was less clear why. 'There are still enormous gaps in the science: how much you need to do, what is redundant and what really makes a difference,' she said. 'It is a very murky scientific area because most places, including us, threw everything at it at the same time. So you never really know what does and doesn't work.'

Catherine Bennett's biggest regret of 2020 is that we didn't do more to fill in those gaps. Had we done so, it might have spared Melbourne what we endured in 2021: another four lockdowns, including a second long COVID winter which took the city and its people to breaking point. Bennett, an epidemiologist with Deakin University, has throughout the pandemic provided steady, apolitical, science-based commentary about Victoria's response. She says the most important thing to understand about Melbourne's second-wave epidemic is how and why outbreaks kept occurring. A statewide or city-wide lockdown assumes the virus is being spread uniformly throughout the community; the only way to stop the spread is for everyone to stay at home. Brett Sutton repeatedly told us, at the height of the second wave, that two-thirds of our cases could be traced back to a specific source: health care and aged care. According to Professor Sutton, about one-third of community transmissions were occurring within hospitals and residential aged-care facilities, and about one-third of infections were being passed between health and aged-care workers to their friends and families. The federal government, on the other hand, most notably Brendan Murphy and the minister responsible for aged care, Richard Colbeck, regularly talked about aged-care infections as being a direct consequence of the virus circulating in the community. While this is true, it doesn't account for the role that aged-care facilities and hospitals played in seeding the virus back into the community.

This might sound like a circular argument but it is a critical distinction. One perspective assumes that the only way to keep our oldest and most vulnerable people safe is to stop all community transmission. The other assumes that the way to stop community transmission is to get on top of outbreaks in hospitals and nursing homes. Bennett likens Victoria's public health response to drenching with water the area surrounding a bushfire, instead of dousing the flames. 'Some of our main aged-care facilities had a continual outbreak for three months,' she says. 'They were seeding the virus back into the population. The reality is we didn't stay in lockdown because we had this uncontrollable outbreak in the community. We had to keep an entire population in lockdown to stop the constant feeding back into the community that was coming out of these long, rolling outbreaks in aged care.'

A team of journalists from the ABC, with the help of epidemiologists including Bennett, produced in early 2021 a compelling, graphically illustrated breakdown of all significant COVID outbreaks in Australia.[6] It contains a timeline which distils Melbourne's second wave into its different parts: outbreaks in aged care, hotel quarantine, meatworks, hospitals, schools, shops and homes. The timeline shows that, by mid-July 2020, the outbreak from the Stamford Plaza hotel, the second and largest of the two quarantine breaches which seeded the second wave, had been contained. By mid-August, so too had school outbreaks and all abattoir outbreaks bar one. There were no significant outbreaks at shopping centres between the start of lockdown and the start of October. The housing commission towers were the only site of large residential outbreaks, and problems in Coles, Woolworths and Linfox distribution centres were addressed by mid-August. From that point on, the second wave was almost entirely driven by cases linked to forty aged-care centres and two significant outbreaks from the Royal Melbourne Hospital and Frankston Hospital.

Bennett says that if we had focused the state's public health response on stopping the virus at these sources, we might have gotten out of lockdown two months earlier. 'That should have been the talking point, rather than this vague talk about evil viruses or humans not doing the right thing,' she says. It also meant that one of our great public health successes went unrecognised at the time.

Kirsty Buising says it was in late July 2020 that staff at the Royal Melbourne Hospital started getting sick for reasons no-one could explain. Some of them worked in a geriatric rehabilitation ward at the hospital's Royal Park campus, where older patients were recovering from surgery or illnesses other than COVID. Some of them were treating COVID patients on infectious-disease wards. They were all nurses and doctors trained in infection prevention and control. Buising is the hospital's director of medical services and an infectious disease consultant. As more staff kept testing positive, she spent time on the wards to see what, if anything, people were doing wrong. As far as she could tell, they were doing everything right: their use of PPE was by the book, they weren't mixing in areas that presented a heightened risk of infection, and there were certainly no shared cigarettes between nurses. The weirdest thing was there weren't even that many COVID patients in hospital. In-patient numbers climbed steadily through July but at the time of the staff outbreaks, there were still fewer than 100 COVID cases on the wards.

Every time a health worker got infected, the test result would be given to a senior member of staff, who in turn would inform the doctor or nurse involved, their direct manager and the hospital's infection-control team. One weekend, Buising was rostered on as the senior staff member responsible for notifications. Over the space of three days, she handled about twenty-five new positive cases. The virus was spreading at a speed and in circumstances that simply couldn't be explained by people touching a contaminated surface or coming into close contact with another case. 'I remember sitting at my kitchen table at 9 a.m. and still being there at 6 p.m. making these calls,' she says. 'More and more I was thinking, "This doesn't make any sense."'

Buising wasn't the only one who'd started to question our assumptions about the virus. At about this time, a Polish-born researcher working at the Queensland University of Technology in Brisbane, Professor Lidia Morawska, was leading a global campaign by scientists to reshape our thinking about how COVID-19 spreads. On 6 July, Professor Morawska was the first named author among 237 infectious disease experts, engineers and aerosol scientists on an open letter to the Clinical Infectious Diseases Society of America calling for national and international bodies, including the WHO, to recognise the potential for the airborne spread of SARS-CoV-2. The letter argued:

> There is significant potential for inhalation exposure to viruses in microscopic respiratory droplets (microdroplets) at short to medium distances (up to several metres, or room scale), and we are advocating for the use of preventive measures to mitigate this route of airborne transmission.[7]

The WHO's position since the start of the pandemic had been that, although airborne transmission couldn't be ruled out, the virus was predominantly transmitted by droplets. The difference may seem subtle but for medical staff looking after COVID patients, the ramifications are enormous. If the virus is predominantly spread by droplets, then it will tend to collect on surfaces within 1.5 metres of the patient. This is why the regular cleaning of surfaces and the careful donning and doffing of PPE was thought to be so important. If it is spread by airborne particles, an entire room, any interconnecting hallways and other rooms are potentially infectious. More pressingly for staff at the Royal Melbourne Hospital, normal surgical masks don't provide much protection against airborne spread—these were the default masks that doctors and nurses were wearing on COVID wards, as recommended by both the WHO and the US-based Centers for Diseases Control and Prevention.

Buising and other members of the hospital's infection-control team had read the Morawska letter. In late July, after the hospital recorded more than thirty staff infections over the space of two days, they decided to mandate the use of N95 respirator masks across all clinical areas, including COVID wards; properly fitted, they gave hospital staff protection against infection they hadn't had for the first six months of the pandemic. The Royal Melbourne Hospital was the first health service in Australia to take that step. It was the start of nationwide overhaul in how masks were used in healthcare and residential aged-care facilities. On 2 August, the hospital's senior management took the additional precaution of closing four wards at its Royal Park campus. 'I don't think you can overestimate how difficult that decision was because we were in the middle of a pandemic,' Buising says. 'It was a tremendously brave thing to do and in retrospect, it probably saved lives.' The Royal Park outbreak was one of the deadliest that Melbourne experienced outside nursing homes. A total of 104 patients were infected and thirty-two died. Between 1 July and 31 August, 262 staff were infected at the hospital.

The size and severity of the outbreak convinced the hospital to do a deep dive into how to better protect its staff and patients from the airborne spread of COVID-19. It brought in aerosol scientists and engineers from the University of Melbourne and asked them to assess its wards. They conducted particle counts and CO_2 monitoring while the nursing staff showed them how patients were managed. They started experimenting with portable air cleaners in rooms where patients had been infected. This led to a number of potentially life-saving changes. Patients were treated one to a room, where possible, to reduce the potential viral load in any given room. Wards with higher ceilings and better ventilation were prioritised for COVID patients. Instead of doors being left open to help nurses keep an eye on patients, they were shut to limit aerosol spread. The outbreak and the hospital's response had quite literally opened a window into how to reduce the risk from an airborne contagion. The results were striking: in 2021, when the virus returned with a vengeance, there were hardly any cases among hospital staff. 'It was chalk and cheese,' Buising says. 'It was a completely different experience.'

Brett Sutton says the international reluctance to accept the idea of COVID as an airborne disease and the relatively simple things that can be done to mitigate its spread, is another example of the stubbornness of orthodoxy. He says there was clear evidence of airborne transmission in Victoria in quarantine hotels and at a supermarket in Epping, where one person infected another by using the same check-out space three minutes apart, but this was not accepted until New South Wales reported similar observations. He says the work of Buising and others at the Royal Melbourne Hospital was central to shifting how we think about COVID. He believes that changes to ventilation and the use of high-efficiency particulate air (HEPA) filters in schools and other places will be the key to how Australia and other countries respond to future waves of infections.

* * *

Melbourne entered the second year of the pandemic as well prepared as any city in Australia and most cities on earth. We had contained a deadly second wave and eliminated, for a time, local transmission of the virus. We had rebuilt our public health defences and established a network of metropolitan and regional public health units that were better placed and better resourced to identify, test and trace local outbreaks. Our hospitals and aged-care facilities better understood how the virus spread and had adopted better precautions to stop it. And at an advanced manufacturing facility in Broadmeadows, a suburb in Melbourne's post-industrial north where six-cylinder sedans used to roll off the Ford assembly lines, the Commonwealth Serum Laboratory had started manufacturing the life-saving Oxford/AstraZeneca vaccine. Why, then, did we not trust these things to keep us out of lockdown?

CHAPTER 7
VAXXED AND VEXED

THE YOUNG NURSE said her name was Sujata. It was difficult to tell whether she was smiling behind her perspex shield and face mask, but on a grey Melbourne afternoon she seemed happy enough to have a patient to attend to. We were standing together in a row of otherwise empty cubicles in a cavernous pavilion at Melbourne's showgrounds. For two weeks in any non-pandemic year, the showgrounds provide the setting for the Royal Melbourne Show, a town-meets-country festival of dairy cows, carnival rides and dagwood dogs. On this day, it was just the two of us in a temporary mass-vaccination centre opened a month earlier to encourage more people from Melbourne's northern and western suburbs to get inoculated against the virus. It was June 2021 and the city was clinging grimly to COVID-zero. We'd had two snap lockdowns in response to outbreaks. The more-infectious Delta variant that was stretching the resources of Britain's National Health Service had been bubbling away in Sydney for at least a couple of weeks. It felt inevitable that Sydney was headed for lockdown, and everyone in Melbourne knew we were living on borrowed time until the premier called another of his afternoon press conferences.

Sujata's job was administering the AstraZeneca (AZ) vaccine, which was manufactured just twenty minutes away at the Commonwealth Serum Laboratory (CSL) biotech facility in Broadmeadows. Since May, CSL had been producing more than one million doses a week. The problem was, no-one wanted them. When I asked Sujata how many doses she had administered that day, she held up a flat hand with fingers splayed. She had been working since 8 a.m. and it was now past 4 p.m.—that was five doses in eight hours. I was there to get my second dose, but so far fewer than 5 per cent of Australians had done the same. After a painless prick I sat for fifteen minutes in a deserted observation area before leaving with an orange sticker that said I was fully vaxxed. Vaxxed and vexed. Given what Melbourne went through the previous year, how were we not rolling up our sleeves for a vaccine that would protect us from death and serious illness and, just maybe, stop us from going back into lockdown?

The simple answer was that, on 8 April 2021, prime minister Scott Morrison held a late-evening press conference which killed public confidence in AZ and turned the second year of Australia's pandemic on its head. That wasn't his intention, of course. Rather, he announced a 'recalibration' of the national vaccine program following new advice from the Australian Technical Advisory Group on Immunisation (ATAGI) that AstraZeneca was no longer the preferred vaccine for adults under the age of fifty. The ATAGI advice was carefully balanced, and the four men fronting Australia's national COVID response—the PM, Health Secretary Brendan Murphy, health minister Greg Hunt and Chief Medical Officer Paul Kelly— were similarly measured in explaining what it meant. They pointed out that the ATAGI advice didn't preclude people under fifty getting an AZ shot; they would just need to consider the risks with their doctor. The news was devastating nonetheless.

For the previous month, reports had emerged out of the United Kingdom and Continental Europe about AZ being linked with a rare but very serious blood-clotting side effect. At first, the UK's

Medicines and Healthcare Products Regulatory Agency and its EU counterpart, the European Medicines Agency, urged everyone to keep getting inoculated with AZ, saying the benefits of the vaccine outweighed the risks for all adults. Within England, where the AZ vaccine was developed by Oxford University scientists, a decision by Danish, Norwegian and Icelandic health authorities to temporarily suspend their AZ programs was at first seen as further evidence of EU payback for Brexit. The origins of this conspiracy theory can be found in a comment made by French President Emmanuel Macron where he described the AZ vaccine as 'quasi-effective'. The notion of AZ being an inferior vaccine to Pfizer, the first mRNA (messenger RNA) vaccine available in Australia, had taken root locally, with the ABC's influential science commentator Norman Swan describing AZ as a second-rate and underperforming vaccine. While this was technically correct according to clinical trials showing that Pfizer was 94.5 per cent effective at preventing symptomatic illness compared with AZ's trial score of 70 per cent,[1] it undersold the benefit of people getting inoculated with whatever vaccine was readily available. In the first half of 2021, that was AstraZeneca, a vaccine that was locally produced, easy to store and simple for GPs to administer at their clinics.

Nick Coatsworth, the face of the federal government's vaccine rollout, accused risk-averse academics and medical commentators of waging a campaign against the vaccine, which he dubbed 'AstraZenecism', and he remains furious about some of the things written and said. 'It is going to take me a long time to forget the people who undermined that vaccine,' he says. Victorian Deputy Premier James Merlino, who led the state during those agonisingly slow, first months of the vaccine rollout, describes the story of AZ as heartbreaking. 'We knew that vaccinating our community was our path out of this and we just saw its reputation trashed.'

* * *

For all the popularity of Norman Swan's podcasts, the ATAGI advice did more to damage the vaccine rollout than the musings of a physician–journalist ever could. ATAGI, a group of fifteen leading infectious-disease and epidemiological experts, led by Professor Allen Cheng, represents the national scientific consensus on vaccine policy. As soon as it cautioned people under fifty against taking AZ, demand for the vaccine collapsed. Health department figures show that, in the two months between February 2021 and the night of Morrison's press conference, the percentage of people who said they were planning to get vaccinated dropped from 80 per cent to 68 per cent.[2] This is why, at a time when Australia had an abundant supply of AZ and not enough Pfizer, nurses like Sujata were standing around in mass-vaccination centres with nothing to do. This wasn't ATAGI's intention. To this day, its members consider AZ a very effective and safe vaccine against COVID-19. Its reasons for taking such a cautious line reveal an unintended consequence of COVID-zero.

'It's a difficult message,' Professor Cheng began. As the co-chair of ATAGI, a member of AHPPC and the most authoritative infectious-disease expert within Victoria's public health response, Cheng had a fair bit on his plate when we first talked about this in May 2021. Despite that, he was patient on the phone as he explained the rationale of ATAGI's advice on AZ. The advisory group's task wasn't to assess the safety or otherwise of the vaccine. That had already been done by Australia's drug regulator, the Therapeutic Goods Administration, which assessed on a weekly basis any new information about the vaccine. The job of ATAGI was to weigh the relative risks and benefits of taking AZ with the risks of COVID. The risk of developing thrombosis with thrombocytopenia syndrome (TTS), the rare combination of blood clotting and low platelet counts linked to the vaccine, was tiny. As of 2 May 2021, 1.4 million doses of AZ had been administered and eleven likely cases of TTS reported. To put this into context, potentially dangerous blood clots occur in about fifty Australians every day.[3] By the end of 2021, when the AZ vaccinations had largely ceased, 13.7 million doses had been administered and 170 cases of TTS had been reported. Of those, eight people died. In the same year, 1317 people died from COVID in Australia. The dilemma ATAGI faced was that, when it met on 8 April to finalise its advice on AZ, there was no COVID in the community. Australia had recorded only four deaths in as many months. In Victoria, we were living in the middle of the good times promised by Tony Blakely and Jason Thompson's model. So long as things stayed this way, the risk of anyone getting seriously sick or dying from COVID was negligible.

'If you get AstraZeneca and you are under fifty, you are probably going to be fine,' Cheng explained. 'It's just that [when] these complications do occur, it seems to be at a higher rate in people under fifty, and because COVID isn't such a severe disease under fifty, that is where we start to worry about the risks and benefits. If we had a huge outbreak like Germany we would probably change that advice.'

At the time I spoke to Professor Cheng, Germany was battling a wave of Delta infections and, in an effort to boost vaccinations, it had scrapped its previous limit on AZ only being available to people aged sixty and over. In the United Kingdom, where a Delta wave was receding, the advice on AZ had shifted the other way, with the age limit increased from thirty to forty. In Australia, our attitude towards AZ reflected the absence of urgency that had infected our vaccination program from the start, when the federal government had taken from July to November 2020 to place its initial order of Pfizer vaccines, and Scott Morrison had repeatedly declared: 'It is not a race.' It was always a race. We just didn't see a need to start running.

Ian Gemmell, an expat Australian doctor who witnessed firsthand the life-saving impact of the AstraZeneca vaccine on his adopted southern England town of Salisbury, was alarmed at the vaccine complacency in Australia, and particularly in Melbourne, where our winters are colder and more likely to bring respiratory illness. 'If you have got the ability to vaccinate now, prior to the cold weather coming on, now is the time to be doing it,' he warned in May 2021. 'If people delay getting their vaccination or choose not to have it because they don't consider it an issue, it is going to come back and it is going to bite you on the backside.' When Allen Cheng talks to me about this again in May 2022, he says that, with the benefit of hindsight, ATAGI might have taken a different view. 'If someone had of said we were going to get a huge outbreak in the second half of 2021 and it will come in before we get an additional supply of vaccine, then we might have made different judgements,' he says. 'But the assumption we had made was that if we had an outbreak in 2021, we would be able to control it as we had in 2020.'

Brett Sutton isn't critical of the ATAGI decision. He points out that the group's job was to assess the risks and benefits of the vaccine for individuals, not the broader benefits and risks for a largely unvaccinated population. Still, at the time, he knew it left us badly exposed to another wave of infections. 'I tried to champion it,' he says. 'I got the AstraZeneca vaccine by choice. I wanted to be promoting it. I knew we had millions of doses that were available and could have gone into people's arms if they were ready to step up for it. I also knew that messaging was poisoned by the way the clots had been overplayed. It was front-page news when the front-page news should have been that we might have 500 to 1000 deaths like the UK if you don't get vaccinated. It is an awful case of the drama of the rare side effects of AstraZeneca vaccine becoming the story, rather than the wonder drug that it was.'

Professor Nathan Grills sees the spurning of AZ as the missed opportunity we had in the first half of 2021 to get vaccinated and avoid the devastating outbreaks and consequences of lockdown that followed. Professor Grills knows how effective the AZ vaccine is because it saved the lives of people he worked with in India's hospital system during that country's Delta epidemic. Grills is a public health expert with the University of Melbourne's Nossal Institute for Global Health. His research work is focused on a series of collaborations in India, including with the Christian Medical College (CMC) in the city of Vellore. At the height of the Delta wave, CMC Vellore had 1000 COVID in-patients and was treating another 400 in their homes. Despite the hospital being stretched beyond capacity, hardly any of its staff got sick—they had all been vaccinated with AZ. Only one staff member died and they were unvaccinated. Grills says he heard tragic stories of good doctors and nurses at other hospitals in India dying with COVID after refusing vaccination. Some of them had been fed misinformation about AZ. The power of vaccines to transform the pandemic experience was clear by April 2021 to anyone paying attention, but in Australia, we were warning people off a vaccine we had in abundant supply.

'I could see that people weren't getting vaccinated because of the information that was out there,' Grills says. 'I knew those people being scared off were going to face COVID at some point and if they weren't vaccinated, they had a 90 per cent greater chance of dying from it or being in ICU. We needed to show the danger of Delta, and governments to say, "This is coming to us. We can't prevent it forever."' Grills is not critical of Allen Cheng and the people who make up ATAGI, but he is critical of its narrow membership, which is heavy on infectious-disease expertise but light on broader public health experience. He says that ATAGI's advice on AZ underestimated the risk of what should have been seen as inevitable future outbreaks: 'We thought we were safe from it. That was never the case. We were going to have infiltrations, outbreaks and waves. To think we could have a slower vaccination campaign until we had more information from other countries was ignorant. We had a very good vaccine that was very safe and effective, and we had a lot of people getting COVID in July, August and September who weren't vaccinated because they had been scared by some of the advice.'

Greg Hunt disagrees. He believes the ATAGI decision on AZ was the right one. 'They probably saved twenty to thirty lives,' he says. 'It was a blow to the program but in the end, we believe they got the settings right based on the evidence.'

If we'd ordered and received more Pfizer earlier, this might not have mattered. Whether we could have ordered more Pfizer earlier remains far from clear. Pfizer first approached the federal government on 30 June 2020 about its vaccine, and on 10 July, company representatives met with Lisa Schofield, a health department bureaucrat. Schofield says there was no offer of vaccines at that meeting, only an agreement to keep talking.[4] In July 2020, no-one knew for sure whether the Pfizer-BioNTech vaccine would be safe and effective against COVID-19. The vaccine's stage 3 trials—the first time they were administered to people—only began on 27 July and were not completed until November. Yet, in the rush to inoculate their populations, other countries were willing to gamble that Pfizer would come up trumps. By the end of the month, the United States had placed an advance order for 100 million doses, Japan for 120 million doses, the United Kingdom for 30 million doses and Canada for 20 million doses. Australia ordered its first shipment of 10 million doses in November 2020, once Pfizer had announced the vaccine worked. The first shipment, a token 142 000 doses, did not arrive in Australia until 15 February 2021, by which time the federal government had a further 10 million doses on order.

Brendan Murphy says there were never more doses available to Australia, nor any prospect of getting the ones we ordered any earlier. He also makes it clear that, even if this wasn't the case, the federal government didn't think we needed them. He says that, to ensure Australia had access to enough vaccines at a time of intense international demand and with the spectre of vaccine nationalism—larger nations like America cornering existing supply with big priority contracts—the government's vaccine strategy was weighed heavily towards domestically manufactured AZ and another vaccine being developed by University of Queensland researchers. Within this strategy, Pfizer was a 'backstop'.[5]

As it turned out, the backstop became the most important player on the field. The University of Queensland vaccine candidate was abandoned in December 2020 after a number of people who took the drug in clinical trials returned false tests for the AIDS virus, HIV. By that stage, surging demand for Pfizer, the first COVID-19 vaccine to come on the global market, left Australia scrambling to secure more doses alongside Northern Hemisphere nations battling winter epidemics. From that point on, Australia's vaccination program became AstraZeneca or bust. When ATAGI cautioned against the use of AZ, it went bust. A charitable view of Australia's vaccination strategy is that we were unlucky. The bigger problem was that, once the federal government realised it didn't have enough vaccines to meet demand, it sought to reduce demand rather than admit its own failing. 'One of the systemic failures of the Australian pandemic response was a disconnect between the Commonwealth and the states, where the Commonwealth just did not have the same level of urgency,' says Jeroen Weimar, the operations manager who led Victoria's COVID response through 2021. This ensured that blame shifting between Canberra and the states would endure as a defining feature of Australia's approach to the COVID crisis.

We kept being told throughout the pandemic that Australia was special, that there was no place on earth you would rather be to ride out the COVID storm. Perhaps that is true, but Australia in 2021 also discovered something that other countries already understood: a little bit of COVID goes a long way to curing vaccine hesitancy. Ian Gemmell experienced this in Salisbury as the postcard, medieval-cathedral town was counting down to Christmas 2020. On 23 December, there were only thirty COVID patients at the small district hospital in Salisbury; two weeks later there were nearly 300. Dr Gemmell, a former British Army medical officer who was now in charge of the National Health Service's vaccination program, commandeered the city's thirteenth-century cathedral, which was closed to worshippers, and soon had people lining up beneath its gothic arches and beyond its front steps for a shot. One of the people he vaccinated was his own teenage son.

A Resolve survey conducted in May 2021 examined the reasons for vaccine hesitancy in Australia. One in two people who weren't planning to get vaccinated said they were worried about side effects, a third said they were waiting for more people to get vaccinated first, and one in five said that, with international borders shut, there was simply no rush.[6]

The promise of our long 2020 lockdown was a COVID-free Christmas. When the time came to open our presents, it didn't quite work out as planned. On 13 December, NSW Health Minister Brad Hazzard called a press conference to reveal that a man who drove flight crews to and from Sydney International Airport had tested positive for the virus—it was the state's first positive case in two weeks. Seven hours later, Hazzard was standing before the TV cameras again, talking about two more cases. These ones had been picked up in Sydney's northern beaches, a spit of land that has Pittwater on one side, the big blue of the Pacific on the other, and some of the world's most affluent coastal neighbourhoods in-between. It is hard to imagine a more Sydney outbreak, with the Avalon Beach RSL and Avalon Bowlo, the local lawn bowls club, both declared exposure sites. It is also hard to imagine anything more crushing for local restaurant, bar and hotel owners who, at the end of a wretched 2020, were desperate to get their tills ringing again.

A week after the first case, NSW premier Gladys Berejiklian announced a lockdown of the northern beaches, with local residents told to stay at home for Christmas. As luck would have it, the Avalon outbreak had already reached the peak of a very small wave by the time the lockdown was called. Although NSW Chief Health Officer Kerry Chant didn't know it at the time, a combination of geography, demography and a rapid response by the local public health unit caught the outbreak before it built into something more threatening.

In Victoria, having just marked our fifty-first straight doughnut day, we weren't taking any chances. On the day that Berejiklian announced the Sydney lockdown, Daniel Andrews ordered 700 police, supported by military personnel, to protect the state's northern border against a new enemy: anyone who had been in greater Sydney or on the NSW Central Coast in recent days. People were given until midnight the next day to get home to their families or alternatively welcome the new year in hotel quarantine. The following day, Jeroen Weimar further toughened our border defences, warning that anyone who hadn't crossed into Victoria by the end of the day would be turned back. 'If you turn up at our land border after midnight you will not be able to enter Victoria,' he said. 'You will be turned around and asked to find alternative accommodation in New South Wales or wherever you have been.' Weimar also encouraged Victorians to refrain from hugging or kissing people recently returned from New South Wales. At the Victorian border that night, and at the Queensland and South Australian borders where similar snap policies had been put into force, there was no mood for any such affection. Instead, it was bedlam, for days on end, as families were divided over Christmas and new year holidays. Australia at the start of 2021 was split into its pre-Federation parts according to dotted lines on a map and the shifting vagaries of public health orders.

We quickly learned that life in a COVID-zero state wasn't all sugary doughnuts. We were told over and over again by our premier that we had built something precious, but it felt as though the state was made of glass. When you didn't have a COVID case, any new case became a crisis. More than one was a dangerous outbreak, and before you could count them on one hand you were back in lockdown again. The result was heightened fear about the virus, bordering on paranoia. Even if you were unlikely to get seriously ill from COVID, you knew that even a small cluster of infections would force us all back into our homes. The emergence of new cases brought a rush to apportion blame, as though every infection in a pandemic is someone's fault. Journalists pointed accusatory fingers at government. Government, meanwhile, looked for someone or something else to blame. A new, more infectious variant of the virus. Another state government. A slower-than-planned vaccination rollout. Or a chronic asthmatic who had just gotten off a long-haul flight with his partner and three-month-old daughter and needed the help of a nebuliser to breathe.

In late January 2021, a 38-year old man returned from overseas with his family. They were taken through Customs and placed into the custody of Victoria Police, who escorted them into quarantine detention at the Holiday Inn at Melbourne Airport. They were checked into adjoining rooms 322 and 323 and told they could not step outside those rooms for two weeks. While inside his room, the man used a nebuliser, a small, portable machine which turns liquid medicine into a fine mist, allowing him to breathe in the Ventolin medication he used to control the symptoms of his asthma. He thought he had permission to use it—a health department review later confirmed that, during the SkyBus ride from the airport terminal to the hotel, a nurse offered him the use of his nebuliser if he needed it.[7] As the man and his family started counting down the days in quarantine, his breathing became more laboured. He didn't realise that his airways were infected with COVID-19. The man's partner and daughter, two other guests on the same floor of the hotel and two hotel staff had also been infected. The most likely explanation appeared to be that the man's nebuliser had pumped the virus in aerosol form around his room and out into the corridor, and that hotel staff had then taken the virus out of the Holiday Inn and home to their families.

Daniel Andrews said the man had been told not to use the nebuliser and that, short of barging into people's hotel rooms, there was only so much hotel staff could do to make sure people followed the rules. The inference was that the man hadn't. 'You are left feeling like a criminal or that you've done the wrong thing,' the man later told *The Age* health reporter Melissa Cunningham from his intensive care bed in hospital. 'That has been the hardest thing in all this.'[8]

A review by Safer Care Victoria, an agency within the Victorian Government's health department, subsequently confirmed that nebuliser guy, who was eventually discharged from hospital back into quarantine, was a victim of another quarantine breach in the same hotel. When infectious-control experts traced the likely spread of the virus, they found the sentinel case—the assumed first case in the outbreak—was a woman who had returned from Sri Lanka with what we now know as the Beta strain variant. After reviewing hotel security footage, the experts identified a routine PCR (polymerase chain reaction) test, where nurses take a mouth and nasal swab from a hotel guest in the doorway of their room, as the likely moment the virus escaped and was pushed by air-conditioning down the corridor, towards rooms 322 and 323.[9] Hotel quarantine guests aren't allowed to leave their rooms but they have to open their doors several times a day to receive food and put out garbage. Any of these episodes could have let the virus into the room of the man with the nebuliser.

On 12 February, on the basis of the five new infections produced by this fluky sequence of events, the entire state of Victoria was pitched back into a stage 4 lockdown. This led to one of the most bizarre episodes of Melbourne's entire pandemic experience. At 11.30 p.m. that night, as the world's best male tennis player, Novak Djokovic, and American Taylor Fritz were heading into the final set of an epic third-round match at the Australian Open, chair umpire John Bloom announced that, due to the imminent imposition of COVID restrictions, all spectators had five minutes to vacate Rod Laver Arena. For five-and-a-half hours, people had sat next to one another, laughing and cheering and shouting and jeering through two tennis matches. Now that the clock was approaching midnight, Victoria's public health orders deemed it too great a risk for those same people to stay in those same seats to watch the deciding set. The bemused spectators cleared out and rushed home, like Cinderella fleeing the ball.

Lockdown number four introduced us to the man from Wollert, a new suburb on the northern edge of Melbourne. In April 2021 the man was trying to get home from India, where a new variant of the virus, soon to be renamed Delta, was driving a deadly epidemic, but international flights into Tullamarine were severely limited, with only 10 000 people arriving for the entire month. The biggest constraint on the airlines wasn't seat availability but hotel quarantine. To secure a flight, every passenger needed a corresponding two-week stay booked in a hotel. The only way for the man to get home was to fly into Adelaide, quarantine there, and then fly into Melbourne. For fourteen days he stayed in Adelaide's Playford Hotel, in a room near the end of a corridor, seemingly without incident. On 4 May he flew to Melbourne and drove home to Wollert, unaware that he was infected with the virus. A little over three weeks later, Victoria was in lockdown again.

This time, our lockdown was ordered by a substitute premier. Two months earlier, Daniel Andrews was leaving a holiday house in Sorrento, the favoured beachside retreat of Melbourne's A-list businesspeople, TV celebrities and political class, when he slipped on stairs wet from overnight rain and fell flat on his back. Andrews says he knew he was in trouble when he heard an 'almighty crunch', with X-rays later confirming he'd fractured five ribs and crushed a vertebra halfway up his spine. While Andrews recovered at home, James Merlino filled in as Victoria's acting premier. When the state's public health team reported a new cluster of COVID cases to their new boss, they offered him good and bad news. Genomic testing confirmed that the virtual strain which infected the man from Wollert originated in a hotel room in Adelaide, not Melbourne. This was the good news—it was another quarantine stuff-up, but this time it was someone else's. The bad news was that it wasn't until 23 May that a second case was linked to the outbreak. The man hadn't infected his family or any mates at work, but for twenty days the virus had potentially spread throughout the state undetected. Another winter was almost upon us and our COVID response had been blindsided. When Merlino announced we were heading into lockdown once more, he feared more what we didn't know than what we did.

Melbourne's third lockdown lasted for five days and our fourth for two weeks. When you say it now, it sounds like a small thing. What was five days or two weeks of further inconvenience given the many months of lockdown we had already endured? In February 2021, the winter epidemic in Europe and the United States was still near its devastating peak. In May 2021, Indian health authorities were recording 4000 deaths a day, and parking lots in New Delhi were being used as makeshift crematoria for families to burn the bodies of their loved ones. Melbourne, like all Australian jurisdictions, remained lightly touched by a virus which, by that stage, had killed close to four million people. Yet, it wasn't a small thing for Melbourne to lock down again.

The February lockdown was announced the day before Valentine's Day. For Melbourne's restaurant owners and staff, this was the biggest day of bookings they'd had since our COVID winter. Valentine's Day fell on a Sunday, which meant the lunches would be long, lovebird diners would order a second bottle of wine, and the waitstaff serving them would be earning double time. Instead, thousands of staff were stood down without notice and all the food crammed into coolrooms had to be thrown out. Ben Logan was working at Di Stasios that day and says the mood in the city was mutinous: 'The entire hospitality industry wanted to pick up anything they could get their hands on and run up Spring Street. It was the first opportunity hospitality had to get people back out. To be thrown to the wind, literally at the eleventh hour, people were just angry.'

Brett Sutton agrees that the use of precautionary lockdowns and the public-health goal of COVID-zero are intrinsically linked.

'Once you have achieved elimination, it is very clear that acting immediately is the right way to do it because it gets on top of it in the shortest period of time,' he says. He also points out that reported case numbers reflect only a small part of the battle. 'The numbers that you have reported on a particular day are always three to four times less than the true number of cases that are incubating on that day. In a setting of ongoing transmission I think Dave Nabarro is right: you use all of the more-sustainable, less-intrusive mechanisms to do what you can without using lockdowns as your only or largest tool. But he is really talking about Europe or North America and not the so-called COVID-zero states.'

Jason Thompson, the University of Melbourne researcher whose work helped inform the roadmap out of our long 2020 lockdown, maintains an electronic dashboard which maps Melbourne's COVID cases and restrictions against the extent to which people move around the city; the last measure is taken from Facebook data. As Thompson explains, the data shows that, during the mostly COVID-free stretch between November 2020 and what became our final lockdown in August 2021, we bought ourselves months of COVID-normal living. Thompson supports Victoria's use of lockdowns—he points to the months we enjoyed with relatively low restrictions and high movement and says this never could have happened if the virus had circulated more freely and thousands of people a day were getting sick with COVID. The dashboard shows that, from mid-November 2020 through to the nebuliser lockdown in February, and from mid-February through to the man from Wollert in mid-May, the echo of regular community and family life returned to Melbourne. It also shows that every time we went into lockdown, even when it was for just a week or two, it took us a while to get back to where we had been: the health restrictions would lift, but workers wouldn't return to the office straight away, our shops and restaurants would remain mostly empty, and everyone would be reminded of our wretched experience the year before. It was only in late March 2022 that people started moving as freely as they had been in May 2021, before the man from Wollert.

Some lockdowns were relatively short but they were never painless. It is also not clear they were all necessary. By 2021, Victoria had developed world-class trace, contact and case-management systems to respond to COVID outbreaks. The data from those outbreaks suggests that these systems—and a bit of good luck—rather than lockdowns were the crucial factors in controlling both the February and May outbreaks.

On the Saturday night before Melbourne went into its two-week lockdown, a young man infected with the virus had a night on the tiles down Chapel Street, an urban strip of boutiques, bars and botox. He started with a few drinks with friends at Three Monkeys, walked across the street to Somewhere Bar and ended up at Circus Bar on nearby Commercial Road, a place of rich velvet drapes and leather booths. All the while, the man drank and laughed and shared close conversations with his companions, oblivious to the fact he might be passing on the virus. In the end, no-one else got sick. For all his close-quarters bar hopping, the man didn't infect one other person.

Professor Rhonda Stuart from Monash Health says we don't know why some people are highly infectious and some people are not at all, but throughout the pandemic, all variants of the virus have behaved in this way. Notwithstanding that we got lucky that night in Chapel Street, the improvements within Victoria's response were clear. Throughout the February and May outbreaks, our contact tracers kept pace with the virus to the point where potential contacts were put into isolation before they'd had a chance to pass it on. The time it takes for an infectious person to infect someone else means it takes at least a week for the impact of any public-health interventions to be reflected in case numbers. From the day Victoria's third lockdown started, the state only recorded a handful more cases. In the fourth lockdown, cases never got beyond a dozen in one day.

While Professor Sutton cautions that reported case numbers don't reflect the full COVID picture, Melbourne's experience in the first half of 2021 nonetheless showed us that pre-Delta variants of the virus, if we responded well enough, could be contained with a classic public-health response—what the WHO's David Nabarro, calls 'alert, detect and respond'. This isn't an argument for sitting back until case numbers rise to alarming levels. As Nabarro puts it: 'You have to act before the thing starts to build up. Any remark by a government that says, "We are going to watch and wait and see and try to do a proportionate response," you know they are going to get it wrong.' This also doesn't mean you have to lock down a major city every time you record a handful of cases. Yet, throughout 2021, the Victorian Government was adamant that this is what we had to do. There are differing theories about why.

Public-health expert Nathan Grills argues that, despite our success in running down the nebuliser and Wollert outbreaks, Victoria's public health capacity at the time still wasn't where it needed to be. He says that the local public health units, although run by highly capable infectious-disease experts, and administratively backed by major hospitals, struggled to find enough trained people to do the work. 'A lot of it was optics,' he says of our improved response. Grills, who oversees a government training program for public health physicians at the University of Melbourne, observes that the root cause of the city's problems in 2020—underinvestment in public health—had not been rectified by the start of 2022: 'They were doing the best they could, but it was a pretty big ask to turn around and develop a functioning system without the necessary staff, expertise and training. I think that did impede us in 2021, to be able to respond and maybe trust our contact tracing system.'

Former federal health minister Greg Hunt says vast improvements were made to Victoria's public health response, but by 2021 the Andrews government had developed a pathological reliance on lockdown. 'It had a feel of captain Ahab chasing Moby Dick,' he says. 'There was a belief at the highest political levels that we had to exterminate this disease invader. By this stage, most medical authorities around Australia and the world were saying, as history has subsequently shown, that this disease would be endemic, it would continue to mutate, and we were on a vaccination path. I felt just terrible for what we were seeing.'

On 24 June 2021, Victoria Police got a hot tip: a woman from Sydney was having dinner at the Botanical Hotel. In a city where on average one person was murdered a week in 2021 and nearly 15 000 serious assaults and 10 000 rapes and indecent assaults were reported to police, a thirty-year-old woman sharing a few drinks and a meal with a group of family, friends and work colleagues at a popular South Yarra pub might not sound like an offence serious enough to dispatch two police officers on a Saturday night to detain the culprit. That is what happened to Jessica Jackson, a media and advertising consultant who'd come to Melbourne thinking she had just left an orange zone when, according to information received by Victoria Police and passed on to the state's health department, she'd left a part of Sydney now flashing red. Jackson was oblivious to this as she sat with her companions with her back to the front entrance of the pub, deciding what to order. She'd lived in Melbourne until seven months earlier, when she'd fled the drudgery of lockdown to work remotely from Sydney. The Bot was a familiar haunt and she'd been there for most of the day. At about 6.30 p.m., she was seated with her boss, her brother, his girlfriend and some of her favourite clients when a waiter came over and said there were two police out the front asking for her by name. Jackson was perplexed as she walked outside into the cold air but it was clearly no mistake—one of the cops was holding a 'WANTED'-style photo of her. 'They told me that I had come from a red zone,' she says. 'They were berating me: "You live in a red zone, you are from Bondi." I was completely caught off-guard. They had my licence photo on an A4 piece of paper. They were coming to get me.'

On the night before her flight, Jackson had gone to bed with rumours swirling that Sydney was about to go into lockdown. About two weeks earlier, a limousine driver named Michael Podgoetsky had driven from his Bondi apartment to Sydney International Airport to pick up a three-man FedEx freight crew who'd flown in from Guangzhou. Podgoetsky was born in the former Soviet republic of Azerbaijan and had emigrated to Sydney with his wife Eliana to raise their two sons. Throughout the COVID crisis, as his regular work doing weddings and hen's nights dried up, he shifted to transporting flight crews between the airport's international terminal and hotel quarantine. He always wore a mask when he drove and insisted that his passengers do the same, but somewhere on the road with the FedEx crew, he became infected with the Delta variant of COVID-19. He tested positive on 16 June, by which time the virus was spreading through Bondi and Sydney's other exclusive eastern suburbs: a woodfire pizzeria in Paddington, a celebrity hair salon in Double Bay, a supermarket in Potts Point. Then, on a Saturday night, a Bondi manicurist travelled across town to a birthday bash in West Hoxton, in the heart of Sydney's west, and brought the virus as an uninvited guest. Of the thirty people at the party, twenty-four became infected. By the time the candles were blown out on the cake, the virus was on a tear.

The NSW Government initially backed its COVID response, led by the exacting Kerry Chant, to contain the outbreak, as it had done with previous clusters. Other than a three-week shutdown of Sydney's northern beaches, New South Wales had not gone into lockdown since the first months of the pandemic. Even back then, the state had adopted a less-prescriptive approach than Victoria. Although premier Gladys Berejiklian, like Daniel Andrews, had ordered all non-essential businesses shut and encouraged everyone to work and study from home, her government did not issue stay-at-home orders. Throughout March and April, people living in New South Wales could still leave their homes whenever they wanted to. It was a lockdown of sorts, but people were entrusted with the key.

On 23 June, the day Jackson flew into Melbourne, Berejiklian was still holding out against pressure from other state leaders and a growing epidemiological chorus to shut down Australia's largest city. The NSW Government announced new restrictions requiring everyone in greater Sydney to limit the number of guests in their homes and to wear a mask whenever they went into public places; in addition, people living in Sydney's east were prohibited from travelling outside the city limits. We were also introduced to a curious prohibition against 'vertical consumption'—drinking while standing. But for the time being, businesses could remain open and people could still go about their lives. There was even an exemption to allow dancing at weddings. Berejiklian explained that, although the situation was serious, she was determined to limit restrictions to what was absolutely necessary. This was in marked contrast to the 'abundance of caution' Andrews adopted throughout the pandemic. As Berejiklian detailed the new restrictions, she outlined her philosophy about lockdowns: 'We have always said we won't burden our citizens unless we absolutely have to. We ask people to make individual decisions on their own circumstances. We have put these rules in place, there will always be exceptions, there will always be certain situations which, perhaps, every single health order doesn't cover. We rely on people's common sense as much as what the health orders say.'

In Melbourne, Brett Sutton and his public health team were looking north with increasing concern and frustration. After the Christmas and New Year's Eve border debacle which left families stranded on the wrong side of the Murray, Victoria had adopted a traffic light system to regulate interstate travel. To enter the state, you needed a permit. If you were coming from a green zone, there was no other requirement. If you came in from an orange zone, you needed to quarantine at home for fourteen days. Victorian residents could return from a red zone but had to spend two weeks in hotel quarantine. Jackson says that, at the time of her ill-fated Melbourne trip, she was staying in the central Sydney suburb of Pyrmont with her ex-boyfriend and her listed address was in North Bondi. The night before her flight, she went to bed in an orange zone. While she was sleeping, new orders by Professor Sutton turned the lights to red. This meant that, when Jackson arrived in Melbourne early on the morning of 23 June, she was entering the state on the wrong permit and, according to the rule change which had come into force a few hours earlier, shouldn't have been entering at all. She wasn't the only person apparently oblivious to this. She says that when she was questioned at the airport by DHHS officials wearing full protective clothing, the only instruction they gave her was to get tested if she showed any symptoms. There was no mention of having to quarantine or isolate. She gratefully picked up her bag and caught a taxi to her South Yarra office. The next day, she settled in for a long day at the Bot.

It was a cold night in Melbourne and Jackson had been outside for more than an hour talking to police, dressed in a light silk dress and heels, when someone came from inside the restaurant to give her a blanket. She says she explained to the police that she no longer lived in North Bondi, that she didn't know she'd been in a red zone, that she had done what she was told by the health officials at the airport. She told them she only realised the traffic lights had changed after she landed in Melbourne. She describes a humiliating experience, huddling beneath a blanket on Domain Road, under police watch, while the rest of the pub gawked through the windows at the curious scene outside. 'I thought it was a bit of a joke and that I'd be let go and have a funny story to come back to dinner with,' she says. But after three hours of sitting in the cold, whatever the police were doing seemed to be taking an awfully long time. 'It was getting close to 10 o'clock and I'm like, "Ladies, what's going on? I need to go to sleep, I have meetings tomorrow,"' says Jackson.

One of the policewomen apologised for the delay. She explained they were trying to work out who was going to drive Jackson into hotel quarantine. A message then popped up on Jackson's phone with a link to a detention order from DHHS declaring her a serious risk to public health. She read it in disbelief. She asked to go to the toilet but the police explained that if she went back inside, the entire hotel would be declared an exposure zone. The absurdity of this, if it occurred to the police, did not distract them from their duties. It was only when a divisional van pulled up, driven by two more police, that it dawned on Jackson that she was under arrest. The police swung open the rear doors and ordered Jackson to climb inside. 'I couldn't get in,' she says. 'I just started crying. It all became so real that this was actually happening.'

Jackson was taken to the Novotel Hotel on Collins Street and told to stay in her room for two weeks. In the end, she was only required to stay one night. When word of the episode reached senior people within Victoria's public health team, they were incensed at how she had been treated. They could see that she should have been isolating, rather than drinking with friends, but understood how ridiculous it was to detain someone who'd spent two days moving freely around Melbourne. She had been tested when she was taken into hotel quarantine and didn't have the virus. What was the point in holding her? 'It just highlighted the idiocy of it all, everyone following rules without any common sense being applied,' Jackson says. 'None of it made any sense and basic human kindness went out of it all. I get that this virus had everyone scared to death but the way people carried on was just barbaric.'

Jackson's exit from hotel quarantine, like her entry, was comically officious. Although she wasn't sick, she was loaded into an ambulance and given a police-car escort to a friend's place in Middle Park, where she was told to quarantine for fourteen days. By the time she was free to leave she had nowhere to go. Melbourne was in lockdown again.

Gladys Berejiklian made the call on 25 June 2021: central Sydney and the city's eastern suburbs would be subject to stay-at-home orders. The following day, all of Sydney and the surrounding regional areas were included in the lockdown. The case numbers were still modest: the entire Bondi cluster had caused just sixty-five infections. But for the first time, Kerry Chant could see the virus was getting away from her. Berejiklian described it as the scariest time that New South Wales had faced throughout the pandemic. Sydney would spend the next 107 days in lockdown, just shy of Melbourne's long stretch in 2020, as we all waited for vaccination rates to blunt the edge of the Delta outbreak. In doing so, it recast the politics of the pandemic, both in New South Wales and Victoria. As Victorian Senator Andrew Giles later reflects, nothing happens in Australia until it happens in Sydney, and this is certainly true of lockdown. When Melbourne endured our previous, lonely COVID winter, the rest of the nation was detached from, if not oblivious to, what this meant. We listened with teeth clenched while the prime minister contrasted the 'gold standard' pandemic response of New South Wales with the failings that led to our second-wave epidemic. We watched the AFL shift the grand final away from Melbourne to Brisbane, while our own stadiums sat empty. Sydney heading into lockdown didn't erase those months of isolation but it gave the NSW capital, a city not prone to empathy, some insight into what we'd gone through.

The Andrews government welcomed the NSW Government's decision to lock down but was dismayed about how long it took. 'New South Wales didn't learn from our experience in 2020,' says James Merlino. 'Looking from Victoria at what was happening with the Bondi outbreak was like watching a car crash in slow motion.

You knew what the outcome of this would be, and you had the extraordinary circumstance of the prime minister being the cheerleader for not taking action, for staying open, for doing something different to what we did in Victoria. We could see this outcome happening, day after day, and it did. The outbreak got away from them and it was inevitably going to cross borders into Victoria and elsewhere.'

They had driven all night by the time they got to Craigieburn on the outskirts of Melbourne: three men, a delivery truck full of furniture, and at least one case of COVID-19. They'd started out in Sydney just after midnight on 8 July and cruised down the gun-barrel-straight Hume Highway, stopping only for fuel and food, to make their first delivery. Then they were off across town to an apartment complex in Maribyrnong, in Melbourne's west, before driving on to Adelaide and back to Sydney. Being a long-haul delivery driver is hard work and not particularly well paid. The pandemic meant there were traffic snarls and bureaucratic delays at the border, and at every stop you were supposed to disinfect your hands and put on a mask while you were wrangling sofas, shelving units and coffee tables. They'd driven back to Sydney by 11 July, a round trip of nearly 3000 kilometres in three days, when the first of the crew tested positive to the virus; then a second man returned a positive test. Jeroen Weimar was desperate to find out exactly where they had been, where they had stopped and who they had spent time with. He became frustrated, along with health officials in New South Wales and South Australia, when the crew and their employer were less than helpful with the information they provided. Within a few days, their trail became all too clear: an infected family in Craigieburn, and confirmed positive cases at an apartment complex at Maribyrnong with an additional two at the MCG, where a man from the apartment building had gone with a friend on the Saturday night to watch Collingwood lose to Geelong—the man's companion lived in Barwon Heads and took the virus back with him. There weren't many cases but Delta was already spreading across the breadth of the city.

On the night of 15 July we were back in lockdown. In a not-too-subtle dig at New South Wales, Daniel Andrews declared: 'Victoria will not wait to act. We know that not much good comes from waiting.' He said that Victoria was entering a five-day lockdown. We'd stay there, save for a few days, for another three months.

Lockdown number five was very different for me. Where I had experienced the others confined by stay-at-home orders and 5-kilometre limits, I saw this one from the outside looking in. Two days after the Victorian premier held his evening press conference, I took a PCR test, packed a bag, popped on a mask, and called a taxi to Melbourne Airport's deserted international terminal to board a plane to Tokyo, a city which had decided to host the Olympic Games at the start of its own Delta epidemic. On the day I left, Melbourne was in lockdown with eighteen new cases, and Tokyo, with 1400 new cases, was welcoming thousands of athletes, coaches and journalists from around the world. It was a surreal experience boarding a near-empty Singapore Airlines flight close to midnight. It felt as though we were travelling in the wrong direction, at the wrong time, to a city that would prefer it if we weren't coming at all.

Once I spent some time out on the streets of Tokyo and saw how locals were dealing with the pandemic, it brought a sense of clarity. Tokyo, like Melbourne, was in a state of emergency, but unlike the Andrews government, Japan's national government is prevented by its postwar constitution from wielding coercive powers—it cannot enforce a lockdown, it can only ask. There were no stay-at-home orders in Tokyo, merely a request from the government of then prime minister Yoshihide Suga for people to go home at night instead of heading out to bars. In turn, there were no laws against the city's bars staying open, but rather an expectation that most would close at 8 p.m. The locals referred to these soft restrictions as *manen boshi*: 'prevention of the spread'. It is a practical phrase, stripped of embellishment or hyperbole, which captures the Japanese attitude towards COVID. There was no talk in Japan of COVID-zero or crushing the virus, just doing what was necessary to suppress each epidemic in order to limit sickness and loss of life. During the day, the city operated much the same as it normally did, with businesses allowed to trade and shops allowed to sell things. The big difference was that, unlike in Melbourne, everyone wore a mask without needing to be asked—inside and outside, whether walking, talking on the phone or riding a bike. At night, if you were desperate to find a place open for a drink or something to eat, you still could, but most people didn't go looking. There were no crowds at the Olympic venues, and the massive screens around the city that ordinarily would have broadcast the games remained blackened. If you wanted to see Japan's nightly domination of judo, you were better off staying at home.

Some of the smartest epidemiologists in Japan thought it was reckless for the government to allow the Olympics to go ahead. On the eve of the opening ceremony, Tokyo's vaccination rate was tracking slightly ahead of Victoria's, but not by much. Only 40 per cent of people had had their first shot compared to 30 per cent of people back home. Hitoshi Oshitani, a member of the Japanese Government's COVID advisory panel, told me he was less worried about athletes or other people bringing the virus into Japan than he was about the mixed message the decision to host the Olympics was sending to Japanese people, particularly young people. Oshitani desperately wanted young people, who were mostly not vaccinated, to remain socially distanced, but it was hard to convince them to do so when their home city was throwing the biggest sporting party in the world. 'They have not had any social opportunities for more than a year and now we are having this huge global sports event,' he said.

'They are going out, more restaurants are open at night, many are having parties at home. We cannot stop them.'

Throughout the two weeks of the Olympics, Japan's COVID response had one foot on the brake and the other on the accelerator. To the surprise of no-one, case numbers started to smoke. A few days after the closing ceremony, the Delta wave peaked in Tokyo with 6000 infections in a day. Yet, for all that, a truly remarkable thing happened: in a city of fourteen million people, only ninety-one died from COVID throughout the entire Delta wave.

Tokyo has never entered lockdown and its per-capita death rate from COVID is lower than Victoria's.[10] Japan's largest city presents a striking counterpoint to what Melbourne experienced. It demonstrates that with strong adherence to less-restrictive public health measures and a very good health system, it was possible to preserve life in the pre-vaccination pandemic and still function as an open society. There are complex social and cultural reasons for this which, to examine properly, would require a separate book. Oshitani would be an excellent person to write it. He explained to me that a unique aspect of Japan's approach in the first year of the pandemic was to admit nearly all COVID cases to hospital, even mild ones. Although this put enormous pressure on the hospital system, it ensured that people with COVID were not only quarantined, they were treated for the disease with antiviral drugs. He believed this prevented mild cases from becoming more-severe ones and kept Japan's death toll low.

Oshitani was concerned during Japan's Delta wave when, due to the weight of infections, the Suga government abandoned this policy and instructed that only people vulnerable to severe COVID disease should be hospitalised. But the outcomes in Tokyo were nowhere near as dire as Oshitani feared. This reflects Japan's success in vaccinating its older population and continuing to treat the virus. The high case numbers seen in Tokyo during the Delta wave, although alarming at the time, were mostly made up of younger Japanese passing mild and asymptomatic disease to their friends.

As I prepared to fly back to my home city, which was still malingering in its sixth lockdown, I realised that what Tokyo had shown me was the importance of agency in an effective and cohesive public health response. Japan was able to ride out the COVID storm because people took the necessary steps to protect their own health. And when they got sick, there was a world-class health and hospital system to look after them. The Victorian Government neglected public health for thirty years, and when the COVID crisis arrived, it decided the best way to stop people from getting sick and dying was to implement a series of draconian public health orders, enforced by an overt police presence and the threat of fines. Daniel Andrews kept telling us there was no other way, but there was. You just had to look beyond our closed borders to find it.

CHAPTER 8
OUT OF LIVING MEMORY

TIM WAS SITTING on the slope of the grassy hill that runs beside the steps of Melbourne's Shrine of Remembrance. The Shrine, designed by architects who'd returned from the Great War, speaks to the careful planning and sense of order that underpins Melbourne. When you sit where Tim sat, you look back down St Kilda Road, a broad, tree-lined avenue which becomes Swanston Street and dissects the neatly waffled streets and laneways of the Hoddle Grid. There is something reassuring about the idea that, nearly ninety years ago, smart, purposeful people climbed this hill on the edge of the city, looked around them, and knew they'd found just the spot for people to come and remember our war dead. There was nothing reassuring about it on the day Tim was there. Only 10 metres from where he was sitting, riot police stood in a line brandishing batons and shields. Behind them, reinforcements were waiting for the signal to move in. At the bottom of the Shrine forecourt, a police BearCat was parked. It is an armour-plated, blast-resistant tactical vehicle purchased by Victoria Police in case Melbourne ever came under siege—at the time, they were thinking about terrorists, not tradies.

The BearCat and police were there on that clear spring day in late September 2021 because Tim and hundreds of people like him had been pushed to breaking point by our pandemic response. Some of them worked in construction, an industry that had been abruptly shut down on the orders of the chief health officer. Others were furious at being told they had to get vaccinated against COVID-19 to work again. They'd all had a gutful of lockdown, but it went beyond the frustration and tedium we'd all experienced at different times. There was within these men—and they were nearly all men—a simmering, self-destructive rage. They felt emasculated. And they were being egged on by opportunistic, anti-social agitators who were drawn to the heat and spittle, the promise that something might go horribly wrong. We didn't know if that would happen that day, but the one certainty was that it wouldn't end well. There at the Shrine, you could see that as clearly as the elegant expanse of St Kilda Road.

A reckless and at-times violent mob had been baiting Victoria Police for the past five days. On the Saturday, they'd broken through police lines in Richmond and put six cops in hospital. On the Monday, they'd turned on the leadership of the Construction, Forestry, Maritime, Mining and Energy Union (CFMMEU), an industrial organisation which is normally at the head of militant protests, not in their sights. The next day they'd rampaged through the city, taunting police and blocking traffic all the way to the top of the West Gate Bridge, where a bunch of them sang a drunken rendition of Daryl Braithwaite's 'Horses', the time-to-go-home anthem for twenty-first birthday parties and bachelor and spinster balls. It was one of the wildest and seemingly most aimless protests ever staged in Melbourne, and it terrified the people stuck in their cars on the bridge. Victoria Police had vowed they would never let it happen again. Now, the mob had retreated to the Shrine for what would become their last stand.

There were about 500 of them. Some were drunk again and others were intoxicated by delusions of revolution. Tim was neither of these things as he sat on the grass, shaking his head at the overwhelming police presence. He explained that he'd served in Afghanistan and felt betrayed by how timid his home city had become. He was in his thirties and physically fit, and he didn't want to get vaccinated. He said he'd take his chances with the virus and it shouldn't be his responsibility to stop other people from getting sick from it.

It was a cold, hard-nosed view starkly at odds with the paternalism that had shaped our public health response, but as the crowd at the Shrine showed, Tim was not alone in thinking it. 'Enough is enough,' he said. 'We've sat idle for eighteen months and watched this state deteriorate, people losing their jobs and kids not going to school. I'm a parent, I'm a husband, I'm a veteran and I have completely lost faith in this government. I'm not sure what else needs to happen before people start standing up. I am not here for violence. I couldn't think of anything worse. There are a few people who ruin it for the rest of us but people just want to be heard. I've said to my wife, "I am almost ashamed to have served my country." What did we go there for? Freedom? Jesus Christ, I'm not feeling very free. We've been led down the garden path by the federal government, now the state government is keeping us locked in our houses. No thank you.'

Tim was clear-eyed enough to see what was coming next. As the police cordon started to tighten around the Shrine, he got up, shot a final glare in the direction of the police, and walked off. He said he had had enough of Victoria and was planning to sell his house and move his young family to Queensland.

Throughout the afternoon, other protestors drifted away. The September sun had a bite to it and being outraged makes for hot and thirsty work. Some got bored, some couldn't be bothered anymore. But after they'd left, there was still an angry rump that refused to go. That was when riot police moved in with military-style rifles loaded with non-lethal rounds. Moving in combat formation, they fired foam baton rounds—projectiles the size of squash balls that land with a punch—and discharged canisters of pepper spray, obscuring the Shrine in an orange haze. After the smoke had cleared, I found a man sitting quietly on a park bench. He had a pair of goggles around his neck and a supply of baby wipes and milk in his backpack—tools of the trade for the protestors who came expecting to be pepper-sprayed by police. He gave his name as Ben Harris and said that he worked as a landscape gardener, talking in a gentle voice which revealed more sadness than anger. He patted his chest and said it felt empty: 'There is just this oppression, this general frustration. I have lost count of the number of times I am driving home and just looking at every telephone pole wondering how could I make it happen.'

If 2020 was the year Melbourne grimly held things together, during the spring of 2021 it felt as though the city was coming apart. There was little public sympathy for what had happened at the Shrine, or on the city streets in the days prior. As Victoria Police Chief Commissioner Shane Patton reflects: 'The hard-core groups you saw assaulting police, throwing missiles, throwing projectiles, that moved out onto the West Gate Bridge, that barricaded the CFMMEU offices, that we were having running battles [with] right throughout the city and up to the Shrine ... that wasn't Mum and Dad. They were hardcore protestors. They were people who came with an intent just to cause trouble.' Yet, as ugly and confronting as the protests were, they were an extreme manifestation of something more widely and deeply felt.

Zeb Jamrozik, the infectious-disease ethicist who spent 2021 working for Victoria's health department inside hotel quarantine, says we shouldn't be surprised people reached this point. He does not mean as a commentary on the restrictions they were railing against but as a reflection on human nature. 'Every study of social-distancing measures had always said, "The longer you do this, the less people are going to comply,"' he explains. 'Health department officials would wring hands about people in western suburbs flouting social-distancing rules. I would be in these meetings saying, "Of course they are. They are used to the idea that families help each other and see each other and for them, that is more valuable than any kind of risk." Every sensible thing that was written about pandemic planning always said, "Look, these are extreme measures, they have a lot of cost, both financial and human, and you just can't do them forever." That is one area where we lost the plot.' At the Shrine, the effect of this social discord, which stayed hidden most of the time, broke into full view.

Throughout the pandemic, I got to know Cate, an intensive-care nurse who works in a public hospital in Melbourne's west. Most mornings, we would run into each other at our local dog park. Sometimes it was just a hello, and on other days we'd fall into step and talk about what was going on at the hospital. Cate's observations and insights became an important touchstone. There was a disconnect between her descriptions of work and the doomsday images evoked by political leaders about intensive-care wards being overrun. Although her hospital had war-gamed Italy-style scenarios at the start of the pandemic, the demand for ICU beds there never came close to exceeding capacity, despite the hospital being located in a hotspot for outbreaks. This was not by accident. One of Cate's daily duties is to feed information about cases on her ward into a national reporting system linked to every public and private ICU in Australia. The system, known as CHRIS, is an electronic dashboard which allows anyone working in intensive care to see how many patients there are in units around the country, how many of those have COVID and how many are on ventilators. In Victoria, if one hospital became stretched with case numbers, its ICU director could arrange for stable patients to be transported to another hospital with spare capacity. This standing agreement, known as 'load rebalancing', resulted in patients being shifted from Shepparton as far as Melbourne, and from Melbourne to Geelong.

The Royal Melbourne Hospital's Chris MacIsaac says the movements of critical patients were cited in media reports as evidence of a hospital system at breaking point, when in truth, they were evidence of a system working to plan. 'We all agreed that no individual hospital in intensive care should become overwhelmed,' he says. 'None of the ICU directors wanted to move to alternative measures like more stringent triaging or what we had heard from overseas about four people being on the one ventilator. Every morning we would meet and talk about the strain each hospital was under, who could admit that day, who felt that things were getting unsafe and wanted to offload. It was great to be able to phone a friend.'

Cate has been caring for critically ill people for more than thirty years. She says that nursing COVID patients, particularly once they are sedated and ventilated, is much the same as looking after other patients in ICU. You rarely get to know them because they are often unconscious when they arrive on the ward, and those who wake up usually do so in another part of the hospital. While they are in your care, you are constantly on the lookout for things that can go wrong when patients are put on a breathing machine: renal failure, cardiac complications, the onset of sepsis. By the time a COVID patient has been ventilated, their reduced lung capacity often has a knock-on effect on other vital organs. The sickest people are on the brink of total system collapse. Where COVID differed from other illnesses in the spring of 2021 was the way in which the families of patients reacted to the critical condition of their loved one. Whereas normally a family puts its trust in the skills and expertise of the doctors and nurses working in intensive medicine, the families of COVID patients questioned standard procedures—like performing a tracheostomy to increase the flow of oxygen—and demanded unproven interventions they had read about via Facebook links, like infusions of high-dose vitamin C. Nearly everyone who became critically ill with COVID that spring was unvaccinated by choice. The saddest thing for Cate was listening to family members pleading for the patient to be given AstraZeneca, the vaccine they had steadfastly refused to take when it would have saved their life. The frequency of violent episodes involving hospital visitors meant that, for six months, security guards were posted at the door of Cate's ward. She recalls one incident when a man became so enraged he picked up a computer, which was bolted to a trolley, and hurled the lot across the ward at a doctor. She says she feels tired and jaded after two years of not having a holiday, training inexperienced replacement staff and dealing with family members of COVID patients. 'If you don't want the treatment, you don't have to come,' she says.

Cate could also see from her vantage point at the sharp end of our pandemic response, that Melbourne in the spring of 2021 was kept in lockdown well beyond the point where our health system was at any risk of being overrun—if indeed it ever was. 'I thought, "You are just taking the piss now,"' she says. The answer was not to let the virus rip. Victoria, like every other state and territory in Australia, had agreed to maintain public health restrictions until 70–80 per cent of the adult population had been vaccinated against the virus. This national plan, based on modelling done by the Doherty Institute, assumed that, until then, lockdowns would be a part of our COVID response.[1] What Victoria needed in the meantime was a less-rigid, more-compassionate set of rules. In August 2021, even though our daily case numbers were lower than New South Wales's, we were the only jurisdiction in Australia subject to a curfew and an arbitrary 5-kilometre rule limiting the distance we could travel from our homes to shop or exercise. The following month, when our case numbers climbed past those in New South Wales, we kept our northern border shut and under police guard, as if the Delta strain was still something we were trying to keep out of Victoria, and not a local pathogen spreading rapidly through our suburbs. Everyone could see there was a public health imperative to keep daily case numbers down until more people were vaccinated, but there was also an inherent illogicality about how we went about it. The central problem was that, although the Victorian Government had declared COVID-zero dead, our pandemic response was still haunted by its ghost.

On the last day of winter in 2021, Victoria's appetite for doughnuts came to an end. For more than a month, Brett Sutton had assured Premier Daniel Andrews that what worked before could work again: that through a combination of lockdown and an expansive program of testing, tracing, isolating and quarantining all COVID cases and the people they came into contact with, the virus could be eliminated from the community. There had already been a false dawn. On 4 August, Victoria recorded no new cases, and an elated Professor Sutton tweeted an image of Australian swim coach Dean Boxall madly gyrating on the Tokyo pool deck. Andrews, although more restrained, posted a single triumphant word on Twitter: 'Zero.' This premature elimination spawned 1000 doughnut memes, with people swapping images of glazed baked goods to mark the occasion. One day later, more cases were detected and Victoria was back in lockdown. Despite this setback, Professor Sutton remained convinced that, with a hard lockdown and a bit of luck, it was possible for Victoria to return to COVID-zero. This assumption underpinned his public health advice—right up until the moment it didn't.

On 31 August, Sutton, Jeroen Weimar and other leaders within Victoria's COVID response briefed a meeting of the government's most senior ministers. They advised them that the epidemiology of the outbreak had changed—that no matter what they did, there would be no more doughnut days. Sutton explained that the Delta variant, due to its faster rate of transmission, could not be contained in the way other outbreaks had. The only choice he saw was for us to stay in lockdown until enough people were vaccinated. That wouldn't happen any time soon. As of 31 August, less than 30 per cent of Victorians were double-dosed against the virus.

The senior ministers at that meeting weren't seated around the Cabinet table. Working-from-home orders meant they were in their studies or lounge rooms or kitchens, dialled into a Teams call. As they listened to Professor Sutton and Weimar explain the situation, they weren't surprised. You only had to look at our case numbers and what was going on in Sydney to understand that our public health response was not keeping pace with the virus. Yet, to finally have it said out loud was deflating. Deputy Premier James Merlino says that, as long as he lives, he'll remember that meeting and the awful realisation of what lay ahead: 'I wasn't surprised but just deeply disappointed. It was the moment we feared would arrive.' Weimar describes it as the lowest point of the entire pandemic response. The next day, Daniel Andrews publicly revealed the change in advice. 'We will not see these case numbers go down,' he said. 'They are going to go up. The question is by how many and how fast.'

This was difficult news to absorb for anyone who had bought into the COVID-zero thinking of the state government. For more than a year, the premier had presented the pandemic as a binary: either you have no cases in the community or you are on your way to a disastrous, uncontrolled outbreak that will overrun your health system. Now that COVID-zero had been consigned to the epidemiological dustbin, where did that leave us? Yet, it also presented an opportunity for the government to change the COVID conversation. Once you abandon the notion of COVID-zero, your public health settings don't need to catch every case, merely enough to keep an outbreak within manageable limits. It is no longer necessary to stop tens of thousands of people from crossing the border to prevent the odd case coming back into Victoria. Once you dump COVID-zero, it opens up the possibility of getting kids back into school and allowing families to reunite. It could have been the start of a serious rethink about the isolation we were inflicting on people like Merle Mitchell in aged care, the damage we were doing to smart young people like Gabrielle, the devastating impact on business owners and the needless restrictions we had in place to stop activities we knew to be overwhelmingly safe. This was Melbourne's opportunity to fundamentally shift our response to the virus. Instead, we got more of the same. Lockdown was extended for another three weeks, classes were shut for the rest of the term, and the curfew and 5-kilometre rules remained in place. The only concession granted was that kids under the age of twelve could go to playgrounds again.

The Age had been largely supportive of the Victorian Government response to the pandemic. The morning after Andrews's announcement, it published an editorial headlined: 'Victoria Can't Go on Like This'. It argued in part:

> Under the national plan, we remain in limbo until full-vaccination rates are at 70, then 80 per cent. That's tough, but it's true, and the libertarians who think 'living with COVID' means that most restrictions should be lifted now are fooling no one. Reaching the vaccination threshold will take until October or November if we're lucky, and even then some restrictions and public health measures will remain. But there comes a point, and *The Age* believes that point has been reached, where the damage caused by the harshest and longest lockdowns in the country needs to be more seriously factored in. Wednesday's announced 'easing' was a harsh and cruel blow.[2]

Merlino says the government saw only one way out: 'We just had to hold our nerve through that period of lockdown, as tough as it was, with a message to the community to get vaccinated. Get vaccinated and we can leave the days of lockdown and severe restrictions behind.'

In early July 2021, when the border between Victoria and New South Wales was still open, Jose drove from his farm in Rochford, a small community outside the Victorian town of Lancefield, to Oberon, a remote town in the central tablelands of New South Wales, to visit his parents. They had moved to Oberon from Sydney about twenty years earlier. His father had dementia and was living in care, while his mother had turned eighty and was having trouble moving around on dodgy hips and knees, but try as he might, Jose couldn't convince them to come and live with him on his farm. His mother was booked in for surgery to try to free up her joints, which is why Jose had driven eight hours up the Hume Highway to look after her. With the virus spreading in Sydney and knocking on the door again in Melbourne, he knew the border could slam shut any day, but he reasoned that, if looking after your elderly mum after surgery isn't grounds for a travel exemption, what is? He had been in Oberon for about two weeks and was planning to come home when he got a call from his dad's doctor. 'It was probably close to midnight,' he says. 'The doctor had just visited my father and he said, "Look, he is at the end stage, he is not going to last much longer." I had a permit to travel the following day but I just said to Mum, "I'll stay." There wasn't even a thought about it. What choice did I have?'

Jose's father died on 17 July and Jose stayed in Oberon for another two weeks to keep his mum company and help sort out his dad's affairs. He then needed to get home to his wife Sonya, who was looking after their farm on her own. That is when he stumbled into a bureaucratic morass. Here is a small sample of it. 'I put in an application and allowed just over two weeks,' says Jose, 'because I know nothing works fast in the public service. The two weeks came and went and I got no confirmation they had received my application. About five days after that day came and went I got a message to say, "We apologise, we have missed your cut-off date, we have cancelled your application and if you want to come back you need to reapply."' Jose did so again, straight away, but it was cancelled again. This went on for three months. Every time someone from DHHS called, it would be a person new to his case. They sounded like they were working in an offshore call centre and no-one seemed to know where Rochford was, how far it was from Oberon, and why Jose had travelled to New South Wales, a state the Victorian Government had declared an 'extreme risk zone'. There were no COVID cases in Oberon and none in Rochford, and even if there were, the practical risk that Jose represented, driving his own car down a highway to his own farm, was negligible.

Jose went to the local police station in Oberon to sign statutory declarations saying he was desperate to come home, and he had so many PCR tests that he was known by name to everyone who worked at the testing centre. The online forms he repeatedly filled out didn't have enough space for him to explain his situation, and no-one seemed to be reading what he wrote anyway: 'I actually got one guy from the call centre telling me, "You were given plenty of warning. Why didn't you come home?" I said, "What is it you don't understand here?" There just wasn't that level of empathy. I am not saying I am special. A lot of people were in that position. It is just frustration and, to be honest, anger at the government. It just didn't seem like there was a plan. I kept on saying to people, "It is one thing to stop people coming into the country"—and even stopping Australians from coming home is just unbelievable—"but we are supposed to be one country."'

The border wars, as they became known, were not confined to the bridges across the Murray River and the more than fifty land crossings which connect New South Wales to Victoria. Queensland guarded its southern border to New South Wales, South Australia shut its eastern border to Victoria, and Tasmania stopped flights coming in from New South Wales and Victoria. Western Australia, a state which had voted nearly ninety years earlier to secede from the federation, did the next best thing and sealed itself off for nearly two years from the rest of Australia. The pay-off for Western Australia, South Australia, Tasmania and, to a lesser extent, Queensland was the preservation of COVID-zero. For most of the pandemic, they were able to operate relatively normally, with people going to work and kids going to school and businesses able to stay open. They protected this prize jealously, as shown by the jailing of two Melbourne men for travelling to Perth to watch a football match. In Victoria in 2021, it led to what Deborah Glass describes as the most heartless decision-making she has seen in her eight years as the state's Ombudsman.

Victoria had not closed its border to New South Wales since Federation. Even at the height of the Spanish flu pandemic which hit Australia with deadlier consequences than COVID-19, Victoria did not impose travel restrictions on people wanting to enter the state. When Deborah Glass reflects on Victoria's decision on 23 July 2021 to close its border to protect itself against the Delta epidemic, she isn't critical of the choice but remains appalled at how it was implemented, with an at-times callous disregard for the consequences for people like Jose. Her subsequent investigation and report were prompted by a slew of complaints from people who found themselves trapped in an administrative no-man's-land. The most damning statistic in her findings is that, of 33 000 applications made for exemptions to cross the border, only 8 per cent were granted. Like assessors working for a shonky insurance company, the default position of the Victorian Government was to deny all claims.

'It was a kind of reverse onus,' Glass says. 'Rather than assuming people who were in dire situations—dealing with seriously ill relatives, needing to deal with their livestock—had genuine, compassionate reasons to cross the border and go home, here was this team of people looking for ways to stop them.' When the Ombudsman's office began investigating, it expected to find an under-resourced system overwhelmed by circumstances. Instead, it found huge resources deployed to keep people out. 'What you get a sense of is that fear factor: "What if we let this person in and they spread the virus?"', says Glass. 'You can sort of justify that fear when you are dealing with a COVID-zero policy but by August, that should have been blown out of the water. There was still this fear that someone who crossed the border might seed an outbreak, even though outbreaks were being seeded all over the place. What comes across, certainly with the borders, was this excessive caution, that we will be blamed if there is another wave as a result of our failures. I can only assume that it came from the experience of 2020.'

To understand what it was like to push back against this bureaucratic force, I drive to a farm about 100 kilometres outside Melbourne, near the town of Birregurra. There, I meet Amanda Garner and Nerida Sadler, two formidable country women who, when confronted with the news that their children would not be able to travel home from agricultural college in the tiny NSW town of Leeton and quarantine at their farms, decided to raise hell. When I sit down with this pair on the back patio of Garner's farmhouse, it quickly becomes clear that, when it comes to wrangling governments, Garner and Sadler are not ordinary mums. Garner works in Indigenous relations and has advised National Party senators, while Sadler is a nurse and hospital administrator who helped Geelong Hospital coordinate its COVID response. Their kids, Harriett Garner and Angus Sadler, were two of ten students enrolled at the Yanco Agricultural High School when New South Wales closed its schools and Victoria shut its border. This led to a protracted dispute with the Victorian Government, which would allow the kids to come home only if they agreed to spend two weeks in hotel quarantine.

The episode highlighted the irrationality at the heart of some of our border policies. The students were boarding in a remote NSW town which had no COVID cases. Their families wanted to drive them home and quarantine at rural properties. The Victorian Government wanted the kids to travel to Sydney, the epicentre of the Delta epidemic, and then fly into Melbourne, now engulfed in its own wave of Delta infections, and spend two weeks in a quarantine hotel. Amanda Garner wrote to the Victorian health department to point out that this would increase, rather than decrease, the risk of the Yanco students bringing COVID into the Victorian community: 'We have the greatest respect for the urgency to curtail this disease's spread, but we desperately implore you to review the uniqueness of the children's school, the location of their homes and the commitment offered by their families.' Despite an intervention by the Ombudsman, and a month-long lobbying campaign by the families, their political contacts and journalists taking up their cause, the department was unmoved.

The families thought about smuggling the kids across the border in the back of a cattle truck, or making the crossing in the dead of night near Cann River, a remote Gippsland town where the local border patrol was known to leave their post at night because Victoria Police hadn't paid the council to keep the lights on at their roadblock. Eventually, Harriett Garner agreed to book into hotel quarantine with her dad. Angus Sadler, who'd injured himself on a motorbike, received a medical exemption to go home for medical treatment. His saga came to an end in a scene resembling a John le Carré novel. On a cold August morning at Cann River, a car approached from the north along the deserted road on the NSW side of the border. Nerida Sadler watched from her car, which was parked on the Victorian side, as the police pulled the car over and instructed Angus to hobble the remaining distance on his crutches. A woman who'd generously looked after Angus for the past four weeks walked alongside him carrying his bag, but she was not allowed to make any contact with Nerida once she reached Victorian territory. 'I was sitting there on the other side, and the policemen sat in their car opposite and watched the exchange,' Sadler says. 'I was seeing this lady that I had met once, who'd had my son for over a month. I couldn't even hug her. She opened the back, I opened the back, we helped Angus into a car, he gave me his bag and I gave her a flower and some wine and a slab and she drove off.'

Victoria was not the only state where a fear of border incursions brought out the worst in our pandemic response. Queensland Premier Annastacia Palaszczuk, after her government refused entry to a woman from New South Wales requiring medical treatment, declared: 'People living in New South Wales, they have New South Wales hospitals. In Queensland, we have Queensland hospitals for our people.' Jeroen Weimar says the Ombudsman's criticisms of Victoria's approach are 'disingenuous' given what the state was confronting. 'We were dealing with a rapidly moving pandemic in an environment when there was no national agreement or consensus about how to deal with transmission across borders,' he says. 'We shut the border because we were desperately worried about stopping the COVID bushfire that was already roaring in New South Wales.'

Deborah Glass doesn't argue that Victoria should have kept its borders open. Her concern is the disregard we showed, both at the border and in high-rise towers, for people who, due to the vagaries of a fast-moving virus and fast-changing public health orders, found themselves on the wrong side of a rigidly enforced line. The failures she identifies are not the decisions taken but the lack of consideration offered to people dreadfully impacted by those decisions and circumstances beyond their control. 'Leave aside my feelings as an Ombudsman on this,' she says. 'When I have looked at so many of the directions here, I have thought about the absence of nuance. There was this fixation on the pandemic and the epidemiological response rather than a holistic, "What are we doing to our people here? Where is the balancing of risks?" I found that personally really troubling. If you are not a resident of public housing towers, would you prefer the towers to be locked down to keep the risk away from you? Of course you would. You want the government to take that kind of strong stand because to take a nuanced stand that considers everybody's human rights is more difficult and is maybe less popular. On the whole those strong measures were supported by the vast majority of the population, which is in itself disturbing.'

Nerida Sadler puts it more bluntly: 'I think COVID has divided people. It has divided friends and families and states.'

* * *

Melbourne's pandemic experience today is barely recognisable from what it was. The city is open and kids are back in school. The morning roads are jammed with commuters, offices are beckoning people back to abandoned workstations, and the MCG, after so many silent months save for the echo of an umpire's whistle through empty stands, has regained its voice. The city is reconnected with the rest of the state and Victoria with the rest of Australia, even its distant west. I recently boarded a plane and flew to Perth without permit or permission to watch Labor leader Anthony Albanese launch his successful campaign to become our next prime minister. Had I tried that at the start of the year, I would have been scratching my initials on the same jail cell wall as the football supporters who conned their way into the previous year's AFL grand final.

The election of a new federal government has knocked the pandemic off the front pages. On the day the votes are counted, nearly 50 000 new cases of COVID are recorded in Australia and forty-five people die with the virus, but the numbers barely rate a mention. As we enter our third COVID winter, nearly 2000 people have died with the virus in Victoria this year—more than the total deaths from 2020 and 2021 combined. People are dying from COVID most days in every mainland state. A death from COVID today is no less tragic than it was two years ago but everything has changed. There is no public clamour to go back into lockdown and no-one within government is pushing for this to happen. Having sent us into lockdown six times, Daniel Andrews now baulks at the idea of reintroducing mask mandates. The massive bureaucracy built to administer and enforce our public health response has been disassembled and the people who led it are adamant that lockdowns are a thing of the past. Vaccinations and improved treatments mean that COVID deaths are more preventable now than at any time since the virus first emerged in Wuhan, but we accept that people are dying from it, and probably will continue to die from it as long as any of us live.

The impact of the pandemic is still felt in our neighbourhoods, local businesses, workplaces and families, but there is a disconnect between this and what we are willing to do to reduce the spread of the virus. We know that properly fitted particle-filtration masks help prevent infection but most of us have stopped wearing them, even when we are in crowded indoor spaces. We know that vaccine boosters are an effective way of stopping people from getting seriously ill, but in Victoria, three out of ten eligible people haven't bothered to get one. If we look back to Tokyo, which is heading into its summer, COVID infections and deaths are running at an order of magnitude lower than ours and cultural adherence to basic public health measures remains strong. Could it be that having stripped people of all agency over the past two years, the Victorian Government left us unable to take responsibility for our own health?

On a cool, late-autumn day, I talk to Victoria's chief health officer via a video call as he sits on the back deck of his Dandenong Ranges home, the steam from a fresh cup of tea rising into the cold air. I ask Brett Sutton how we should make sense of the tolerance we now appear to have for death and disease from this virus, which, though less virulent than it was, is killing and putting more people in hospital in Victoria than it ever has. 'It remains an awful toll and a tragedy,' he says of the rising COVID death toll. 'That hasn't changed. But there is a community change in perspective which is, in part, about being as protected as we can be. We are getting more deaths on a daily average now but in 2022 it is one death per 1100 infections. It is only the sheer weight of numbers that has made that death toll so high. We had very few tools that we could manage through 2020 and lockdown was the thing that would protect all of those who were in aged care and otherwise very vulnerable individuals. It was the right thing to do when you consider how significant that toll was, but we are rightly moving to the sustainable, acceptable, tolerable things we can do now.'

Professor Sutton rejects the notion that the Victorian Government's attitude to COVID deaths has changed. He says our resort to lockdown in the first two years of the pandemic didn't reflect an 'ideological puritanism that we couldn't tolerate a single death', but rather the judgement that it was our best way of protecting lives and allowing society to operate normally while we waited for a vaccine. Having signed the public health orders that took Melbourne in and out of lockdown six times, he recoils at what the Chinese Government recently did in Shanghai, where a largely vaccinated city of twenty-six million people was locked down for two months. 'We are not locking down now and we wouldn't lock down in a highly vaccinated population,' he says. 'The reality is a lockdown wouldn't work with the Omicron variant, in my view, anyway.'

Allen Cheng says that, although the virus is still with us and, in raw numbers, as deadly as it has ever been, the overwhelming public sentiment is that the pandemic is over. 'Everyone knows someone who has gotten sick and they seem to be doing OK,' he says. 'The other thing is, what is the alternative? I don't think there is any appetite to go back to what we would need to get numbers down and keep them there. You can't put the genie back in the bottle now. We can't get back to zero ever again. You would have to have a year-long lockdown to do that. When we didn't have a vaccine we were buying time to get one. Now that we have got it, the population is substantially protected and in the public's mind, things have just moved on and we have got to deal with it.'

I put the same question to Martin Foley. Having previously served as the Victorian minister responsible for housing, disability, ageing and mental health, he has as good a grasp as anyone of how the pandemic has dug into the social fault lines which determine who gets sick, who carries the burden of chronic conditions like diabetes and obesity, and who gets to live a prosperous, healthy life. The numbers show that, despite what we were told, we were never really in this together. If you were born in Australia, you are eight times less likely to die from COVID than if you moved here from the Middle East and five times less likely to die than someone who moved here from North Africa. If you are among the wealthiest, most educated people in our society, you are between three and four times less likely to die from the virus than if you are among the most socioeconomically disadvantaged.[3] Foley doesn't agree that our tolerance for COVID deaths is greater than it was. He says that knowing what we now do about the importance of prompt treatment for COVID, the challenge for our health system is to break down the social barriers that prevent people from accessing the timely treatment they need. He agrees with Professor Sutton that, whatever path the virus takes from here, lockdowns are no longer the way to stop it. 'The restrictions and public health measures of 2020 and most of 2021 are no longer fit for purpose,' he says. 'It is not proportionate or necessary to have those restrictions anymore.'

James Merlino is emphatic: 'Every death is genuinely a tragedy for their family and friends. We don't have a level of acceptance of a mortality rate.' But the plain truth is that we do. In 2020, according to the Australian Bureau of Statistics, there were 905 registered deaths from COVID. In the same year, 16 587 people died from ischaemic heart disease, more than 5000 people died from causes related to diabetes, more than 3000 people died from breast cancer, and 3139 people took their own lives. None of these figures relate to the pandemic. They are a usual, annual snapshot of end-of-life statistics in contemporary Australia. In 2020, the year in which Melbourne spent more than 100 days in lockdown to contain the second-wave epidemic, COVID was the thirty-eighth leading cause of death. Three times as many people died from an accidental fall than died from COVID that year.[4] In January 2022, COVID was Australia's second-leading cause of death,[5] but we didn't order people to stay in their homes—we removed the requirement for them to wear a mask in schools, shopping centres and cinemas. On 18 November 2021, shortly before Victoria reached a vaccination rate of 90 per cent,

Daniel Andrews declared that normal life would return: 'We have saved lives, we have kept people safe. We have opened the place up, we are going to keep it open. Victorians have kept their end of the bargain and the government will do the same.'

The COVID mortality statistics from the lockdown years don't capture the lives saved. Cheng calls this the prevention paradox: 'If public health does a really good job, things don't happen and the question is did we need to do that?' Figures provided by the Victorian health department go some way to filling in this gap. In an attempt to quantify the most important outcome of our pandemic response, department officials calculated Victoria's excess mortality between January 2020 and December 2021 and what that figure might have been had we adopted the policy settings of other countries. According to this modelling, 2706 people died in Victoria in the first two years of the pandemic beyond what would have been expected in pre-COVID times. Had we mirrored the COVID response of Sweden, the country most readily identified with a laissez-faire approach to the pandemic, that figure would have been 7185. Had we copied France's approach, the toll would have been 8394. The British approach pushes our excess mortality to 13 964 people. And if we'd followed the lead of the United States, an additional 21 102 people would have died in Victoria.[6]

This modelling, although helpful in placing Victoria's response in a global context, is not necessary for understanding what Melbourne's pandemic experience might have been had we taken a less-cautious approach. As Professor Cheng puts it: 'If we hadn't taken the chance to get it down to zero, it would be a very different place and we would be missing a whole lot of people. What we could have had was 20 000 dead from COVID. There is probably no other situation where it is so obvious what could have happened. And it wasn't pretty.'

What did happen to Melbourne wasn't pretty either. There was a scarring from the isolation, atrophy and absence of agency that lockdown brings which now runs deep through this city. If you were able to share lockdown with family, if you had a job that allowed you to keep getting paid while not going to work, if you were able to push down your own frustrations and buy into the larger bargain on offer, then it was bearable. But like the sickness and death caused by the virus, the impacts of lockdown were unevenly spread. How you fared depended greatly on where you lived, whether you had a university education and how financially secure you were before the pandemic arrived. We can be thankful for the lives saved, but no-one could think the past two years were good for our sense of community, self-worth or happiness. For the city and its people, this was a traumatic experience. It will take many years for social researchers to fully understand the full implications of this but, as a moment-in-time snapshot of how we felt coming out of the pandemic, the day we walked into polling booths to cast our votes in the recent federal election is a revealing place to start.

On 21 May 2022, Australian voters brought to an abrupt end the Coalition government of Scott Morrison, the prime minister who led Australia through its COVID crisis. Morrison's popularity soared in the early months of the pandemic, along with popular support for all state premiers. This was unsurprising: when facing a genuine crisis, most people want their leaders to succeed, we want to feel safe. In March 2021, we saw an emphatic demonstration of this in the Western Australian state election, when Mark McGowan, the premier who shielded his state behind closed borders for the entire pandemic, led the Labor Party to the most lopsided victory in any state or federal election in Australia since Federation. There is also a point in a crisis when incumbency flips from being a political advantage to a curse. We saw evidence of this in March 2022, when South Australian voters turned on the first-term Liberal government of Steven Marshall. Marshall led a competent and effective response to the pandemic but his electoral timing was rotten. South Australia's fixed election date coincided with a surge of Omicron infections and the state's first significant loss of life to the virus since the pandemic began. Marshall, who had diligently followed the plan for reopening endorsed by National Cabinet, was skewered by voters. We saw it again on a Saturday night inside the ballroom of Sydney's Fullerton Hotel, when Morrison climbed onto the stage just before 11 p.m. to concede a crushing defeat to Anthony Albanese.

The election rout of Morrison's Liberal Party redrew Australia's national political boundaries. Seats held by the Liberals and their conservative forerunners since Federation were lost to independents. Josh Frydenberg, the treasurer who during the pandemic spent nearly $300 billion sandbagging the Australian economy and people's jobs, lost his own. The Labor Party secured only a third of the vote but it was enough to take power for the second time this century. 'This has been a time of great upheaval over these past few years,' Morrison told a disbelieving crowd of supporters. 'It has imposed a heavy price on our country and on all Australians. I think all Australians have felt that deeply. We've seen in our own politics a great deal of disruption, as the way people have voted today. That says a lot, I think, about the upheaval that has taken place in our nation.'

Morrison cannot blame his election defeat on the pandemic, yet the pandemic cannot be separated from the election result. Andrew Laidlaw, a political consultant who conducted polling and focus groups in Victoria for political and commercial clients in the lead-up to the election, says the turning point came in the spring of 2021, at about the time that police were tightening their cordon around the Shrine. Put most plainly, this was the moment when we'd had enough. 'It is like sedimentary rock. Layer upon layer of pressure on people finally forced them to crack,' Laidlaw says. 'It had been eighteen months and people just completely lost hope.' Laidlaw says that in the focus groups he conducted, people savaged the prime minister for his lack of leadership and the Victorian premier for failing to acknowledge or ameliorate the consequences of his own sledgehammer approach. When polling day came, people voted for a change of government and something more fundamental: to end an awful chapter in our lives. Yaron Finkelstein, a political adviser who served as Morrison's private principal secretary and travelled with the former prime minister throughout the six-week campaign, explains by way of metaphor the emotive, overwhelming desire of voters to move on. 'It was like a house in which a murder had occurred,' he says. 'You don't blame the house, but you want to get out of the house and put some serious distance between you and where the crime took place.' The rejection of Morrison was visceral and, for now, many people feel much the same about Daniel Andrews.

Australia's pandemic scoreboard, when compared to that of nearly all other nations, is extraordinary. Heading into the 2022 winter, we have a low death toll, a high vaccination rate and a recovering economy with historically low unemployment. Inside these headline metrics are the stories of what two years of lockdown meant for us: the dislocation from family and friends; the disruption to normal work and schooling; the isolation from other states and the rest of the world; and the overbearing presence of restrictions, rules and edicts governing everyday life, when government officials and politicians became the arbiters of when we could leave our homes, how far we could drive, who we could share a cup of coffee with, and whether we were allowed to have any fun. When the time to vote came, it didn't matter whether people blamed Scott Morrison for the troubled vaccination rollout, the chaotic summer when the state borders reopened or any other decisions his government took—we just wanted him gone, along with the past two years. There was also a resolve to change things for the better.

Social researcher Rebecca Huntley says this reflects a classic human response to a crisis. 'People's weaknesses have been exacerbated; friendships have been lost and marriages fallen apart,' she says.

'People have also re-evaluated. All crises have positive effects. Yes, they were cranky at him but they were cranky for a reason.'

In our determination to move beyond the pandemic, we shouldn't ignore its lessons. After deadly bushfires ravaged Victoria in 1939, Supreme Court justice Leonard Stretton was asked to conduct a royal commission. As a judge, Stretton would have made a wonderful novelist. In his findings about the fires, he writes with clarity and a lyrical turn of phrase. In his opening paragraph, he makes the point that the problem of a once-in-a-century disaster like the devastating fires of Black Friday—or the COVID pandemic—is that critical lessons fall out of living memory:

> The rich plains, denied their beneficent rains, lay bare and baking; and the forests, from the foothills to the alpine heights, were tinder. The soft carpet of the forest floor was gone; the bone-dry litter crackled underfoot; dry heat and hot winds worked upon a land already dry, to suck from it the last, least drop of moisture. Men who had lived their lives in the bush went their way in the shadow of dread expectancy. But though they felt the imminence of danger they could not tell that it was to be far greater than they could imagine. They had not lived long enough. The experience of the past could not guide them to an understanding of what might, and did, happen.[7]

The experience of 1939 had fallen out of living memory when the 2009 fires burned much of the same country seventy years later, and it was long forgotten by December 2019, when the Black Summer fires burned up and down the east coast. More than likely, we won't have to wait that long for the next pandemic. When it arrives, we can accept our response to COVID-19 as the template for how a modern, well-resourced society should respond: shut the borders, shut all businesses, shut all schools, shut our front doors, and wait until the government says it is safe to come out again. There is no question that if we are willing to do these things, it is a recipe for low case numbers and relatively few deaths. The lesson from this pandemic is that, if a modern, well-resourced society invests properly in public health and trusts its people to protect their own, a government shouldn't have to play on people's fears and impose draconian restrictions on everyday life to limit death and disease from a respiratory virus. Melbourne's status as the world's most locked-down city should be cause for neither pride nor shame. Nor should it be forgotten. We never want to be that city again.

ACKNOWLEDGEMENTS

MELBOURNE'S PANDEMIC EXPERIENCE is for many people a blur. One of the difficult tasks in researching this book was bringing people back to moments in which critical events took place and decisions were made. I am grateful to all my interview subjects for their generosity and forbearance. I am also indebted to the epidemiologists, infectious disease and public health experts who from the start of the pandemic made themselves regularly available to an inexpert journalist. A personal thanks to Susan Sawyer for her passion and dedication to adolescent health, and to my fellow dog walker Cate, whose identity I changed to protect her employment. It was my privilege to write about the pandemic alongside a crack team of journalists from *The Age* newspaper. Although the conclusions in this book are my own, many of the facts they are based on emerged from their dedicated reporting. I am grateful to the editor of *The Age*, Gay Alcorn, for giving me time to write this book, to Louise Adler for convincing Monash University Publishing to take on the project, and to Paul Smitz for his considered advice and deft editing. Thanks are not enough for my darling Nicole, whose love and companionship made lockdowns bearable—well, almost. To our three children, Max, Amelie and Jasper, I enjoyed spending more time with you but would give anything for you to have that time back.

NOTES

Chapter 1 This Is Australia
1. Inner Melbourne Community Legal, *Submission to the Victorian Ombudsman Investigation into the Treatment of People and Conditions of Detention at 33 Alfred Street, North Melbourne*, 2020.
2. Deborah Glass, *Investigation into the Detention and Treatment of Public Housing Residents Arising from a COVID-19 'Hard-Lockdown' in July 2020*, Victorian Ombudsman, 17 December 2020, p. 105.
3. Inner Melbourne Community Legal, *Submission to the Victorian Ombudsman Investigation*, pp. 3, 6.
4. Maddy Savage, 'Did Sweden's Coronavirus Strategy Succeed or Fail?', *BBC News*, 24 July 2020, https://www.bbc.com/news/world-europe-53498133 (viewed May 2022).
5. *The Argus*, 'The Commission Meets: War on Slums', 2 March 1938, p. 2.
6. JB Paul, 'Dunstan, Sir Albert Arthur (1882–1950)', *Australian Dictionary of Biography*, 1981, https://adb.anu.edu.au/biography/dunstan-sir-albert-arthur-6055 (viewed May 2022).
7. Glass, *Investigation into the Detention and Treatment of Public Housing Residents*, p. 57.
8. TS Ignatius et al., 'Evidence of Airborne Transmission of the Severe Acute Respiratory Syndrome Virus', *New England Journal of Medicine*, vol. 350, 22 April 2004, pp. 1731–9.
9. Glass, *Investigation into the Detention and Treatment of Public Housing Residents*, p. 55.
10. *Official Gazette of the Republic of the Philippines*, 'Rodrigo Roa Duterte, Third State of the Nation Address, July 23, 2018', 23 July 2018.

Chapter 2 The Man from Wuhan
1. Dana McCauley, Eryk Bagshaw and Rob Harris, 'Australia Prepares for 50 000 to 150 000 Coronavirus Deaths', *The Sydney Morning Herald*, 16 March 2020.
2. Stephen Donnelly, 'Bloody Proud to Be Victorian with Dan Andrews', *Socially Democratic* podcast, episode 116, November 2021.
3. Rob Harris, 'Inside the Crisis that Changed Australian Government', *The Sydney Morning Herald*, 9 June 2020.

NOTES

4   Peter Conran, *Review of COAG Councils and Ministerial Forums*, Department of the Prime Minister and Cabinet, October 2020, p. 3.
5   Jodie McVernon, Tania C Sorrell, Jenny Firman, Brendan Murphy and Sharon R Lewin, 'Is Australia Prepared for the Next Pandemic?', *Medical Journal of Australia*, vol. 206, no. 7, 17 April 2017, pp. 284–6.
6   Julian Rait, 'The 1919 Influenza Pandemic in Australia', 8th Annual Graduate Summer Program in Epidemiology, Johns Hopkins University, Baltimore, June 1990.
7   Geoffrey Blainey, 'The Centenary of Australia's Federation: What Should We Celebrate?', Papers on Parliament, no. 37, Australian Parliament House, November 2001.
8   Wei-jie Guan et al., 'Clinical Characteristics of Coronavirus Disease 2019 in China', *New England Journal of Medicine*, vol. 382, 30 April 2020, pp. 1708–20.

Chapter 3 Woefully Unprepared
1   Helen Garner, 'The Lockdown Diaries', *The Monthly*, October 2020.
2   Christine Roder et al., 'Area-Level Social and Economic Factors and the Local Incidence of SARS-CoV-2 Infections in Victoria During 2020', *Medical Journal of Australia*, vol. 216, no. 7, April 2022, pp. 349–56.
3   Jennifer Coate, *COVID-19 Hotel Quarantine Inquiry Final Report and Recommendations*, December 2020, p. 223.
4   Ibid., p. 186.
5   Leah Grout et al, 'Estimating the Failure Risk of Quarantine Systems for Preventing COVID-19 Outbreaks in Australia and New Zealand', *Medical Journal of Australia*, July 2021.

Chapter 4 An Unconscionable Delay
1   Doherty Institute, *Doherty Modelling Report for National Cabinet*, 30 July 2021.
2   Katherine B Gibney, Lucinda J Franklin and Nicola Stephens, 'Infectious Diseases Notification Practices, Victoria 2013', *Communicable Diseases Intelligence*, vol. 40, no. 3, 2016, pp. E317–25.
3   Australian Bureau of Statistics, 'Regional Population: Statistics about the Population and Components of Change (Births, Deaths, Migration) for Australia's Capital Cities and Regions, 2020–21 Financial Year', March 2022.
4   Australian Bureau of Statistics, 'COVID-19 Mortality in Australia, Deaths Registered to 31 October 2021', December 2021.
5   Professor Lyn Gilbert and Adjunct Professor Alan Lilly, 'Independent Review of COVID-19 Outbreaks at St Basil's and Epping Gardens Aged Care Facilities', Australian Department of Health, 30 November 2020.
6   Peter Rozen QC, 'St Basil's Aged Care Facility COVID-19 Outbreak Coronial Inquest, Opening by Counsel Assisting', August 2020.
7   Ian Norton, 'Expert Witness Report', Coroners Court of Victoria, 11 November 2020.
8   Professor Lyn Gilbert and Adjunct Professor Alan Lilly, 'Newmarch House COVID-19 Outbreak Independent Review,' August 2020.
9   Gilbert and Lilly, 'Independent Review of COVID-19 Outbreaks'.
10 Christine Golding, 'Statement to the St Basil's Aged Care Facility COVID-19 Outbreak Coronial Inquest', undated.

NOTES

Chapter 5 The Lonely Run
1. Commonwealth Department of Health, 'Coronavirus (COVID-19) Case Numbers and Statistics', 5 April 2022.
2. Jim Reed, 'Youth Mental Health: Covid Mental Health & Well-Being Research', Resolve, March 2022.
3. Nicholas Ho et al., 'Systems Modelling and Simulations of Strategies to Mitigate the "Shadow Pandemic" of Mental Ill-Health in Victoria', Brain and Mind Centre, University of Sydney, November 2020.
4. Nicholas Ho et al., 'Optimising Strategies for Improving Mental Health in Victoria, Australia during the COVID-19 Era: A System Dynamics Modelling Study', unpublished.
5. Monash University Accident Research Centre, 'Injuries during the COVID-19 Pandemic', monthly bulletins July 2020 to October 2020.
6. Samantha Batchelor et al., 'Use of Kids Helpline by Children and Young People in Australia during the COVID-19 Pandemic', *Journal of Adolescent Health*, vol. 68, no. 6, June 2021, pp. 1067–74.
7. Reed, 'Youth Mental Health'.
8. Drew Desliver, 'Millions of People in US and EU Are Neither Working Nor Learning', Pew Research Center, January 2016.
9. N Brennan et al., *Psychological Distress in Young People in Australia: Fifth Biennial Youth Mental Health Report—2012–2020*, Mission Australia, 2021.
10. Vivek Murthy, *Together: Loneliness, Health & What Happens When We Find Connection*, Harper Collins, New York, 2020.
11. Michelle Lim, 'Ending Loneliness Together in Australia White Paper', Ending Loneliness Together, 2020.
12. Murthy, *Together*.
13. Eliza Littleton and Jim Stanford, 'An Avoidable Catastrophe: Pandemic Job Losses in Higher Education and Their Consequences', The Australia Institute, September 2021.
14. Chip Le Grand, 'Melbourne Uni Chief Says Victoria Must Address Difficult Ethical Questions', *The Sydney Morning Herald*, 19 September 2020.
15. *The Connexion*, 'Covid: New Measures Decided Friday, Set to Be Regional', 11 September 2020.
16. Boris Johnson, 'Prime Minister's Statement on Coronavirus (COVID-19)', 22 September 2020.
17. Australian Bureau of Statistics, 'COVID-19 Morbidity in Australia, Deaths Registered to 31 January 2022', 15 February 2022.
18. Merle Mitchell, testimony to Royal Commission into Aged Care Quality and Safety, 10 August 2020.
19. Jon Faine, 'Merle Mitchell: Community Activist Colossus', *The Age*, 7 October 2021.
20. Witness UY, testimony to Royal Commission into Aged Care Quality and Safety, 10 August 2020.

Chapter 6 Dementor's Kiss
1. *Public Health and Wellbeing Act 2008*, section 6.
2. Michael Ryan, 'Michael Ryan (WHO Health Emergencies Programme) at Daily Press Briefing on COVID 19 March 13th 2020', YouTube, 16 March 2020.
3. Peter Godfrey-Smith, 'Covid Heterodoxy in Three Layers', *Monash Bioethics Review*, November 2021.

NOTES

4 Jennifer Westacott, *Insiders* ABC TV, 6 September 2020.
5 Jodie McVeron and James McCaw, 'Sorry Melbourne: The Chance of Reaching 5 COVID-19 Cases by Mid-October is under 50%', *The Conversation*, 8 October 2020.
6 Inga Ting, Nathanael Scott, Alex Palmer and Katia Shatoba, 'Anatomy of Our Battle against COVID-19', *ABC News*, 25 January 2021.
7 Lidia Morawska et al., 'It's Time to Address Airborne Transmission of Coronavirus Disease 2019 (COVID-19) , July 2020.

Chapter 7 Vaxxed and Vexed
1 Shane Huntington, 'The Oxford Vaccine Has Unique Advantages, As Does Pfizer's'—Using Both Is Australia's Best Strategy', *The Conversation*, 13 January 2021.
2 Commonwealth Department of Health, 'Operation COVID Shield COVID-19 Vaccine Sentiment Summaries', June 2021.
3 Therapeutic Goods Administration, 'COVID-19 Vaccine Weekly Safety Report', 6 May 2021.
4 Lisa Schofield, testimony to Senate Select Committee on COVID-19, 21 June 2021.
5 Brendan Murphy, testimony to Community Affairs Legislation Committee, 6 April 2022.
6 Resolve Political Monitor, produced for *The Age* and *The Sydney Morning Herald*, May 2021.
7 Ewin Hannan and Damon Johnston, 'What Caused the State's Third Lockdown?', *The Australian*, 4 May 2021.
8 Melissa Cunningham, 'I Feel Like a Criminal: Traveller Says He Told Authorities about Nebuliser', *The Age*, 12 February 2021.
9 Hannan and Johnston, 'What Caused the State's Third Lockdown?'.
10 Author's calculations as of 3 May 2022, based on 4336 recorded deaths from COVID from a population of four million for Tokyo (0.031 deaths per 100 000 people) and 2987 deaths from COVID from a population of 6.68 million in Victoria (0.045 deaths per 100 000 people).

Chapter 8 Out of Living Memory
1 Jodie McVernon et al., *Doherty Modelling Report for National Cabinet*, 30 July 2021.
2 *The Age*, 'Victoria Can't Go on Like This', editorial, 1 September 2021.
3 Australian Bureau of Statistics, 'COVID-19 Mortality in Australia: Deaths Registered until 31 March 2022'.
4 Australian Bureau of Statistics, 'Causes of Death, Australia, 2020'.
5 Australian Bureau of Statistics, 'Provisional Mortality Statistics, January 2022'.
6 Victorian Department of Health, unpublished calculations on excess mortality between 1 January 2020 and 1 December 2021.
7 Leonard EB Stretton, *Report of the Royal Commission to Inquire into the Causes of and Measures Taken to Prevent the Bush Fires of January, 1939, and to Protect Life and Property and the Measures to Be Taken to Prevent Bush Fires in Victoria and to Prevent Life and Property in the Event of Future Bush Fires*, 1939.

Chip Le Grand is the chief reporter for *The Age*. He has worked as a journalist with *The Australian* and *The Age* newspapers for thirty years, and has spent most of that time writing about the people and politics of Melbourne. During the pandemic, he worked from home with his wife, three teenage children and two large dogs, reporting on Melbourne's singular experience throughout the COVID crisis. His previous book, *The Straight Dope*, an investigation into the Essendon and Cronulla doping scandals, won the 2015 Walkley Book Award and William Hill Australian Sports Book of the Year.